ROUTLEDGE LIBRARY EDITIONS: ARCHAEOLOGY

Volume 40

ANCIENT IRELAND

ANCIENT IRELAND
A Study in the Lessons of Archaeology and History

R. A. S. MACALISTER

LONDON AND NEW YORK

First published in 1935

This edition first published in 2015
by Routledge
2 Park Square, Milton Park, Abingdon, Oxon, OX14 4RN

and by Routledge
711 Third Avenue, New York, NY 10017

Routledge is an imprint of the Taylor & Francis Group, an informa business

© 1935 R. A. S. Macalister

All rights reserved. No part of this book may be reprinted or reproduced or utilised in any form or by any electronic, mechanical, or other means, now known or hereafter invented, including photocopying and recording, or in any information storage or retrieval system, without permission in writing from the publishers.

Trademark notice: Product or corporate names may be trademarks or registered trademarks, and are used only for identification and explanation without intent to infringe.

British Library Cataloguing in Publication Data
A catalogue record for this book is available from the British Library

ISBN: 978-1-138-79971-4 (Set)
eISBN: 978-1-315-75194-8 (Set)
ISBN: 978-1-138-81386-1 (Volume 40)
eISBN: 978-1-315-74785-9 (Volume 40)
Pb ISBN: 978-1-138-81799-9 (Volume 40)

Publisher's Note
The publisher has gone to great lengths to ensure the quality of this book but points out that some imperfections from the original may be apparent.

Disclaimer
The publisher has made every effort to trace copyright holders and would welcome correspondence from those they have been unable to trace.

ANCIENT IRELAND

A STUDY IN THE LESSONS OF ARCHAEOLOGY AND HISTORY

BY

R. A. S. MACALISTER, Litt.D.

PROFESSOR OF CELTIC ARCHAEOLOGY, UNIVERSITY
COLLEGE, DUBLIN

WITH 24 PLATES
AND 18 OTHER ILLUSTRATIONS
AND MAPS

METHUEN & CO. LTD. LONDON
36 Essex Street W.C.2

First Published in 1935

PRINTED IN GREAT BRITAIN

CONTENTS

CHAP.		PAGE
	INTRODUCTION	ix
I	THE FALLOW LAND AND ITS EARLIEST INHABITANTS	1
II	THE MEN OF THE HALBERD	16
III	THE MEN OF THE SWORD	54
IV	THE MEN OF IRON	75
V	SHADOW-SCENES	126
VI	THE MEN OF THE CROSS	160
VII	THE MEN OF THE BAYS	204
VIII	MORE SHADOW-SCENES	221
IX	THE BUILDERS OF CHURCHES	245
X	THE BUILDERS OF CASTLES	266
	NOTES AND REFERENCES	283
	INDEX	301

MAP OF IRELAND, SHOWING THE PLACES MENTIONED IN THIS BOOK

ILLUSTRATIONS

FIG.		PAGE
1.	Specimens of badly-made Stone Hatchet-Heads . . . . . *facing*	26
2.	A Halberd-Head . . . *facing*	26
3.	Sketch Map showing the Commercial Relations of Ireland with Europe in the Early Bronze Age	28
4.	Specimen of Halberd-Period Pottery . .	32
5.	A Dolmen, Inismore, Aran Islands *facing*	34
6.	Plan of Carnagat	42
7.	Plan of Cullamore.	43
8A.	Scribed Stone from Tornant, Co. Wicklow *facing*	46
8B.	Stone Covered with Cupmarks, Donard *facing*	46
9.	Inhabitants of Central Australia standing around a Ground-Drawing. . *facing*	48
10.	A Section of the Bog of Allen Roadway *facing*	50
11.	Forts on the Aran Islands . . *facing*	58
12.	Interior of a Chambered Carn, Seefin Mountain, Co. Wicklow . . . *facing*	62
13.	Burial Cist at Keenogue . . *facing*	66
14A.	Alignment at Barachauran, Co. Cork *facing*	70
14B.	Circular Structure beside Loch Gur, Co. Limerick . . . . . *facing*	70
15.	Gorget from Gleninsheen, Co. Clare *facing*	72
16.	Pottery Figure from Ballintoy, Co. Antrim *facing*	80
17.	Bronze Cauldron, Co. Tyrone . *facing*	84
18.	Wooden Cauldron, Altartate, Co. Monaghan	86

FIG.		PAGE
19.	PLAN OF THE PRINCIPAL STRUCTURES ON THE HILL OF UISNECH	103
20.	THE UISNECH HOUSE	105
21.	PLAN OF A STRUCTURE AT TOGHERSTOWN, CO. WESTMEATH	108
22.	THE SHERCOCK FIGURE . . . *facing*	114
23.	THE HOLDERNESS BOAT	115
24.	OGHAM STONE AT AGHASCRIBBAGH, CO. TYRONE *facing*	118
25.	EARLY GREEK ALPHABET ON WHICH THE OGHAM ALPHABET WAS BASED	119
26.	IRELAND AS KNOWN TO PTOLEMY	124
27.	DUK-DUK DANCERS . . . *facing*	146
28.	THE ORNAMENTATION OF THE MULLAGHMAST STONE	180
29.	THE CHURCH OF KILDARE FROM THE DESCRIPTION OF COGITOSUS	182
30.	DEVELOPMENT OF AN ORNAMENTAL CROSS FROM THE CHI-RHO SYMBOL	184
31.	THE KILNASAGGART STONE . . *facing*	184
32.	THE WHITE ISLAND SCULPTURES. I–IV *facing*	194
33.	THE WHITE ISLAND SCULPTURES. V–VII *facing*	196
34.	THE SLAB OF FEIDLIMID . . *facing*	212
35.	THE BALLINDERRY GAMING-BOARD . *facing*	218
36.	AN IRISH BISHOP, OR ABBOT, ON A STONE AT KILLADEAS, CO. FERMANAGH . . *facing*	226
37.	FRAGMENT OF MEDIAEVAL INTERLACING *facing*	226
38.	THE DOORWAY, CLONFERT CATHEDRAL *facing*	250
39.	THE NETWORK OF CISTERCIAN FOUNDATIONS IN IRELAND	257
40.	WINDOW, KILCOLMAN, CO. KERRY . *facing*	260
41.	A PELE-TOWER, DUNGOREY, CO. GALWAY *facing*	274
42.	THE CLIMATE-CURVE AND THE HISTORY OF IRELAND	278
MAP OF IRELAND, SHOWING THE PLACES MENTIONED IN THIS BOOK. . . . . *after Index*		

INTRODUCTION

ARCHAEOLOGY as a science is still comparatively young: and the Archaeology of Ireland, for all that the country has had a succession of antiquaries for many centuries, is one of the youngest of its branches. Indeed, just because there has been such a succession, rooted in remote and pre-scientific days, the threshold of the subject is cluttered up—the aptness of the word will condone its inelegance—with a mass of rubbish, which ought to have been cast into the scavenger's bucket long years ago. Even yet, the pagan origin of the Round Towers; St Patrick's homiletic use of the shamrock; St Kevin's assassination of his admirer (who is dubbed with the entirely modern and essentially un-Irish name 'Kathleen'); the existence in various places of symbolic groups of 'seven churches'; these and the like fictions make their appearance in the most unexpected quarters, and illustrate afresh the universal experience that an error, once started, can hardly ever be overtaken. Even yet, Dublin residents call Speaker Connolly's shooting-lodge in the mountains 'The Hell-fire Club'. Even yet, the *Irish Melodies* of Moore, to say nothing of the inspirations of lesser bards, are accepted as authorities for archaeology and history, of equal value with the works of a Montelius or a Mommsen. It is high time to shake off all such *incubi*.

I remember, once on a time, reading a letter in a newspaper, written by a man who ought to have known better, to the effect that 'we are not out for scientific research; we wish to keep our belief in the greatness of our ancient civilization'. If any one who feels thus should chance to take up this book, let him read no further. It is written in the conviction that delusions are always bad; that popular delusions are superlatively bad; and that their badness increases in direct ratio to their popularity. It is also written in the conviction that a virile application of Science to the study of Ancient Ireland is a truer patriotism than the only too common saccharine sentimentalism; which provokes a reaction to the opposite extreme by its monotony and indifference to scientific truth, and for this very reason cannot lead, in the end, to anything but disillusionment.

This book is intended as a supplement to a previous book, *The Archaeology of Ireland*, issued by the same publishers in the year 1927. In that work, what may be called a 'museum' standpoint was adopted; it consisted essentially of descriptions of such types of buildings, weapons, implements, and so forth, as are characteristic of the country. In the present work a more 'anthropological' standpoint is adopted; an attempt is made to work back, through the artifacts, to the men who made them, and to reconstruct the conditions in which they lived. Except where it is absolutely necessary, particulars set forth in the preceding volume are not repeated in these pages; and for references, &c., the reader is sent back to the earlier work.

There are, however, a number of points in which, during the past seven years, I have gradually discarded opinions to which in the earlier volume I gave expression; and here a retracing of old ground cannot be avoided. Among these points may be mentioned the continuity of the Bronze Age: the date of the Aran and other great western forts: the date and manner of the introduction of the Celtic language: the nature of the iron-age invasion, and the ethnological affinities of the invaders: the significance of 'the stone of Fāl' at Tara: the origin and development of the Ogham script: and some other matters, which the attentive reader of the previous volume will not fail to notice. Knowledge is steadily growing: but in Irish Archaeology it has not grown far enough to enable us to attain finality in any of our conclusions. The author feels, however, that the present book may claim to be a nearer

INTRODUCTION

approximation to finality, in these and certain other matters, than its predecessor.

To those who may find matter for expostulation in some comparisons instituted between the ancient people of Ireland, and the aborigines of the islands of the Southern Seas, I reply, why not? The South Sea Islanders were a fine people, before they were reduced to their present degraded condition by the iniquities of 'civilized' European intruders. To those who complain that admired heroes and heroines, about whom there are so many pretty picture-books, are here shown as mere human beings—as the saying goes, no better than they should be—I reply that no one regrets this more than I do, but I cannot help it; I have gone for my information to original sources, and not to pretty picture-books. Critics may be inclined to protest that I have occasionally looked away from my proper province—the past—and indulged in glances at the present and the future: these I refer to the title-page, where they will find that this book professes to be 'a study in the *lessons* of Archaeology and History'.

There now remains the pleasing duty of expressing thanks to friends and correspondents who have helped me on my way. I owe much to many discussions with my colleagues, especially Dr. Adolf Mahr, the Director of the National Museum, Mr. H. G. Leask, Inspector of Ancient Monuments for the Irish Free State, and Professor Eoin MacNeill, University College. I have also to acknowledge the ready helpfulness of Mr. A. C. Deane, Curator of the Belfast Museum. To Dr. Mahr I owe an additional and very heavy debt, for his generosity in putting freely at my disposal the photographs, here reproduced, of some of the most important recent acquisitions of the Museum (figs. 4, 13, 15, 17, 18, 22, 35) and also for allowing me the use of large plans of Carnagat and Cullamore, executed by Mr. Walter Campbell, and preserved in the Museum Archives. From these I have drawn smaller plans (figs. 6, 7), adapted to the size of this book, and sufficient for the immediate purpose of illustrating the descriptions which it contains. To Mr. Thomas Mason, Dublin, for generous permission to use his photographs (figs. 12, 31, 34) ; to the Lady Dorothy Lowry-Corry for the use of her photograph of the Killadeas stone (fig. 36) and to Prof. Jackson, Manchester, and Mr. A. C. Deane, for permission to include the Ballintoy statuette (fig. 16), now in Belfast City Museum, thanks are also due. I have to acknowledge the favour of Messrs. Macmillan & Co., in allowing me to reproduce fig. 9, from Spencer and Gillen's *Northern Tribes of Central Australia*, published by them ; and of Prof. Hugo Obermaier, Madrid, in permitting me to copy fig. 27 from his work *Der Mensch der Vorzeit*. For providing me with a copy of the sampler-inscription (p. 274) with permission to publish it, I have to thank Mrs. Beverley Ussher, Cappagh : and E. R. Richards-Orpen, Esq., Killanne, Co. Wexford, for allowing me to print the window-pane inscription on the following page. The Rev. T. C. de la Hey, vicar of Bromsgrove, at my request, was so good as to check my memory of the inscription quoted on p. 244.*

R. A. S. M.

July 1934

Postscript. After this book had gone to press, the Free State Government made a grant, as generous as it was unexpected, for archaeological research. It is too early yet to do more than acknowledge an act which will certainly be of incalculable benefit to Science.

---

* The Bromsgrove stone-mason has set out these obviously rhythmic lines as if they were prose, and he has misspelt the first word. As such indiscretions detract from the effectiveness of the epitaph, I have ventured to correct them.

CHAPTER I

THE FALLOW LAND AND ITS EARLIEST INHABITANTS

SLOWLY the ice dissolved, and was lost in the waters of Ocean. Slowly the face of the land, as yet a dull muddy slop with no green leaf to rest the eye, was laid bare once again to the life-giving kiss of the sunbeams. Slowly the curtain rose and revealed the stage, still unlighted and empty, but with scenery set, prepared for the actors destined to play out the chequered drama of Irish history.

The Ice Age had at last come to an end. The stress of its latest rigours had not been so severe as in a former visitation, which had covered the whole land with a block of ice thick enough to submerge the mountain-tops. In the recent glaciation the strip of land bordering on the southern sea had escaped: a few plants, and possibly some lowly species of animal life, had there contrived to maintain their existence. But for the moment all, to the north of that strip, was desolation.[1]

A Prologue to the Play flits across the stage—a solitary human figure, who makes a momentary appearance, and then vanishes. We cannot tell who he was or what brought him hither. All that we are able to say, at the moment, is that a man's bones were found in a cave at a place called Kilgreany, near Cappoquin in Co. Waterford, embedded in a layer of stalagmite, underneath, and therefore older than, a layer of early post-glacial deposit. No implement of any kind accompanied the bones, to indicate their place among the pigeon-holes of the anthropological historian. In the dawning light this vague shadow comes out of the unknown, utters never a word, and passes from our ken.

He may have had comrades, whose bones, in their unknown tombs, still await the posthumous fame which the spade shall confer upon them. When their time comes, perhaps they will be more communicative. Meanwhile we wait, as best we can content, knowing nothing beyond the bare fact of the existence of this earliest man who lived and died in Ireland.[2]

As the lights increase in strength, the scene before us gradually assumes a definite aspect, wherein the strange and the familiar intermingle.

The vertical profile will be much as we know it to-day. We shall have no difficulty in picking out the rugged heights of Connemara or of Kerry, and the gentler upland beauties of Wexford and Wicklow. We shall recognize the strange straight-cut outline of Ben Bulbin; we shall see the graceful cone of Croagh Patrick, awaiting the traditional sanctity in which it is later to be clothed. Over the plains we shall see the rivers that we know—not always in the channels wherein they flow to-day, but sufficiently near to them to allow us to speak over them their familiar names.

But at the beginning of the play, the horizontal outline of the stage will be unrecognizable. It is only by accident that Great Britain and Ireland are islands. Geologically, they are both mere extensions northward of the great continental 'shelf'. A slight elevation of the land-mass would destroy their insularity, and would turn them into inland areas, anything up to a hundred miles from the nearest sea. In contrary wise, a slight depression would turn them into an archipelago of rocky islets, every one the disconnected summit of a submerged mountain. Such conditions passed in alternation, during the ages immediately preceding the occupation of Ireland by Man.

The causes and the direct consequences of these alternations belong to the province of the geologist rather than to that of the archaeologist. There is no evidence that there were any human dwellers in the country at the time of maximum elevation. The rugged mountains of Cumbria and Cambria, the vast inland lake which filled the deeper depths of the basin of the Irish Sea, the majestic river which ran out of it southward, and relieved it of the tribute which the Clyde, the Mersey, the Dee, the Boyne, the miscalled Liffey, and a host of minor streams poured into it—and which was itself swelled by the Severn, the Barrow, the Suir, the Blackwater, the Seine, and countless other tributaries—all these barriers opposed themselves to human advance, as they opposed themselves to snakes, polecats, and other animals, daffodils and other plants, indigenous in Great Britain but unknown in Ireland, or only recently imported thither by human agency. We may indeed assume that these species did not reach Great Britain itself until after the insularity of Ireland—as an island, the older of the two—had been completed. Nor have we any reason to believe, on the other hand, in the existence of Robinson Crusoes, marooned singly or collectively upon the island tops of sunken mountains.

The land, freed from the ice-burden, had to find rest after her long endurance of the load. Before she could be peopled, she had to seek equilibrium after that distorting strain; as an india-rubber ball restores its shape, after it has been pressed in on one side. She rose and fell, and rose and fell again, as a pendulum oscillates with ever-diminishing amplitude before its vibrations cease. Forests of oak and forests of birch and pine grew and passed away. Upon their decaying tree-trunks formed the mosses, which in their turn became the peat-bogs. Bears, boars, wolves, the misnamed 'Irish elk' with its colossal horns, skulked in the forests or ranged over the plains. Man, the universal enemy, the universal destroyer, had not as yet intruded upon their paradise.

As we await his arrival, let us take a rapid glance over the island prepared for his reception. We need not here trouble ourselves with the outlying areas, now sunk in the surrounding seas. Submerged beds of peat, revealed by the dredger, speak of ancient forests, which in their turn tell us of long-lost lands: for forests cannot grow, nor can peat-mosses form, under the sea. We shall take the country as we find it, which is much as its first inhabitants found it.

Ireland is a land of anomalies, not the least of which is its geographical configuration ; the relative distribution of its mountains and its plains. Most islands rise gradually from sea-level to some central peak, or to an axial mountain ridge. In Ireland, however, as in some gigantic lunar volcano, the mountains stand like a bulwark around a low-lying central plain ; over which, rivers of considerable size pursue their winding way, changing so little in level, from reach to reach, that they are navigable for unusual distances. The greatest of them all, the Shannon, rises not much more than twenty miles from the nearest point of the sea-coast ; but so securely is it hemmed in by the marginal mountain barrier, that it has to wander for ten times that distance before it can discharge the burden of its waters.

Lakes abound in the central plain as well as in the hollows of the mountain bulwark. But the lakes that we may see to-day are as nothing compared with the complex network of inland waters which covered the land at the beginning of human occupation. Almost everywhere we may find sunken areas with flattened floors, often of vast extent. These may be, and generally are, marshy, except where they have been artificially drained with the ditches which now disconcertingly interrupt a cross-country excursion. There may be stretches of water within them here and there, often little more than large ponds—the shrunken relics of the lakes which once filled the entire hollow. In the days of her first inhabitants, Ireland might have challenged a comparison with Finland, so many and so great were her lakes.

The mountain coast-line barrier is not unbroken. There are three important gaps in its course, where the central plain, which is essentially a limestone formation, impinges upon the sea. The first of these is the stretch that lies between the city of Dublin and the town of Drogheda, some thirty miles to the north. This has always been the most important gateway into the country, the pathway of invaders, the chosen land of colonists. The other gaps, as they do not face any neighbouring land, are less impor-

EARLIEST INHABITANTS

tant, though not wholly unimportant, historically: these are the inlets between South Donegal and Sligo, and South Galway and North Clare. In addition to these primary gateways, minor but still effective entrances are provided by the principal river estuaries; while the rivers themselves are ready-made highways for the invader. Such a gateway is Waterford Harbour, whence the Barrow, Nore, and Suir spread back fanwise into the region behind the granite wall between Dublin and Wexford. The Blackwater, loveliest of all the Irish rivers, opens the land a little further west; the Lee with its wonderful harbour-mouth, the Bandon—these two afford a clue to the sandstone labyrinths of Cork, which would otherwise present bewildering difficulties to an invader ot South-Western Munster. The Shannon, with its important tributary the Suck, notwithstanding the obstacle of a line of reefs below the site of the town of Killaloe, has ever been the waterway through the central plain; and, shortly before railways were invented, to make older means of communication obsolete, long chains of canal routes had been dug, which widely increased its area of service. The line of lakes running northward from Galway penetrates the mountain fastnesses of Connemara. The island-studded Loch Erne, with its outlet at Ballyshannon, taps the central plain in the north. The volcanic regions of Antrim are traversed by the Bann, which, with its enormous expansion called Loch Neagh, opens up North-Eastern Ulster.[3]

Nature was surely in jesting mood when she fashioned this wonderful island. The people of Ireland appear incomprehensible to their neighbours; it could hardly be otherwise, for they live in an incomprehensible country of paradoxes. Nature has here doubled the parts of the spendthrift and the skinflint. She bestowed rivers upon the country which are great, but just not great enough for the demands which modern industry would fain make of them. She was niggardly in coal, but lavish in its heart-breaking and wasteful substitute peat. The most that can be said for this material is that it is highly effective within its legitimate province, of providing country cottages with a pleasant and sanitary fuel: if there were any excuse for exhausting the supply by commercial exploitation, the day would be hastened when those who depend upon it would be reduced to disagreeable substitutes, such as dried cow-dung. She bestowed abundance of useless gold, breeding covetousness in the hearts of less favoured rivals; but she withheld the tin which at one time in history was absolutely indispensable.[4] Here she laid down beds of richly fertile soil—sufficient to earn for the land the name *Ēriu* (of which the current 'Erin' is the dative case), a word which apparently means 'the fat land': but there, by way of contrast, she left stretches of barren, rocky waste, yielding at best scanty returns, and that only after bitter toil—thus sowing the seed of insatiable discontent. As though she had repented herself of this freak, she saddled the country with an atmospheric moisture which makes the most fertile regions unprofitable except as pasturage; and to complete her jest, she contrived a climate which, though pleasant enough, is probably the most enervating in Europe, except in the bracing north-eastern quarter. As ancient saints are said to have exposed themselves, of set purpose, to divers temptations, 'to increase their fight with the devil',[5] so, in the remaining three-quarters of the country, the world-wide struggle for existence is increased to such a degree of severity by the unconquerable demons of lassitude and *laisser-faire*, that to seek to maintain the country permanently as an agricultural rather than a pastoral land is to run serious risk, sooner or later, of a hideous visitation of famine. 'In the beginning, ere man grew', it was written in the Book of Fate that he who finds a dwelling in the north-eastern quarter has for birthright an energy, quickened by the winds blowing over the northern snows of Scotland, which the rest of the folk must purchase at a great price, and must fight an ever-losing battle to maintain. It was the north-eastern quarter that created the great Dorsey Fort, and the boundary wall called 'The Black Pig's Dyke',[6] in or about the third century A.D., to keep out southern aggression. It was the north-eastern quarter which gave the greatest trouble to England. It was the north-eastern quarter which was first divided into shires, so that the rigours of local government might the more easily be applied to its turbulent inhabitants. It was the north-eastern quarter which in desperation England finally cleared of its inhabitants, and filled with colonists pledged to her own service. To this quite irremediable vice of the Irish climate is due the notorious fact that Irishmen always do better in any country but their own.

Further complications are introduced by its geographical position, in the shadow of another island, larger and economically more favoured. This island has been the barrier which prevented Ireland from becoming the prey, first of the Romans, and afterwards of the Saxons: and but for its shelter, Ireland would have been absorbed and exploited, centuries ago, by one or other of the ruthless military powers of the Continent. Contrariwise, that other island, having become the centre of a gigantic world-embracing Commonwealth, is compelled in self-defence to maintain at least a nominal hold over a land which could so easily be made a platform of attack.

It is not irrelevant to recapitulate these familiar facts. They are the keys to the perplexing maze of Irish history, which is the history of a vain beating against the iron bars of these limitations; and so will it continue till they are recognized and accepted with resignation. Nature may apparently submit to be harnessed, but in fact she never abdicates the seat of the charioteer: for those who rebel against her gentle whips, she has in reserve a scourge of scorpions.

Thus jesting Nature, when she fashioned Ireland, hid within her fair creation a host of insoluble problems which have profoundly affected the country's history. The statesman who has sought to grapple with them has ever been forced to confess defeat: those who have put their trust in his panaceas have ever been forced by bitter experience to the realization that he is merely a man, with a man's limitations, and with no power to work miracles or to bring the impossible to pass.

However, all these complications, with their latent possibilities of turmoil, of hopes ever renewed, ever, and inevitably disappointed, lay still in the future, what time the earliest settlers established their home in the country. Not for them the vain effort to extract tilth from an unwilling soil, or metal from a stony rock. Not for them a wrestle against principalities and powers. Mere food-gatherers they, parasites upon Nature: content with the molluscs of the shores, with trapped birds or captured fish. Thus easily satisfied, they made no effort to explore the interior of the country, where all was unknown and full of dread; nowhere far inland has any trace of their existence been discovered. They shunned the forests, haunted by savage beasts; the noxious swamps, the impassable lakes and rivers. Only by sufferance were they squatters upon a land which, we cannot doubt, their imaginations peopled with demons and hobgoblins. In their time, every strange land was an abode of uncomprehended terrors—the terrors that could be seen, and the yet more terrifying terrors that were invisible.

The remains of these earliest occupants, so far as we know, are confined to the coasts of the county of Antrim. This does not necessarily mean that they never lived anywhere else. The coast of Antrim would doubtless be more attractive to them than elsewhere, for there alone is abundance of flint to be obtained. But even such an elementary and (to them) all-important economic fact was still to be discovered, when the country was first peopled. Colonists might have settled in the southern counties, and there lived and died for generations, before they had heard anything of the chalk cliffs of the north-east corner, with their inexhaustible beds of what was, at the time, the most important of all of the raw materials of industry. Such persons would be obliged to make shift with whatever stones they could get: only by slow degrees would they learn and fully utilize the resources of the country, or discover the not inconsiderable limitations which nature had imposed upon them.

Flint is a tractable material, and in skilful hands can be worked into easily recognizable implements. Other stones are less responsive to the methods of ancient artificers, and the implements made of them would at best be makeshifts, not always to be identified with assurance as products of human manufacture. The tragi-comedy of the alleged implements from Rosses Point, which gave rise to a hot controversy a few years before the publication of this book, is of importance only as illustrating this uncertainty. On the basis of certain criteria, which had been confidently formulated as definitely discriminative between stone fractures produced by human and by non-human agency, a number of broken pieces of limestone, picked up on an entirely modern storm-beach, were taken to be ancient implements, specifically assigned to the Mousterian period of the Old Stone Age—although during that epoch of time the whole of Ireland was so heavily glaciated, that life in any part of its area would have been impossible. The publication of these implements, though a futility in itself, had the extremely valuable effect of showing that the criteria of human workmanship, upon which their champions had relied, are untrustworthy.[7]

In consequence, although there may have been colonies of these earliest inhabitants of Ireland in the south, we cannot point to any traces of them, disregarding the obscure Kilgreany man and his possible associates. The Antrim coast-dwellers, as we shall see in a moment, fall into the period between the Palaeolithic and the Neolithic, to which it is convenient to give the name *Mesolithic*, while admitting the justice of the criticisms that have been levelled against this word. No implements in any stone other than flint, comparable with the flint implements of the early Antrim shore-dwellers, have been found in the southern counties. And neither in north nor in south, once more disregarding the Kilgreany skeleton, have any human bones been found in association with the implement-bearing beds.

There is another cause for the absence of traces of the shore-dwelling population in the South of Ireland. The time to which this colonization is to be assigned is the last period of land-submergence, immediately preceding the establishment of modern conditions. The part of the Antrim coast, where remains of the colony have been found, was then sunk 25 ft below the present land-level. In other words, the shore which they occupied now stands at a height of 25 ft above the level of the sea; and 25 ft depth of water then covered the strip of land which is the shore for us, in these modern days. But this was not the case all over the country. Ireland did not rise or fall as a whole: rather did it move like the surface of a bedroom mirror, supported upon pivots, in which, when the upper part is moved backward, the lower part moves forward. It was balanced thus, on an axis whose poles lie somewhere about Dublin in the east and Sligo in the west.[8] The 'Raised Beach' deposits—the beds of waterworn stones, gravel and shells, interspersed among which are the implements which tell of human occupation—is 25 ft above the level of the sea on the northern coast: but as we proceed southward, on both sides of the country, wherever subsequent erosion has left remains of it for our instruction, we find its altitude gradually diminishing, till it reaches the present sea-level at the two points named. Further south it disappears altogether. Presumably it continues under the sea, as a *sunken* beach, so that the *pied à terre* of early colonists in the south is now as far beneath the waves as that of their northern brethren is above them; and is therefore hidden for ever from our curiosity. We are in consequence compelled to confine our attention to the Raised Beach in the north of the country.

At Larne, Kilroot, Portrush, and other points upon the coast, the gravels contain artifacts in flint, mingled with the ordinary beach deposits. Seeing that the manufacturers of these implements are as yet known only by their handiworks, no human remains having anywhere come to light in association with them, we are unable to say anything about their physical character: and as the sea has apparently washed away all their midden refuse, we can say no more of their mode of life than can be inferred by analogy with the huge shell-heaps, left by their contemporaries and probable kinsmen upon the Baltic shores of Denmark. This absence of the debris of occupation has been taken as an indication that the raised-beach sites were merely factory-sites, where artificers congregated to make tools; departing at nightfall to dwellings further inland. But this is not convincing. The artificers would probably have required occasional sustenance in the course of their daily labours, the preparation of which would have left traces in beds of ashes or piles of shells; and if they lived away from the immediate source of flints, they would be more likely to carry home with them the raw material, broken no doubt into manageable sizes for transport, and there to shape out their finished implements where these could be stored in safety. If they had gone away at night, they would have run the risk of losing the fruit of their labours by theft: for, as we shall see presently, there were rival settlers almost at their doors. We must suppose that they threw their refuse into the sea, and that it was washed away.[9] Besides, if they did live inland, some of their habitation sites ought to have come to light.

The criticism may be made that in deducing the existence of a colony from implements alone, we are violating a principle which follows naturally from what we have laid down a few pages back. If the discrimination of human workmanship in the ruder stone implements can be legitimately called into question, there can be no certainty in assuming the fact of an undeveloped stone-age human occupation, unless we discover human bones. This is a sound and safe rule: certainly when the rudimentary flint chips from Tertiary gravels are brought forward to prove the existence of Tertiary Man, it is reasonable to demand that Tertiary human bones should also be produced before any conviction on the subject can be admitted. But flint, unlike most other stones, can within well-defined limitations be fractured, by the methods of stone-age Man, to standard forms: and when a site yields a large number of flint tools, conforming to definite and well-established types, then we are justified in accepting the presence of a being capable of designing those types, even though natural decay may have utterly destroyed the relics of his bodily constitution. The flints from the raised-beach sites conform thus to fixed standards, and therefore permit us to accept them as evidence for early colonizations.

They tell an interesting story. It has ever been the fate of Ireland to be the cockpit of two opposing peoples, which, after they have come together and fused into one, presently find themselves obliged to meet a fresh opponent. Halberd-Pict and Sword-Celt : Picto-Celt and Iron-Teuton : Picto-Celto-Teuton and Scandinavian : Picto-Celto-Teuton-Scandinavian and Anglo-Norman : Picto-Celto-Teuton-Scandinavian-Norman and Tudor or Stuart English colonist —and, peeping into a future which some of us conceivably may live to see, but which none of us can possibly hope to survive, Picto-Celto-Teuton-Scandinavian-Norman-English-Hebrew (for the last-named element is already a conspicuous, and apparently an increasing, ingredient in the mixture) and whatever Power will hereafter commandeer the soil of a would-be independent ' Republic ', to serve as a platform from which to challenge the might of England, thereby bringing upon the land a destruction that shall stamp her flat—from the first we ever find two peoples, living a cat-and-dog life within the household of Ireland. It could not be otherwise : Ireland was the *cul-de-sac* of the ancient world, until Columbus (or whoever was the real discoverer of America) perforated the bottom of the bag. Refugees might enter, but could not leave : they must stand at bay or perish. It has been so throughout history, and it was so at the very beginning.

The coast deposits, in fact, reveal remains of at least *two* peoples, differing in cultural relationship, differing, we cannot doubt, in language and in religion : strangers and—a natural consequence at their level of civilization —antagonistic each to the other. The Raised Beach at Larne has for many years been the classic site in Ireland for remains of the *Campignian* culture. On Island Magee,

EARLIEST INHABITANTS 13

within sight of Larne, there have been found remains of the *Asturian* culture. Both of these are aspects of the civilizations belonging to the intermediate, transitional phases between the Old Stone Age and the New: filling in the time, so to speak, that intervened between the final disappearance of the glaciers of the Ice Age and the establishment of modern climatic conditions.

The Campignian culture seems to have originated in the lands bordering upon the southern end of the Baltic Sea. Implements similar to those yielded by the Antrim raised beach have been found at Nöstvet in the south of Norway, in the famous shell-heaps of the Danish coast, and then, spreading westward through Northern Europe, as far as the hill called Le Campigny (Seine-Inférieure) in France, whose name this phase of culture has inappropriately borrowed. The typical implements are the 'Campignian pick', a roughly chipped bar of flint, some four to six inches in length, with a blunt point at each end; and the 'kitchen-midden axe' or *tranchet*—a sort of chisel, having a straight sharp edge, intercepted between two plane faces. Both types of tool appear among the shore debris of the Antrim Raised Beach; they are sufficient to identify the dwellers on that beach as settlers from an area of Campignian culture—presumably from the Baltic area, whether they arrived by a direct or an indirect route.

On the other hand, the Asturian culture, as its name implies, is of western origin. Excavations in the caves of Asturias, in the north of Spain, have revealed a local facies of Mesolithic civilization, more or less contemporary with that of Campigny. The typical implement is a roughly fashioned flint point, trimmed to a pyramidal or conical shape. This form of flint reappears at Island Magee, in sufficient quantities to justify us in assuming an Asturian colony to have settled there.

This is all that we know about the first men in Ireland. We can guess that fish and shell-fish, sea-birds and their eggs, afforded them a sufficient, if monotonous and not ideally hygienic diet: but for the rest, their memorial has perished with them. Their lives, their loves, their hates, their speech, their manners, customs, and scheme of society, their deaths, their gods, all have faded as in a dream. It will be a day of great and glad surprise when any explorer is so fortunate as to discover one single fact, however insignificant, in all this store of forgotten knowledge. Whether they vanished before invaders, or perished by pestilence or otherwise, or whether they persisted so far as to bequeath some drops of the blood now coursing in the veins of the people of Ireland, it is as yet impossible to determine.[10]

Our knowledge of ancient peoples can never be complete. At every turn we are confronted by the barriers set up by broken traditions, decayed wood or textiles, metal melted down, manuscripts lost, inscriptions defaced and chipped. The process of annihilating the materials of the historian is going on perpetually: a gradual but ruthless process, sometimes flaring up into a monstrous catastrophe, such as the destruction of the Dublin Public Record Office in 1922. The historian too often finds himself in the unhappy position of some ancient Roman augur, at the moment of realization that the guidance which he was seeking in a time of public emergency must have been written in one of the books which the Sibyl had destroyed!

But though our knowledge can never be complete, it is ever growing; it will continue to grow, even after the last ancient grave in the world has been opened and duly classified. The foregoing statement of facts regarding the earliest settlers in the country claims no finality: it may be antiquated even before it reaches the reader's hands. Researches in this region of Irish Archaeology, carried out, as we write, by specialist investigators, promise to open many new doors, and to reveal many surprising things behind them. It would not be right to say more, however, until they have completed the publication of their results.

A word of caution is necessary in conclusion. The Campignians and Asturians were not the only shore-dwellers of Ireland. Throughout the whole of her history there have been people living the same mode of life; only a few of the shore sites can be ascribed to these earliest colonists. For example, the Whitepark Bay settlement, also in Co. Antrim, is of the Bronze Age at earliest : and other settlements are later still, some of them of quite modern times.

CHAPTER II

THE MEN OF THE HALBERD

WE must therefore wait for some unexpected future discovery if we are ever to know definitely whether the Campignian-Asturian colonists died out; or continued their existence by the shore, till superseded, and, as a natural consequence, in time extirpated, by newcomers, who imported the fully developed neolithic and bronze-age civilizations; or gradually climbed up the ladder themselves, penetrating inland the while, to find that the dreaded *Hinterland* was not so impossible a place for habitation after all, and learning new arts as they conquered new lands. Within our present knowledge there is no transition between the culture, such as it was, of the Raised Beach, and the culture of the Bronze Age. Nothing is known of the history of the expansion of Man over the interior of Ireland.

There ought to be a chain of settlement-sites, leading from the middens of the shore-dwellers to the central Hill of Uisnech, which a legend, unsubstantiated by fact, asserted to be the central point of radiation for all the provincial boundary-lines.[1] There may actually be in existence such a chain of sites, buried and unrecognized: the fortunate accident that Ireland is essentially a pastoral and not a tillage country has withheld the devouring plough from violating her soil, to any serious extent, so that (apart from the dampness of climate and of soil) the archaeological records of history have a chance of being preserved there better than anywhere else. For the present, all that we know is that the Campignian-Asturian settlers are confined to the sea-coast, while the bronze-

THE MEN OF THE HALBERD 17

age culture is spread over the whole land ' from the centre to the sea '—or, if we may amend the logic of the old doggerel at the expense of its rhythm, from the sea to the centre.

The most pressing necessity for the student of Irish archaeology is a series of distribution maps, showing the range of various types of antiquities. But the time for the preparation of such an atlas is not yet. Archaeological study has not been endowed hitherto with the liberality which its importance demands, but has been left to uncoordinated efforts of amateurs, whose individual work is often, but not universally, excellent. No archaeological synthesis of permanent value can be undertaken until we have a complete Archaeological Survey of the whole country, which shall include a description of the extant monuments, county by county ; a judiciously edited synopsis of the bewildering mass of heterogeneous material already accumulated, in printed books, proceedings of societies, MS. collections, and so forth ; and a classified index of all the archaeological ' finds ' that have ever been made, so far as it is now possible to construct such an index. When this work has been done, but not till then, it will be time to begin to consider such questions as the influence of forest-lands and bog-lands, fertile regions and wastes, isothermic and rainfall lines, upon the population at the successive stages of its history. For the present we have mere detached fragments of knowledge, which cannot be fitted into a consistent scheme. The private enterprise of individuals and of societies could not finance such large undertakings ; the spare-time energies of amateurs could not compass them ; indeed this national work, involving, as it necessarily does, acts of trespass upon private property, could not be undertaken at all, except as a department of the duties of a government.

We have said that there is no direct evidence to help us in deciding between the alternatives stated in the opening sentences of the present chapter. But when we consider probabilities, the chances are enormously in favour of the new culture being the importation of a new people. The weavers of history during the early Christian centuries, whose work is embodied in *The Book of Invasions*, and in the later compilation of Geoffrey Keating, have preserved scraps of tradition which, when critically examined, are found to contain much precious metal hidden away in their obvious dross. One of their stories is to the effect that the first men who came from Ireland were three fishers from Spain: Capa, Luigne, and Luasad were their names.[2] A contrary wind had blown their boat away from the shore of their homeland, and had carried them to Ireland. When they saw that the land was good, they determined there to establish themselves; and accordingly they returned to Spain to fetch their wives. This happened in the days immediately preceding the universal Deluge. (There were not wanting carping critics who wondered how the story could have been transmitted across that catastrophe.) But even in holy Ireland—although, as another legend would remind us, Ireland, being free from serpents, *ought* to have been as safe as Eden before the Fall [3]—even there, the Flood overwhelmed them, when they were in the very act of setting foot once more upon the shore where they had thought to make their home.

Disregard the names of these fishers. Disregard their wives. Disregard their antediluvian existence: a singular oversight, by the way, on the part of our worthy historians, who, seeing that they accepted the early chapters of *Genesis* as literal history, should have remembered that these outlying regions of the world were not inhabited at all, until after the dispersal at Babel. Leave these trimmings out, and what have we left? The most probable occurrence possible: a small company of seafarers—it may well be, of fisher-folk—driven in their cockle-shell curachs across the wild Bay of Biscay, by a combination of winds and ocean-currents which set in that direction; and cast ashore, more dead than alive, on the rocky coast of an unknown land. Where they were, they knew not. How to get home again, they knew not. To their friends left behind they were lost for ever. Like the Lotos-eaters

THE MEN OF THE HALBERD 19

in Tennyson's poem, they sat on the shore, dreaming of home, but dreading the waste of waters that lay between —till one said that they should nevermore return; and although the land which had received them may have been in certain particulars less delectable than the Land of the Lotos, they perforce consented to the suggestion, accepted the situation, and made the best of it.

They were better able to cope with the dangers which confronted them than their Campignian-Asturian predecessors had been, many centuries before. They had a better equipment of tools and weapons; and they probably had sloughed off most of the primaeval fears which for the earlier folk had barred the way to the interior of the country.

From time to time 'new blood' joined the colony, at first, perhaps, by a series of similar accidents. But only at first; for as they gradually spread over the surface of the land, there dawned inevitably the fatal day when somebody discovered a rich store of gold in the gravels of one of the south-eastern stream-valleys. We can scarcely imagine how rich it was. It had been accumulating for the thousands upon thousands of years that had elapsed since the Tertiary Period; it is, indeed, unlikely that a more abundant supply was known at the time, in the whole of Europe. Let the wealth of bronze-age gold ornaments in the National Museum in Dublin bear its testimony; taking into the reckoning the fact that it is probably not the tenth, nor yet the hundredth part of the objects in gold which have been found from time to time in cutting peat-bogs or in agricultural operations, and of which the rest have been carried off post-haste to the nearest goldsmith, turned into money, and summarily melted down. The feeble traces, which are all that now remain in the auriferous gravels after their reckless exploitation during the Bronze Age, cannot give us the least conception of the sight that gladdened the eyes of the earliest prospectors.

We have called it a fatal discovery. The secret could not be hid. The thousand tongues of Rumour carried the tidings, not only through the land but beyond the seas : and as it happened, the discovery coincided in time with a period of great unrest over the western half of the known world—to this we shall return later. There were many homeless wanderers : it is not surprising that they should be drawn in ever-increasing numbers to this almost virgin island, by the mighty magnetism of its new-found gold.

Thus the population increased more and more rapidly, and in time a network of village communities became established upon plains, in fertile valleys, or in forest clearances. Each of these might maintain marital and other relationships with its neighbours ; might perhaps be forced, by aggressive communities further off, into mutually defensive alliances. But each group would soon lose touch with groups at a greater distance. The dwellers in the centre might speak the same language, might worship the same gods, as those who lived on the coast ; but before long, both alike would forget their old kinship ; and, as a stranger was as a matter of course an enemy, their mutual relations would be hostile rather than friendly.

In any case, an uneven distribution of wealth would be inevitable in a country where the resources of nature are distributed so capriciously. Villagers whose lot was cast upon a rocky sea-coast would not have been much better off than the Campignian shore-dwellers : we can see this by an analysis of the relics from the Whitepark Bay and other shore-dwellers' sites.[4] Those who lived in metal-bearing or fertile regions, would prosper. And thus the universal struggle between ' haves ' and ' have-nots ' would arise, automatically and inevitably : that eternal struggle, the mainspring of human progress. There can be no progress in a competitionless Polynesian Isle of the Blest, where the gifts of nature drop automatically into the hand stretched out for them. ' The Golden Age,' we are told, will return with the establishment of some sort of Communism : an ambiguous promise, for what, after all, is ' The Golden Age ', more than a pretty dreamland name, contrived (with indefensible optimism) by poets, for days which witnessed the untrammelled charmlessness of a precursor-creature, not yet graduated into Manhood? Amid, if not by means of, the struggle of 'haves' and 'have-nots', Ireland, like all the other lands of the world, had to fight her way onward, and upward.

The division of the country into provinces, a division which still survives as a meaningless fossil upon the maps, may perhaps be as old as these early settlers, and their battles for the good lands. The dwellers in the rugged west must have fought many a fight to gain a share in the fertile plains and the auriferous mountain-streams of the east: those whom a kindly fortune had established in these more desirable centres, must have fought with equal vehemence to keep them out. In such circumstances, frontiers, depending usually upon mountain-chains, river-courses, and similar natural boundaries, must early have become established; and, once established, must have been jealously guarded.

Until the site of a village of these early settlers, with its cemetery, shall have been discovered and scientifically excavated, we can never hope to know much about their physical character and their manner of life. The osteological material at our disposal is as yet of the scantiest; it is presumed rather than determined that they were a short-statured people, with long narrow heads. That they were dark in complexion is attested by the Irish literature of a later day, which always ascribes dark hair to the despised and enslaved aborigines (as they had by then become), in contrast to the fair hair of the patrons who made the literature possible.[5] These data lead us to assign them to the 'Mediterranean Race' of ethnologists, which is found in its fullest purity in Spain and Italy. It was a true instinct which made the story-teller bring his fisher-colonists from Spain: the ethnological connexion between the two countries is confirmed by the archaeological evidence, such as it is.

At what stage the colonists began to work the metals which they found in the country is uncertain: it cannot have been very long after their arrival. As discovery follows discovery we are obliged to be more and more guarded in our assertions: and we cannot now, with any confidence, assert that there was ever a period of human occupation in Ireland (apart from the Campignian-Asturian episode) during which the use of metals was entirely unknown. If the newcomers had a Spanish origin, they were natives of one of the most richly metalliferous countries in Europe, and may have been fully prepared to deal with the metals of Ireland so soon as they found them. On the other hand, the virtual absence of tin put the population of Ireland, throughout the Bronze Age, in a position of serious disadvantage; for until they had obtained access to the Cornish mines they were obliged to make their metal tools and weapons of pure copper, an unsatisfactory substitute for bronze. Even after the Cornish tin had become available, the difficulty of procuring it from oversea must have added considerably to its costliness; in consequence of which, metal tools and weapons must always have been of the nature of a luxury. Those who could not afford them were obliged to content themselves with flint: so that flint was used in the country as late as the Iron Age,[6] and was worked with perennial skill. Usually the art of flint-chipping declines, both in quality and in quantity, with the arrival of the metal which supersedes the older material: but in Ireland the Neolithic and the Bronze Ages may be said to have been contemporary, not successive, phases of culture. Many, perhaps most, of the inhabitants remained Neolithic; only the wealthy few were able to indulge in metal artifacts.

The flint implements found in Ireland conform, as a whole, to the types common to Western Europe. It is here unnecessary to go over well-trodden ground, and to describe, for the hundredth time, the various forms of flakes, knives, scrapers, arrow-points, and so forth. There is a wide range of variety of these, as we might expect, considering the extended range of the time during which they were manufactured and used. There is also a wide range of technical skill. Flint chips are found so rude that it is next to impossible to be assured of their human workmanship, and quite impossible to classify them or to determine for what purpose their maker designed them. On the other hand, some of the knives and arrow-points are miracles of technical skill, and indicate a rare command of the artificer over his material. Naturally, where flint was not available, as was the case over most of the country, and other stones were employed, the implements are technically less perfect. Chert was the next-best material, though it is very capricious in its qualities, and is not always capable of being fashioned into shape by the flint-chipper. But a number of implements in chert, including arrow-heads, scrapers, hollow-scrapers, saws, and knives, found in the neighbourhood of Kells, Co. Meath, have been described by Mr. Crofton Rotherham.[7] They seem to have come from an early dwelling-site, although no remains of huts were identified : a hammer and anvil stone were found, as well as a sandstone spindle-whorl : but the site was not systematically examined, the relics being collected for Mr. Rotherham from the tillage-fields by ploughmen.

But a fully detailed description of Irish stone weapons and implements must be left to those whose duty it shall be, to compile a corpus of flint implements found in the country, in connexion with the Archaeological Survey of the future. Such a volume, fully illustrated, would be an essential part of the publications of a properly organized Survey ; the same may be said of similar compilations, of bronze implements, of pottery, of skull-measurements, and indeed of all the other classes into which the antiquities of any country can be divided. In a work like the present there is no room for minute details ; and the main outlines have already been laid down so completely that in a general treatment of the subject it is impossible to add anything new. We need do no more here than to underline the *caveat*, already formulated, against assuming that a tool of flint, or for that matter a tool of stone, is necessarily to be classed as Neolithic.

A flint implement in Ireland may be as late as the Iron Age : flint implements may be found in those essentially iron-age structures, *crannogs* ; and for the present we are without any satisfactory evidence, other than the associations in which individual specimens may be found, to help us to distinguish between tools of early and those of late origin. It is one more paradox in the history of the country, due once again to the peculiar climatic and other conditions prevailing, that while we cannot absolutely assert that the country ever had a pure Stone Age (apart from the shadowy first inhabitants described in the preceding chapter), there is a sense in which it never really emerged from the Stone Age, until the coming of Christianity. There was always an aristocratic and a pauper civilization side by side—the one following out the historical succession of bronze and iron; the other perforce remaining content with flint.

But while in this place we merely refer the reader to such studies of flint implements as have already been published,[8] we must not pass over the rhomboid javelin-point in silence, on account of its historical importance. This beautiful weapon is chipped into the shape of two isosceles triangles, placed base to base: one of them with an acute apical angle, forming the point, the other more obtuse, forming the butt. The two sides of the weapon, after shaping, were ground flat, so that it assumed the appearance of a metal blade. The weapon links Ireland to Spain, as it is a characteristically Peninsular type.[9]

Such a continued use of flint must have had an important effect upon the development of internal communications. Flint had to be procured from the only certain source of supply, the chalk cliffs of Antrim, where the quantity was inexhaustible. It was there collected and conveyed to the flintless regions of the south and west. In what form it was transported, whether as unworked raw material or as implements already manufactured, is doubtful: probably the latter. There are hardly any known flint factory sites, indicated as such by the presence of piles of waste flakes, in any of the non-siliciferous regions. Lambay affords an exception: upon that island a pile of flint flakes was discovered in the course of some building operations, although there is no local supply of flint.[10] If the raw material was fashioned into shape at a distance from the flint beds, we should have to assume that it was so highly prized that the minutest particles were utilized, in one way or another, to account for the absence of waste material: so that it is more reasonable to suppose that the Antrim people, being fully aware of the value of their possession, kept the monopoly of the flint trade in their own hands; that they themselves manufactured the tools required by the rest of the inhabitants of the country, and bartered them away in return for other commodities.

Another consequence of this uneven distribution of flint was the great use made of the polished stone hatchet, a tool found in large numbers throughout the country. It is made, not of flint, but of one or other of the more generally accessible hard compact rocks, such as basalt. In fashioning the tool, a block of the stone was chipped roughly to the required shape, and then polished smooth. Specimens have been discovered in every county of Ireland; for all who could not afford metal, it served the double purpose of chief tool and chief weapon.

We here repeat the wish, expressed in our previous essay,[11] that the ghost-word 'celt' as a name for this tool should be abandoned. It has no legal right to exist (having been derived from a misinterpretation of a misreading in one group of MSS. of the Vulgate version of the Book of Job). It falsely suggests a special association with the people called 'Celts'. It gives no information as to the purpose or nature of the tool. And it tends to obscure the fact that the object which it designates is not a complete implement, but only part of an implement: the *head* of a hatchet, which requires to be supplemented with a wooden haft. This can be expressed, and all the foregoing objections avoided, by calling the tool a 'hatchet-head'. The alternative 'axe-head' may conveniently be reserved for types in which the stone is *perforated* for receiving the haft.

The hatchet-head, in its final form, is triangular in outline, a flattish oval in section, thickest in the middle, and tapering forward to a double bevelled edge. The apex of the triangle, which forms the butt of the tool, is either brought to a point, or else trimmed off, so that there is a small oval plane surface at the termination. This is not always at right angles to the axis of the tool: sometimes it is sloped obliquely. It is possible that the purpose of the slope is to furnish a support for the thumb, whenever the tool, for any special purpose, was taken out of its haft and grasped in the hand: experiment shows that the thumb rests comfortably upon the sloping plane, when the stone is grasped in this way. But undoubtedly the normal way of using the tool was as the head of a hatchet with a wooden handle. The handle was perforated, and the butt of the tool was thrust into it: specimens of such handles have been recovered from peat-bogs. Doubtless the handle was bound round tightly with thongs to prevent the haft from splitting; but none bound in this way have been preserved.[12] In some, a wooden pin passed through the side of the hole in the haft, and penetrating into a corresponding hole bored for a short distance into the side of the stone head, helped to keep it rigidly in position, and prevented it from being driven backward through the socket in the haft by the blows which its use rendered inevitable.

As is always the case in stone implements, there is much variety, as between tool and tool, in the skilfulness with which these objects are made. Human equality is an ideal so unattainable as to be idiotic: as one star differeth from another in glory, so, by the inexorable laws of Nature, one workman differeth from another in competence. Some of these tools are beautiful examples of perfection, in shape, evenness, polish, and efficiency. Others are irregular in outline, and have been made by an artificer too lazy to grind them down far enough to efface all the chip-matrices, produced in the first process of rough shaping. The two specimens here figured (fig. 1), which are in the author's possession, have been specially chosen for illustration as examples of inferior work.

The best-made and most highly polished examples can hardly have been intended for ordinary industrial use.

FIG. 1.—SPECIMENS OF BADLY-MADE STONE HATCHET-HEADS

FIG. 2.—A HALBERD-HEAD

THE MEN OF THE HALBERD

They are works of art, made of stones which, beyond doubt, had been specially selected for their ornamental veining, and polished to the highest degree attainable. Such objects must have been ceremonial in their intention, to be used as objects of cult, as instruments of cult, or as the insignia of important officials, carried by or before them upon special occasions.

We turn now to implements and weapons of metal. We have seen that the metal workers in bronze-age Ireland were handicapped by the scantiness of the available tin supply: though this metal is not unknown in the country, the quantity is so small as to be commercially negligible. Tin is necessary to harden copper—or, to put the fact in a more accurate form, tin is the most convenient of a variety of materials which can give copper tools the toughness necessary to make them efficient. Pure copper can be hardened by hammering after it has been cast: but hammer-hardened copper is a poor makeshift for the copper-and-tin alloy called bronze.

An admixture of tin not only toughens the copper: it also makes it fusible at a lower temperature, and renders it capable of being cast in a closed mould. Pure copper, melted and poured for casting into a closed mould, comes out with so many air-bubbles that the product would be almost, if not quite, useless. Consequently, until tin was procurable, nothing could be made in copper except flat axes and flat daggers, both of which could be shaped in an open mould. A depression was sunk in a smooth surface of stone, of the outline and depth of the tool which it was proposed to cast; the molten copper was poured into it; and after it had cooled, the resultant tool was rendered compact by hammering and so was complete. Ireland has been called 'the home of the flat axe'; and the name is justified by fact.[13] Everywhere through the country these rudimentary metal tools have been found: and as the accompanying map (fig. 3) shows, when they come to light in Great Britain, they lie along lines of march which have Ireland for a radiant point. Irish merchants, laden, we may presume, with Irish gold, though bearing

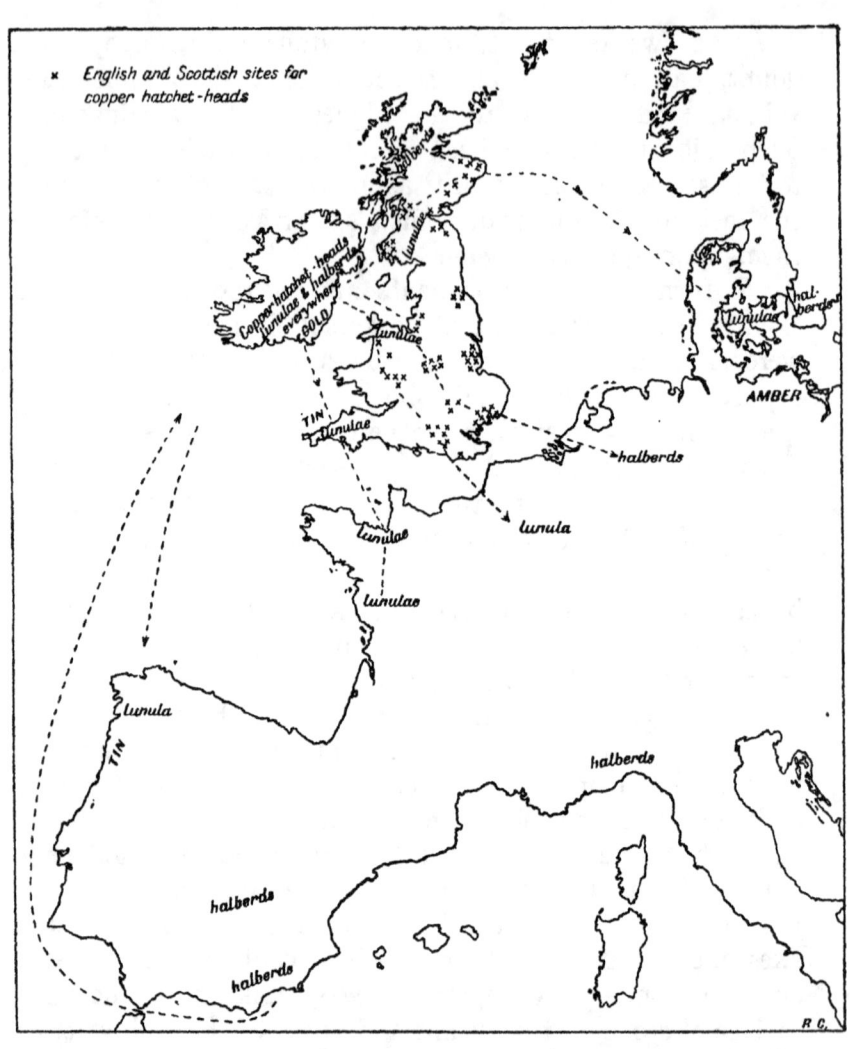

FIG. 3.—SKETCH MAP SHOWING THE COMMERCIAL RELATIONS OF IRELAND WITH EUROPE IN THE EARLY BRONZE AGE

THE MEN OF THE HALBERD

their flat copper-headed hatchets for their protection and use during the dangerous journey before them, cannot have been always exempt from misfortune. The hatchets may have been lost in crossing a ford, or in a fight with a man or a wild beast : and where they fell they lay, till the wood crumbled into dust and the copper was recovered by antiquaries in modern times.

But naturally, wealthy metal-users would not remain permanently satisfied with inefficient copper tools : especially as they had at hand the best of all materials for barter, in the gold of the Wicklow river-gravels. The inexhaustible tin supply of Cornwall was almost at their doors : to Cornwall they must have turned in their necessity, so soon as they heard the news of its existence and of its resources.

Dr. Walther Bremer made the attractive suggestion that the early bronze-age folk of Ireland, not content with trading, actually for a time possessed themselves of the Cornish mines [14] : or, if we may suggest a slight modification of the theory, that the tin-region of Cornwall was held by a cognate colony, part of the same movement, and coming from the same region, as the people who had colonized Ireland. It is a fact that Irish objects of this period are found in Cornwall : and (what is equally suggestive) there is little or no evidence there of the presence of the Beaker-People, the characteristic metallurgists of early bronze-age England. There must have been a powerful body of squatters in Cornwall to keep these invaders at bay : while, on the other hand, the Irish metal-workers must have had free access to the tin of Cornwall—their nearest and most probable source of supply—for otherwise it would be impossible to account for the rapid and successful development of the bronze industry in the country.

It is not proposed here to recapitulate the oft-told tale of the transformation of the copper hatchet-head, under the pressure of hafting exigencies. It will suffice to say that the flat copper hatchet-head gave place to the flanged bronze hatchet-head and this in its turn to the palstave, during the period of the occupation of the Men of the Halberd.[15]

We have chosen this name for the people with whose lives and works we are concerned in the present chapter, because, as the axe was their most important tool, so the axe-like halberd was their most important weapon. The hitherto unpublished example here figured (fig. 2) was probably found in Co. Westmeath : it was formerly part of the collection of Irish antiquities at Killua in that county, and is now in the author's possession.

The halberd is a derivative of the simple triangular-bladed dagger, and is made by mounting the blade, not in a short handle in a line with its axis, but in a long handle at right angles to its axis. The blade thus projects from the handle, not forward like the point of a spear, but sideways like an axe-blade : and probably the axe suggested the idea to its inventors. The weapon was an early attempt at solving the chief problem of warfare —how to attack the adversary while keeping him at a distance. The short dagger forced the combatants to come to grips, and from the point of view of each of them, the wrong man might possibly strike first ! The halberd transferred the action of the dagger to a distance beyond the reach of its wielder, and kept him out of immediate contact with his adversary. There was the further advantage, that the handle into which the blade was fixed could be used on occasion as a fencing-foil, warding off the strokes of the opponent.

The Irish halberd is fashioned with great skill, as befits the chief weapon of the warrior. This is the more remarkable, in that so far as examples of the weapon have been analysed, they show little or no tin. Unlike the halberd-blades of Germany, or those pictured upon the graven rocks of Ventimiglia, the Irish blades are curved scythe-wise in outline, being convex on the upper side ('upper' when the weapon is held aloft) and concave on the lower. There are a few exceptions to this rule, but it applies to the majority of known specimens. There are large rivets at the butt end, usually three in number ; but often more, and in two rows.

Although the halberd is as it were the 'text' of the

present chapter, I must abstain from more than these familiar generalities in dealing with this weapon. I happen to know that a monograph on the subject is in preparation by another hand, and I must not run the risk of anticipating a work which, when it appears, will be a welcome addition to the literature of Archaeology.[16]

It may, however, be legitimate—indeed it is essential—to indicate that the halberd is one of the most important links between Ireland and Spain. Whatever were the names of the first settlers, they were equipped with battle-axes or battle-hatchets of stone; and those who attained to wealth and eminence among them replaced these rude weapons by similar weapons in copper or tin so soon as they were able to do so. The Spanish invaders (or immigrants) who carved their hieroglyphics upon the famous slab at Clonfinloch, in the heart of Ireland, pictured their warriors as equipped with this weapon:[17] whatever may have been their intention in preparing this, the oldest contemporary record of any historical event in Northern Europe.

The surviving pottery of the Halberd-People is scanty, and we cannot record more than that the vessels appear to have been bowl-shaped, with rounded bottoms, and ornamented with impressed hollows: not with the elaborate imitation of basket work which decorated the vessels of their successors. These hollows were sometimes impressed independently, but sometimes with a notched edge of wood or bone, as in an example, one of the most perfect in existence, from Lisalea, Clones [18] (fig. 4).

Their principal ornament in gold was the lunula; a thin disc of gold, cut to a crescentic form, with the ends expanded and turned sideways, at right angles to the plane of the object. It was designed to be worn on the breast, the turned ends being presumably intended for a cord with which the ornament was prevented from slipping off. Lunulae are invariably decorated with faintly incised designs composed of lozenges, zigzags, and other simple geometrical elements, in a great variety of combination. The decoration is almost entirely confined to the horns

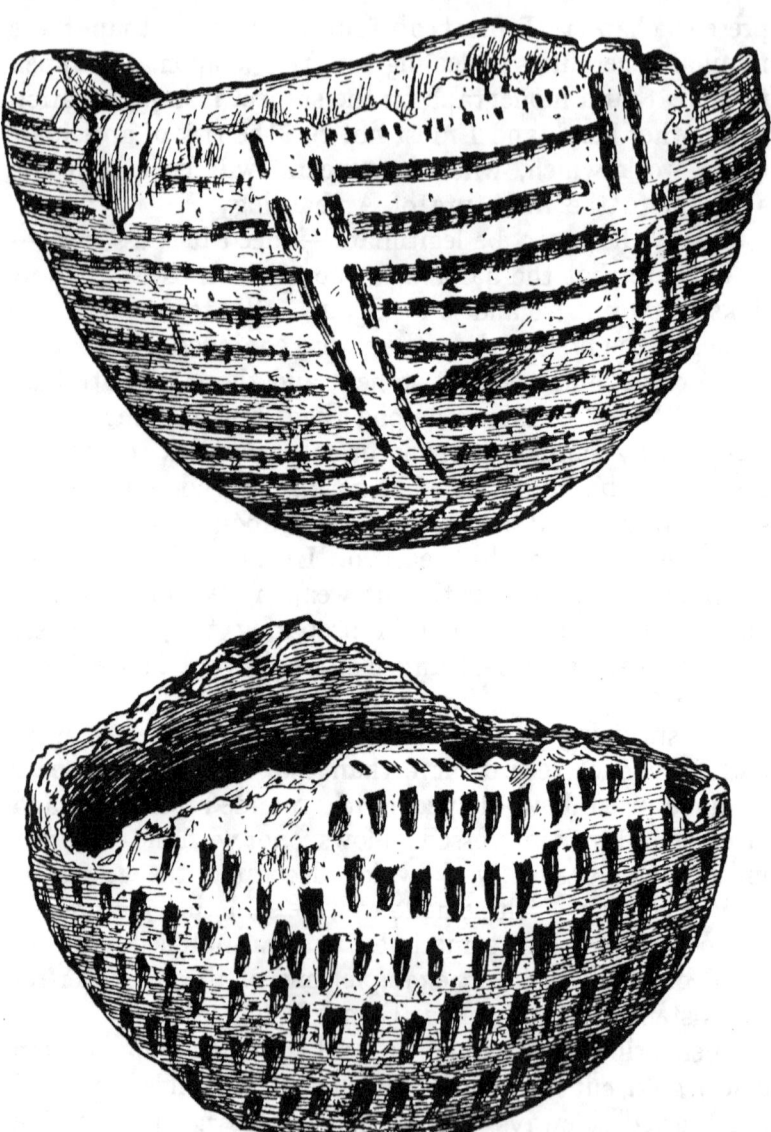

FIG. 4.—SPECIMEN OF HALBERD-PERIOD POTTERY

of the crescent, though the presumably long and tangled hair of the wearer might have been expected to hide it: a slight ornamental emphasis of the margin is all the decoration of the surface that lay exposed on the breast of the wearer.[19]

The theory was first proposed by Coffey that these ornaments were copies of, or at any rate were suggested by, the appearance of a couple of strings of beads, hanging round the wearer's neck.[20] In such collars, the beads would be massed together on the shoulder, but the lower string would hang loose from the upper string in front, leaving a crescentic space between them. Thus Coffey explains the concentration of the ornament upon the horns of the lunula. Chronological considerations are against the acceptance of this explanation: the lunulae precede, in chronological order, such strings of beads as have been found in the country.

The map of the distribution of lunulae,[21] prepared by Coffey, is a very clear indication of the Irish origin of the ornament and of the situation in Ireland of its centre of distribution. The whole area of Ireland is peppered with sites where lunulae have been found: and in Europe, outside the borders of Ireland, the chief sites are in the regions most easily accessible from Ireland. In conjunction with the map of the distribution of copper axes, they tell a consistent story: the lines of axes, prolonged across Britain, end in places where lunulae have been found.

What can we say of the religion of the Halberd-People, or of their social organization? So far as the latter is concerned, we may presume that, like the Picts of Scotland, who represent a later phase in the development of the same people, they reckoned kinship on a classificatory basis—a point to which we shall return later in this chapter. If, in addition, they counted descent through the mother, rather than through the father (for which certain survivals, scattered through the literary material, present some evidence), we may infer that they accorded to women that equality with men which, anthropologically, is characteristic of the less highly developed barbarisms: for it is among these that matrilinear descent is exclusively found, and the one is the concomitant of the other. Of their religion we have only two tangible indications: the care taken of the dead, or at least of the important dead; and the fields of rock-scribings, scattered here and there, which almost certainly indicate places where assemblies of a socio-religious nature took place, analogous to the periodical festivals of such peoples as the aboriginal Australians.

I. The extraordinary labour involved in preparing tombs for the mighty dead, in several of the lands of Western Europe, is well illustrated in Ireland. Chambers were constructed of slabs or blocks of stone, set on end, and roofed with other stones, for the reception of the body and the grave-goods: and were then covered over with a pile of small stones or of earth. The slabs or boulders used in the construction of the chambers were not necessarily gigantic: but even so, it was no mean task to raise them, with the scanty facilities at the disposal of the builders. Sometimes, however, stones of forty, fifty, seventy, or even a hundred tons weight were lifted, and were poised on the upright side stones with such skill that, in most cases, they have stood firm ever since.[22] The example figured, in two aspects, stands on the Great Island in the Aran group, Galway Bay.

There the great man was left alone in his glory, never to be insulted by intrusion. It could not have so much as entered the heads of those who honoured him at the cost of such heavy toil, that people of a later generation would be guilty of the sacrilege of pirating some of his traditional glamour, by interring their own dead upon the slopes of his sacred mound: but 'secondary interments' are common enough, so that this unthinkable thing actually happened, after the memory of his greatness had begun to fade. Still less could they imagine that a yet later day would come when spoilers, blind to the radiance of his forgotten name, would so far set at naught the terrors which his deified person had once inspired, as to break

FIG. 5.—A DOLMEN, INISMORE, ARAN ISLANDS

open the mound, dig it away, and expose and ransack the chamber: yet this portent also happened, to mock human vanity. Gold ornaments and bronze weapons were alike appropriated; even bones of the dead might be taken for charms and amulets, as we learn from a passage in the Brehon Law Tracts:[23] and through the centuries following, the gaunt burial chamber was left, a meaningless skeleton, till the dreamers of the eighteenth century came along to tell the world that it was a 'druid's altar'.

If we may believe our ancient records, saints as well as sinners here met on common ground. Both alike found it in their hearts to 'convey' the gold and the bronze which, in pious self-renunciation, had been laid up for the ancient hero's use in the other world by those who had served him during his earthly life. Benignus, the disciple and companion of St Patrick, having heard that a certain gravemound was believed to contain treasures in large quantities, forthwith possessed himself of them in the company and with the full approval of St Patrick himself, according to the ancient tract known as *The Colloquy of the Ancients*; it seemed to the chronicler such a natural thing to do that he records it as a matter of course.[24] None of the persons concerned spared a thought for the future Man of Science, for whose exclusive use and advantage the treasures were legitimately destined! Nay, even the rude pottery urn in which the great man's ashes had been laid, and the humble food-vessels containing his viaticum, were not exempt from pillage. Manus O'Donnell tells a tale in his *Life of St Colum Cille*,[25] which would be amusing if it were not a gross insult to the intelligence of his readers, and an abominable libel on the saint. It is to the effect that Colum Cille, having been so unoriginal as to turn water into wine for the entertainment of certain guests, was faced with what any ordinary person would have supposed to be the much less difficult task of providing vessels in which to serve it. In this emergency he had the happy thought to open a neighbouring barrow, and to use its pottery as table beakers. Probably by the time they were made available the guests were so thirsty that they were ready to drink without worrying their host with impertinent questions about cleanliness.

To these monuments, in their ruined form, is usually given the name ' dolmen ', which is dog-Breton for ' stone table '—one of several similar pseudo-Celtic names fathered on megalithic monuments by the light-of-nature theorists of a century or two ago. It is useful to have such a word, for convenience of classification and reference : but it should be borne in mind that just as a ' celt ' is only part of an implement, so a ' dolmen ' is only part of a construction. There is no difference between a dolmen and a chambered tumulus, except the accidental fact that the latter has had the good fortune not to be stripped bare.*

These great monuments strengthen the links bound by the halberds and the lunulae between Ireland and Spain. Spain is one of the chief repositories of megalithic monuments in Europe; and only in Spain can some of the greatest of the Irish monuments be surpassed. To Spain we look with increasing confidence for the land of origin of the Halberd-People. The jar-burial found a couple of hundred years ago at Castle Saffron in Co. Cork [26] is still unique in Ireland, doubtless because no others have as yet been found—not because they do not exist. And this mode of interment, found at both ends of the Mediterranean, would most probably have come from Spain to Ireland. It is further suggestive that in association with the great dolmen field of Carrowmore, Co. Sligo, there was found the only bell-beaker—a Spanish type of pottery—as yet discovered in the country.[27] The only two beakers of the Rhineland type have come from Co. Down, at places easily accessible from Britain : they were either importations, or, more probably, the work of captured slaves.[28] Their presence serves to emphasize the general absence from Ireland of all characteristic traces of the Rhineland ' Beaker-People ', who spread like a flood over Great Britain at the beginning

* It is *possible* that some late examples are cenotaphs or ' soul-houses ' or the like, and were never intended to be covered : but this cannot be proved.

THE MEN OF THE HALBERD 37

of the age of Metal, but who were stayed for a season from the further advance into Ireland.

Even at this early date, however, the culture of the country was not homogeneous. Even already, though we are unable to produce distribution-maps of any class of ancient monument with a reasonable certainty of completeness, we can see that there are types which are found in the north and not in the south. The division of the country which has been made in modern times as a matter of political expediency is no new thing: except that the line of frontier now established is scientifically unreasonable. It should follow the ancient boundary line, which runs with the esker-ridges connecting Dublin and Galway. North of that line may be called the 'horned carn' region: for there is a number of these peculiar structures in that part of the country, which are quite unknown in the south.

A horned carn is a burial mound built upon an oval base of considerable length, and consisting of a pile of stones within which is a cist, a chamber, or a series of chambers, constructed of large slabs. At one end of the pile there is what we may call a portico, more or less semi-circular in shape, the sides of which project like 'horns' at the end of the mound: this is the feature which gives the class of monuments its name. In the interior disposition of the chambers, which anticipate the communal burial chambers of the Sword-People to be described in the following chapter, there is a considerable variety in individual cases. The horned barrows of the Cotswolds are closely analogous; they differ, however, in that the inner surface of the 'horns' is convex on plan, not concave, so that the portico is cusp-shaped rather than semicircular.

The analogy between the Irish horned carns and those in Scotland—in which country they are also concentrated in the north, especially in Caithness—is closer: beyond doubt the two groups of structure are the work of the same or of closely related people. As the horned carns of Ireland have not been sufficiently studied, and as some of the most important specimens have been destroyed, it may be useful to expend a few pages on a description of a few of the principal specimens.

1. At Annaghclochmuilinn, parish of Killeevy, county of Armagh, there was a long carn or heap of stones, which was intact till September 1791. In that month the proprietor at the time, Sir Walter Synnott, opened the mound. In order to preserve the structure revealed by the excavation, a ditch was dug and trees were planted around it; but in vain. Less than a hundred years later the land fell into the possession of a farmer who coveted for tillage the site which the carn occupied, and utterly destroyed it, leaving nothing on the site but a stone or two.

Two independent descriptions of the monument survive. The first is by General Charles Vallancey,* the second is by a local antiquary of Dundalk, a Mr. John Bell.† Vallancey's description, so far as it goes, is useful, though *more suo* he wastes much space with speculation as to the use of the structure in the rites of Mithraism. He gives a ground plan and some crude sketches, after drawings by Lady Synnott. Bell gives a more satisfactory illustration, with an extremely small plan. On the whole his description is more detailed than Vallancey's, though in some points I suspect it is less accurate. There is also a lithograph of the façade of the monument in Newenham's *Picturesque Views of the Antiquities of Ireland*, published in 1830, which we need not consider further: the artist seems to have been concerned with the preparation of an effective rather than a true picture, and the result cannot be reconciled with the other two illustrations. All later accounts [29] of the monument are derived from Bell's; Vallancey's seems to have escaped notice.

The carn had the form of a long narrow pile of stones, the major axis lying approximately N.W. and S.E. To judge from the small oval figure which represents it on the first edition of the Ordnance Map (Co. Armagh, sheet 25), it

* In his fantastic *Collectanea de Rebus Hibernicis*, vol. VI, part ii (1804).

† Published in 1815 in a periodical called *The Newry Magazine, or Literary and Political Register*.

THE MEN OF THE HALBERD 39

was broader at the north-west than at the south-east end. Our authorities are at variance in their statement of its dimensions. Vallancey gives the length as 60 ft; Bell as 44 yds, more than twice Vallancey's estimate. Vallancey gives the height, which Bell does not specify, as 12 ft; on the other hand Bell gives the breadth, which Vallancey does not specify, as 24 yds.

Synnott began his excavation by trenching across the middle of the mound: but he soon turned his attention to a place about 20 ft from the north-western end, where the tops of two standing stones projected some eight inches above the level of the stone heap. Digging down beside these he found them to be part of a curved portico, approximately, but it would seem not quite perfectly, semicircular on plan. The diameter of the portico from end to end of the curved wall is given by Vallancey as 33 ft. In the middle of the curved wall of the portico there was found a doorway, with two standing jamb-stones supporting a lintel. This is shown as perfect in Lady Synnott's drawing, reproduced by Vallancey: in Bell's drawing it appears as an irregular gash, with the jamb-stones displaced and the lintel-stone removed: perhaps the latter had been appropriated in the meanwhile by some one who wanted a long stone for a gatepost or a similar purpose. The dimensions of this doorway are not given. It is described as 'low', but it cannot have been much less than 5 ft in height, for one of the *inner* doorways is shown complete in the background of Lady Synnott's drawing, and the latter doorway is said to have been 4 ft in height.

This doorway gave admission to a passage divided into four compartments by means of slabs, projecting after the manner of *antae*, and forming the jambs of internal doorways. Vallancey describes, and in his plan represents, the four chambers as diminishing from outside inward. He gives dimensions for all four chambers, but the breadth of the innermost chamber is said to have been only 2 ft. This is too small, and it does not agree with the scaled plan. Bell makes the four compartments of a uniform size, 9 ft long by 8 ft broad—practically the same as the dimensions of Vallancey's outermost chamber (9 ft 6 in. by 8 ft).

Bell describes each chamber as being walled on the sides by a single upright slab. Vallancey draws his plan as though the passage was constructed of small-stone masonry; but the section on an accompanying plate corroborates Bell's statement. The latter, in his letterpress, says that each of the lining slabs was about 9 ft long by 7 ft high. The roof was formed in the way universal in this class of monuments—slabs were placed lying horizontally above the wall slabs, others above them and projecting beyond them, and so on, till the space could be bridged with a single slab. The weight of the pile of stones pressing upon the outer ends of the slabs kept them from overbalancing. The total height of the chambers is said to have been 7 ft 6 in.

Bell tells us that the two rows of slabs, forming the side walls of the structure, projected 19 yds into the stone heap. He had already stated that the row of chambers was 37 ft long. There is a difference of 20 ft, which is presumably the length, from front to back, of the circular portico.

This portico seems to have been built of coursed masonry, laid horizontally, except at the place where the two tall pillar-stones were intruded. Even in the height of these stones our authorities are at variance. Vallancey gives the height as 9 ft, Bell as 13 ft. If we accept Vallancey's figure, 12 ft, for the height of the carn, we must take Bell's estimate of the height of the stones as more correct. According to a report recorded by Vallancey, there were indications of two other pillar-stones at the south-eastern end of the mound. It does not appear that these were ever investigated, so we can do no more than record the possibility that like other structures of its class the monument was horned at both ends.

Nothing seems to have been found inside the chambers but a broken urn. Vallancey makes no reference to this; Bell gives us a very unsatisfactory illustration of it. If it had any resemblance to Bell's drawing, it was quite unlike the pottery usually found in sepulchral monuments in Ireland.

It is important to collect all the particulars available about this unique monument, the destruction of which is at once a heavy loss and a heavy disgrace to the country; and also to expose the disagreements in the available descriptions, and the consequent impossibility of ever attaining to exact knowledge as to its design and construction : thus once more emphasizing the necessity of preserving records of everything that still remains.

2. We now pass to another monument at Newbliss, parish of Clones, County of Monaghan. Here the semicircular portico reappears, though in other respects this monument had little in common with the Annaghclochmuilinn structure. It also is now destroyed, and our knowledge of it depends upon the report of a Mr. Stopford, who does not appear to have been highly qualified for such a task : the dimensions which he records cannot be reconciled with the proportions of his sketch-plan.[30] He tells us that it measured 46 ft by about 16 ft; was cut in the peat; and was lined with large rough stones set on end. At one extremity was the portico, which gave admission to an oval ante-chamber measuring 12 ft by 8 ft, and roofed with slabs corbelled in the way which I have just described : the height of the roof above the floor was 6 ft. Another doorway, at the inner end of the chamber, gave admission to a gangway or passage, which led to four other chambers, rectangular on plan.

No finds are recorded from this structure either, to give any idea of its date or purpose; except what Mr. Stopford describes as a round slab of sandstone, with some characters scratched upon it. Of the nature of these characters he offers no information, although the object was in his possession when he wrote the description : where it may be now is unknown. On the whole the structure seems to be residential rather than sepulchral: the plan bears a noteworthy resemblance to that of the Uisneach house described below.

3. The next monument to call for notice is the mound called Carnagat, Co. Tyrone.[31] This structure, which stands on a site some four miles from the town of Clogher,

was originally in the form of a pile of stones, 90 ft in length, 30 ft in breadth, and 10 ft in height (fig. 6). At the northern end there was a curve of standing stones, but no other indication of the enclosed structure. The carn was opened by a local cleric, who did a considerable amount of work of the kind in the neighbourhood, not invariably to the advantage of archaeological science. We have here a development of the horned carn, with two porticoes, one at each end, and each forming an entrance to a chamber or group of chambers. As at Annaghclochmuilinn, the chambers are in passage form, and are subdivided by antae

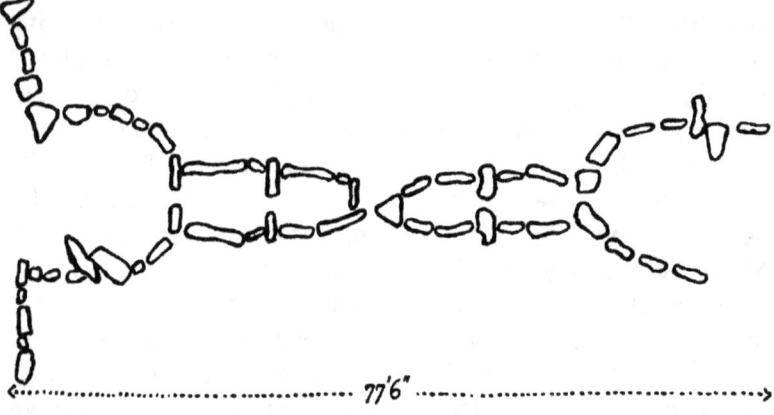

FIG. 6.—PLAN OF CARNAGAT

into compartments: this is a normal feature in Irish structures of its kind. The roof of the chamber had been formed in the ordinary way, with oversailing flagstones; but these had cracked and collapsed. The floors of the chambers were paved with small flagstones: the only objects found by the excavator were a small leaf-shaped arrowhead of flint, and an object of red stone, which seems, from the vague description, to have been an ornament, or amulet of some kind.

4. The foregoing monuments represent what seems to be the normal type of the class under description. We now come to some varieties. First we notice the monument at Cullamore, in the same neighbourhood as the

THE MEN OF THE HALBERD 43

last, which, while essentially belonging to the same group, presents the peculiarity of having an extension of the chamber running at right angles to the principal axis (fig. 7). The portico is roughly laid out. In front of it there is a crooked row of stones, the purpose of which could not be determined without excavation.* The narrow doorway in the middle of the portico leads into a passage-chamber 17 ft 6 in long by 3 ft broad, closed by a cross

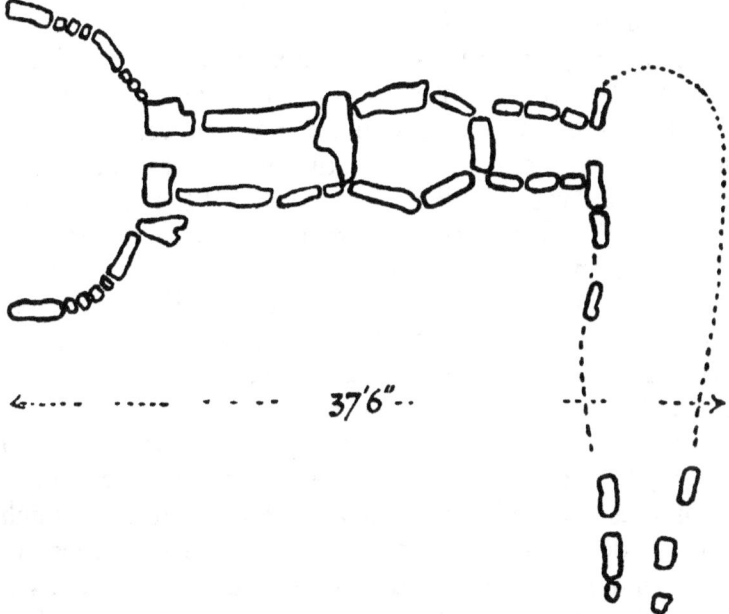

FIG. 7.—PLAN OF CULLAMORE

stone at the inner end. In line with this is a second but smaller chamber, approached, not from the portico but by the right-angled passage just mentioned, which is 21 ft 6 in in length.

This arrangement may possibly be a device to secure secrecy and to baffle thieves. The important personage, for whose benefit the monument was first erected, being buried in the inner chamber, thieves might violate the portico and the sepulchre to which it gave access, without finding him or his treasures.

* Not included in the accompanying plan.

5. We come next to a variety in which there is a portico at both ends, having its circle completed. The best example of this type is at Highwood in Co. Sligo,[32] in which a passage 44 ft long and 6 ft broad, originally divided into four subdivisions, is terminated at each end by a circle, of about 10 ft diameter. This circle does not appear to have been a means of approach to the chamber. In fact the dolmen with a circle at each end at Slievemore in Achill Island,[33] one of which circles contains a standing stone, 9 or 10 ft in height, suggests that these small circles were sanctuary enclosures in connexion with the dolmen. A dilapidated carn at the same place, with a cruciform arrangement of cists and two circular enclosures at one side, deserves passing mention in this connexion.

6. I have now to speak of the remarkable long carn which was found, in incongruous association with a series of ordinary circular bronze-age carns, on the summit of Carrowkeel Mountain, in the County of Sligo.[34] These carns were excavated by the Royal Irish Academy in 1911; the results are briefly described on pages 62–3. They are all circular on plan, with one exception.

This is a heap of stones, 120 ft long, 35 ft in maximum breadth, 8 ft high in the middle. The circumference of the base is marked out with a kerb of boulders which, however, does not run continuously. The long axis lies approximately N.N.W., and S.S.E.—much the same as at Annaghclochmuilinn. At the south-south-east end there is a sort of portico, the plan of which is quite irregular: it is not circular, but seems to have been intended, at the beginning of the construction, to have approximated to that form. The large slabs of which it is made prevented the intention from being carried out: the back slab is 12 ft broad by 3 ft high. Unlike the other porticoes, however, this at Carrowkeel is completely blind. There is no entrance through it, and no chamber behind it. At the opposite end of the structure there is a small cruciform chamber, or, to speak more accurately, a cruciform combination of cists. These had been opened and rifled, and the stones pulled about, before the Royal Irish Academy's

THE MEN OF THE HALBERD 45

Exploration Committee came on the scene. Hardly anything of its contents remained for the purposes of science, but so far as could be judged from the few fragments that remained, the contents of this long carn did not differ in any respect from the contents of the round carns in the same group. The monument is evidently a survival from the horned carn into the chambered carn period.

7. Turning eastward again we re-enter Co. Fermanagh, and stop for a moment at the remarkable carn of Doohat.[35] Here the bifurcations are increased in size at the expense of the body of the carn, and another arm has grown, giving the shape of a five-pointed star to the plan of the monument. In the centre the chamber has dwindled into a cist 11 ft long, subdivided into two unequal parts. To the south of the monument there is a curved line of stones, recalling a similar row in a similar position with respect to the Cullamore monument.

The body of this Doohat carn contains a number of smaller cists scattered irregularly through its structure. This links it to a group of other monuments in the same region, showing the same peculiarity. A carn on the Barr of Fintona, Co. Tyrone,[36] shows a central cist, with a ring of subsidiary cists round the monument.

8. But perhaps the most remarkable of this group is the carn called *Dūn Ruadh*, the Red Fort, near Greencastle in the same county.[37] Dun Ruadh consists of an earthen ring, 100 ft in diameter, enclosing a heap of stones built in the form of a ring, with an entrance having a passage into it, prolonged into what we may call a couple of lips in which we may perhaps see the last degeneration of the portico carn. In the body of the stone heap at least 13 small cists are scattered. These have been pillaged by people looking for saleable antiquities: a number of food-vessels have been found in them. The well-known monument on the Mull Hill in the Isle of Man looks as though it had some kinship to this type of monument.

9. If we call the plan of a normal horned carn 'the Y plan', we could group two Y's together either by making the tips of the stem opposed to one another (➤ ◄)

or by making the tips of the forking points opposed (< >). The first we have already seen at Carnagat. The second form may be called the Deerpark type, from the well-known monument near Sligo.[38] Here two portico tombs, one of them with a double set of chambers, are apposited in the manner indicated. The central space can hardly have been covered in any way, but we may assume that the burial chambers were once roofed in the manner already described. A monument at Ballyglass * in Co. Mayo shows the same form of plan.

Here once more we are confronted with Mediterranean analogies. For a near kinship, at least in external form, exists between the Horned Carns of Scotland and Ireland on the one hand, and the Tombe dei Giganti of Sardinia on the other. Both groups display the semicircular portico, with an opening in the middle leading into a long rectangular passage. In the Irish examples this passage is usually subdivided by projecting 'pilasters' at intervals, and also by sills in the floor, which is not the case in any of the Sardinian tombs of which I have seen the plans.

What remains to be said about the disposal of the dead may be postponed to the following chapter. In cases of doubt, and much doubt still attaches to bronze-age chronology, it is on the whole better to adopt a later than an earlier date as a working hypothesis. But much more intensive work needs to be done on the development of Irish pottery and other grave-goods before we can certainly ascribe any interments other than dolmen-sepulchres to their proper period in the Bronze Age. The evidence for a great cleavage in the middle of the Bronze Age has not hitherto received the attention due to its importance, and not only discoveries of the future, but those already made and recorded, will have to be considered with that catastrophe in view.

II. Rock-scribings are found upon surfaces of rock or

* There are fifty-five places of this name in Ireland, eleven of which are in Co. Mayo. The site of the monument is on the six-inch map no. 7.

FIG. 8A.—SCRIBED STONE FROM TORNANT, CO. WICKLOW
NOW IN THE NATIONAL MUSEUM, DUBLIN

FIG. 8B.—STONE COVERED WITH CUPMARKS AT DONARD
IN THE SAME COUNTY

slabs, or pillar-stones. Similar scribings are found in Great Britain, concentrated in, though not confined to, the more southern counties of Scotland and the more northern counties of England. The patterns consist of various geometrical figures, dotted at random over the inscribed surfaces: they are in no recognizable order; no recognizable picture of anything is to be found among them. We may not unreasonably conjecture (on the analogy of rock-scribings in France and Spain) that such objects of cult as hatchet-heads, bull-roarers, hands, lightning, the sun, and so forth are suggested by some of them: but only a small proportion could be explained in this way, and the rest remain incapable of identification. Unintelligible groups of concentric circles, with or without a radial line cutting across them; cup-marks, zigzags, random lines—these form the majority of the figures. Spirals also appear, but are uncommon, and so far as is known are entirely confined to the northern half of the country. In the two stones here shown (fig. 8), one, from Donard, bears a number of cup-marks: the other, from Tornant, has concentric circles and other devices.

We repeat—for it cannot be too strongly emphasized —that these symbols are scattered over the rocks and the surfaces of stone which they decorate, in no apparent order, and with no assignable significance. In fact, 'decorate' is not the word to apply. Decoration, that is, conscious ornamentation, almost of necessity involves a certain rhythmical repetition of the ornamental *motif*: and the decoration of lunulae and of ornamented bronze hatchet-heads shows that the artists of the Halberd Age were quite aware of this. These random marks are no more a decoration of the rocks than a handful of halfpence flung casually on a table would be a decoration of the table. And even *if* we could extend the definition of the word 'decoration' so as to include these markings, the question would still remain, what is the use of decorating a casual surface of rock? Enormous labour must have been expended in hammering out these figures: why should any one take the trouble?

48 ANCIENT IRELAND

We find a reasonable answer to this question at the other end of the world. When the time comes to initiate the boys of an aboriginal Australian community into manhood, one of the least dreadful of the ceremonies which they have to undergo is their instruction in tribal traditions, which till then have been kept a secret from them.

To that end diagrams are prepared with pipeclay upon surfaces of ground smoothed for the purpose—diagrams which convey nothing to an uninstructed stranger, but which for the initiated are full of meaning. The resemblance between these diagrams and the rock-scribings found in various places in Ireland is amazing (fig. 9). There, as well as here, concentric circles are conspicuous: and though they look all alike to us, we are told that one group is meant to represent a well, another a tree, another an emu's egg, and so forth, according to the exigencies of the story which the diagram is intended to illustrate.[39] They are not, in any sense of the word, pictures, any more than the notches on an Australian message-stick are writing: they are mere mnemonics, aiding the memory of the narrator and of those to whom instruction is being imparted. If, instead of making temporary diagrams, which the first shower of rain after the ceremony washes away, the sages of the community were to batter their diagrams with a sharp stone upon a surface of enduring rock, it would not be many years before there would be as great an accumulation of figures as we find on some of the inscribed rock surfaces in our own country. And though the details of the significance of the two groups of sculpture, for the initiates who fully understood them, would doubtless be very different, to us, who must be content to remain outside the charmed circle, there would seem to be singularly little differentiation between them.[40]

The energy of these early colonists before long began to make itself felt in the neighbouring countries of Europe. They possessed rich stores of gold and of copper. The former, so far as we can discover, they collected from alluvial gravels: no ancient gold mines are known. The

FIG. 9.—INHABITANTS OF CENTRAL AUSTRALIA STANDING AROUND A GROUND-DRAWING IN CONNEXION WITH A CEREMONY OF THE WOLLUNQUA TOTEM

By permission of Messrs. Macmillan]

latter they mined : and remains of ancient metal workings are known from Cos. Waterford, Kerry and elsewhere.[41] A foreign trade began to be established, and Irish goods began to be distributed over Northern Europe. Distribution maps indicate quite clearly trade routes through Cornwall and Brittany or the Cotentin Peninsula into Western France ; and through Scotland to Northern Germany and perhaps Scandinavia. Along the latter route travelled the halberd, which again, like the lunula, is found chiefly in North Britain and is rare in South Britain : but its presence in Britain is merely an incident in a trade with Northern Germany. There the halberd once more becomes naturalized, and its expansion follows along the same line of march as that of the lunula.

But further, the distribution of flanged hatchet-heads tells the same tale. It is a characteristic of the Irish specimens to be decorated on the blade with punched ornament, based upon geometrical figures in combinations precisely similar to those which decorate the lunulae. This decoration is such a regular feature of the Irish specimens that it may be regarded as an Irish characteristic : and the similarity of style to the lunula decoration is further evidence in this direction. When, therefore, we find tools with such ornamentation outside Ireland, especially as we find them with a distribution similar to that of the more certain lunulae and halberds, we are justified in taking them as additional testimony to the widespread trade which centred in Ireland during the Halberd Period. Merchants laden with ornaments, tools, and weapons in gold and copper, and also in bronze so soon as tin became available, crossed the sea to the nearest points of Great Britain, north and south. Those who landed in the south of the island proceeded in a south-easterly direction, and once more crossed the sea on the way to the regions which we call France. Those who landed in the north of the island went eastward, and prepared themselves for the longer voyage over the North Sea to the shore of Germany. We cannot tell if they carried other merchandise besides the products of their metal handicrafts, nor can we tell with certainty what they received in exchange for their goods —amber and jet possibly, but very likely other things as well, which have not survived the corrosion of time to instruct us. Certainly in the present extremely imperfect state of knowledge, we cannot point to any product of these foreign regions as having been imported during the Halberd Period.

In short, the available evidence gives us a favourable opinion of the energy and enterprise of the population of Ireland during the Halberd Period. They exploited the resources of the country of their adoption, and they established foreign commercial relationships, to a quite remarkable extent, considering the inefficiency of means of transport, and the difficulties and danger of the stormy seas. This energy they certainly owed to the climate of the time in which they lived. They belonged to the later stages of the *Sub-Boreal* or *Upper Forestian* Period of climatologists, the 'climatic optimum' of post-glacial Europe; a period when the atmosphere was dry and bracing. The old bogs, which had been deposited during the preceding Lower Turbarian Period, had become dry enough to support framed timber houses, like the well-known specimen found at Drumkelin,* Co. Donegal, many years ago, and roadways like the elaborate specimen (fig. 10), of which a section was exposed in the Bog of Allen in 1932.[42] But this condition of things could not last for ever: the climate was deteriorating all through their time of occupation, and we may reasonably suppose that human resisting power and energy were diminishing concurrently. Never again were the external conditions of life destined to be so favourable in Ireland. Never again could the inhabitants of the country command such a store of physical energy. The Upper Forestian Period came to an end about 850 B.C., and gave place to the moist, clammy climate of the *Sub-Atlantic* or *Upper Turbarian* Period, the epoch of the formation of the later bog levels. A new

---

* So spelt in literary references to the structure, but on the Ordnance Maps called Drumkeelan. Both, strictly speaking, are wrong.

FIG. 10.—A SECTION OF THE BOG OF ALLEN ROADWAY

THE MEN OF THE HALBERD 51

people, the Sword-Folk, entered the country, and, in the fresh vigour with which they landed, crushed the Halberd-Folk. But they, too, had to yield to the curse of the climate, and before the Upper Turbarian Period had come to an end, they had been crushed in their turn, by a comparatively small body of invaders.

The Halberd-People, there can be no doubt, were the aboriginal folk which remained as the substratum of the population in both Ireland and Scotland. They were at a low level of civilization when they dominated both countries; it was inevitable that they should go down before new and vigorous assailants, equipped with better weapons. But their latent intellectual powers were far in advance of those of all their successors: it is not unjust that Great Britain and Ireland should have been grouped together by classical writers under a name that means 'The Pictish Islands'. It is more than likely that most of what is good in the mixed strains that now occupy both countries is a Pictish heritage: that most of the faults are due to the Celtic intrusion. The Picts were in the end squeezed away into a corner of Scotland: there alone for a time they maintained their independence and showed their wonderful receptiveness. They rapidly assimilated Christianity: and with Christianity they adopted the arts of Christianity and soon beat their teachers on their own ground. Already they had high latent artistic gifts, as the carvings of animals upon their earliest monuments sufficiently show. To this they added the interlacements, key-patterns and other ornaments which they learnt from their Irish teachers, and they developed them with a complexity and subtlety which left their masters far behind. To name but a single instance, there is nowhere in all Ireland a work of 'Celtic' sculpture that can stand comparison with the elaborately carved slab at Nigg, in Ross-shire.

Further, they learnt to write, from the Irish colonists who came to share Scotland with them. It is unfortunate that the cumbersome Ogham script was the form of writing which they thus acquired: but even in their adoption of this unadaptable signary they displayed their practical abilities. The Ogham script is not a particularly good medium even for expressing the sounds of Irish: it was quite hopeless for expressing the sounds of the totally different Pictish language. This incompatibility the Pictish people eased by inventing new characters which, for them at least, sufficiently expressed their peculiar sounds, though we unfortunately have no means of knowing what they meant by them.

A few short funerary inscriptions remain in the Pictish region. These are the only relics which we possess of their ancient language, except a few stray words recorded in a probably corrupt form by Bede and other ancient writers. But they are enough to show that in vocabulary and construction it was totally different from any Celtic or even any known Indo-European language. The genitive relationship was indicated by the suffix *-en*, the dative relationship by the suffix *-or* or *-vor*: the possessive pronouns were also indicated by suffixes, *-on* for 'his', *-es* for 'her'. An *-n-* interpolated between the substantive and the suffix seems to have represented the definite article. There was no native word for 'son' or 'daughter': *ipe*, the only relationship word which we certainly know, appears to have been classificatory in its sense, and to have meant both 'son' and 'nephew'. The stories reported to us by ancient writers, of the peculiar marital and other customs of the Picts, are, perhaps, misunderstandings and perversions of the simple fact that, like so many other primitive peoples, they reckoned kinship on a classificatory rather than on a descriptive basis. They read like the efforts of a modern colonist to extract cheap and easy fun out of a black who, quite seriously, applies the word whose nearest English equivalent is 'mother' to a number of different women in his tribe, and makes similar extensions of the meanings of words which, quite wrongly, the colonist supposes to mean specifically 'son', 'brother', and so forth. Not till the Picts had learnt from Celtic missionaries a religion with the theological conception of *Pater et Filius* did they find a specific word for 'son' to be essential; and they adopted the necessary term from their Goidelic teachers. Hence we find the loan-word *maqq* (= *mac*, son), in the Pictish Oghams: and as though to leave no possible doubt that it *is* a loan-word, the corresponding word for *daughter*, which has no theological import, was borrowed, much about the same time, from the increasingly dominant Norse (*dattr*). That the word borrowed is *mac*, not *map*, incidentally shows that the chief evangelizing influence radiated from the Goidelic colony in Iona, not from the Brythonic *Candida Casa*: a place which in recent years has become almost as great a nuisance in 'Caledoniology' as was Macpherson's Ossian, a little over a hundred years ago!

CHAPTER III

THE MEN OF THE SWORD

A FEW years ago it was possible to maintain that the bronze-age population of Ireland had been continuous from first to last, rising gradually with the flowing tide of European civilization; evolving steadily from the 'flat hatchet' stage to the stage of the 'socketed hatchet'. But as new facts come to light, this simple theory becomes less tenable. In the middle of the Bronze Age in Ireland there is a profound breach in continuity, no less real for all that its records, historical and archaeological, are of the vaguest. Nothing short of an overwhelming invasion can explain the facts; an invasion so devastating, that the invaders seemed very gods to the dispossessed, and as gods trod the soil.

It was possible to maintain that the bronze-age people of Ireland derived its bronze culture fundamentally from their Spanish homeland. This is still true in a sense, in that their rivals in Great Britain, the Beaker-People, as such, never made any impression upon Irish civilization. Their characteristic form of pottery is practically unknown in Ireland, so that it was natural to infer that they never penetrated to the country. But the use of the beaker did not endure throughout the Bronze Age, even in England. It disappeared early, though the people associated with it persisted; and it is quite possible that after the Beaker-Folk had ceased to make beakers, they, or at any rate some closely cognate community, pressed into Ireland (doubtless out of Britain) and overturned her people and their civilization.[1]

It was possible to maintain that the bronze-age popula-

THE MEN OF THE SWORD 55

tion of Ireland was uniformly dolichocephalic: but it is so no longer. A striking proportion of the skulls revealed, even in the more or less casual excavations which have fallen within the limits of possibility during the recent lean and troubled years, have been brachycephalic: and we have good reason to expect that when profitless political turmoil ceases, and organized scientific research becomes established, the proportion will be greatly increased.[2]

That such an invasion as we are now considering should have taken place is only too probable. A country upon which Nature has bestowed gold, in quantity sufficient to make invasion worth while, is going to be invaded sooner or later. This is one of the numerous laws of Nature— human nature—against which Utopia-mongers are impotent. If in addition it be really true that the auriferous country has been controlling an important source of mineral supply in a neighbouring region, exasperation is added to gold-hunger. As we saw in the preceding chapter, this may have been the case, as between Ireland and the tin-lands of South Britain. The Halberd-Folk who colonized Ireland from Spain were a little in advance of the Beaker-Folk who colonized Britain from the Rhineland, in laying hold of Cornish tin. And when the invaders of Britain realized this, and learnt that the gold of the land of Ireland was good, they gathered strength and carried out their great invasion of the latter country.

A reminiscence of this catastrophe lived on in memory for generations. Warped and distorted, cut up into a number of incoherent and mutually contradictory folk-tales, it reached the early Christian historians of Ireland, who did what they could to reduce its chaos to a semblance of order. They re-modelled it, after the manner of Procrustes, upon a framework of chronology, which (chiefly following Eusebius among ecclesiastical historians, though not in slavish reliance upon him) they gradually built up from data ultimately of Biblical origin. A student in search of historical actuality might reasonably complain that they had better have left it alone: from his point of view they made a sorry mess in fitting together the pieces of their puzzle. Many of them they lost, or, rather, had already been lost before the remainder reached the hands of their manipulators: and in some cases, perhaps, they contrived new pieces, to fill awkward holes in the quaint picture which they produced out of their material. But such disdainful criticism is not quite fair, even though it contains much truth. The ancient historians, like all of us, made mistakes: but they did the great service of preserving much that otherwise would have disappeared for ever; and beneath all their weird dreamland delirium we can even yet discern real, if elusive, truths.[3]

The history which was thus contrived has been summarized so often that it seems superfluous to go over the well-trodden ground once more. But the most prominent features may be lightly touched upon, so far as these have a bearing upon our present reconstruction. Our historians picture the occupation of the country as a series of invasions. In this, beyond question, they are perfectly right. They begin before the Flood: the story of Capa and his companions is not the only antediluvian invasion of which they tell us: there were others, notably that of a heroine called Cesair, which is quite clearly one of the many ancient cosmogonic flood-myths of the world, artificially fitted into the Biblical scheme by boldly uniting Cesair to the kindred of Noah.

Then, after long intervals, come 'Partholon', 'Nemed', and the 'Fir Bolg'. When we compare the tales told of these three invasions, we realize that they are nothing more than three different versions of one story. The people thus variously designated occupy Ireland; are much persecuted by invaders from overseas, uncanny demons, called 'Fomorians'; and they either die of an annihilating plague (the Partholonians) or flee the country (the Nemedians). The latter take refuge in Anglesey, in Britain, and in 'the Northern Islands of Greece', for which we need not trouble to search a modern atlas. Of their descendants, some are enslaved by the King of Greece: they escape from his servitude and return to the inheritance of their fathers under the name 'Fir Bolg'. The rest learn magic and wizardry, return to Ireland at a later date, oust their former kinsfolk, and under the name 'Tūatha Dē Danann' they hold the land till, in their turn, they are driven out by the 'Children of Mīl'—in other words, by the iron-age invaders.

Criticized as a sober record of historical events, such a farrago would obviously have neither sense nor reason. But underlying it there are grains of history, some of which can be isolated, and, with the help of archaeological evidence, can even be substantiated. We may safely ignore the antediluvian stories: these are either cosmogonic mythology pure and simple, or else they are later scraps of folklore, artificially projected back into the primaeval world. The Partholon-Nemed-FirBolg legend meets us next: we speak in the singular number, for these three groups of stories, as we have seen, are in essence but one. They stand appropriately at the beginning of the tale, even before the gods: for they are undoubtedly a reminiscence of the Halberd-Folk. The last of these three names must not be translated 'Belgae', as has sometimes been done. It means 'Men of Bags', and its most reasonable explanation reveals the people so designated as wearers of breeches.

One tale, less extravagant than that which introduces us to the 'Northern Islands of Greece', makes the Fir Bolg avoid oppression by a flight to Aran, to Islay, and to other islands on the outskirts of the British Archipelago. Here at once we see an explanation, which is actually given us in this story—and the only reasonable explanation available—of the most perplexing buildings in Ireland: namely, the colossal stone fortifications in the West, which are especially conspicuous upon those very Aran Islands.[4] On those barren rocks, peopled by a folk who retained a primitive simplicity until their exploitation in recent years by tourist agencies, we are taught to see the last refuge of a disinherited people, where the Men of the Halberd, driven out by the Men of the Sword, made their last despairing stand. Protected behind the great walls which they built for themselves, they managed at least to keep body and soul together, on the bleak and economically unattractive islands which afforded them an asylum (fig. 11).

The invasion of the 'wizards' who dispossessed the Men of the Halberd was so overwhelming, as we have said, that it seemed a thing supernatural. History has here been thickly overlaid with folklore, with myths derived from ancient legends of the antagonisms of light and darkness, of good and of evil, so that practically nothing of mere mundane affairs is left. A *theogonia* has been substituted for a sordid story of piracy. The very name given by the historians to the invaders—'People of the god, [son] of [the earth-mother] Dana'—ascribes to them a divinity. The archaeologist must here fill the gaps, for the historians cannot produce a single historical record, in the strict sense of the term.

According to the explanation here adopted, the enormous forts of the Aran Islands are silent but eloquent witnesses to the terror inspired by the Sword-Men. Who could have thought it worth while thus to fortify a group of barren rocks, miles out to sea? No one: except people who feared that, even there, ruthless, gold-greedy plunderers might find them out. The old stories of how the Nemedians and the Fir Bolg—in essence one and the same people—fled to certain islands and there in desperation 'dug themselves in', in an all but literal application of the old saying 'Between the devil and the deep sea'—these must be essentially true; for the forts stand to this day, impressive witnesses to their truth. If those mighty walls had proved unavailing to keep out the invaders, armed with their irresistible glaives, the refugees would have had no prospect other than to be hurled, over the towering cliffs of their island sanctuary at the end of the world, into the boundless, fathomless ocean.

These forts, then, are the testimony of the invaded to the might of the invader. To balance this testimony and to confirm it, the self-glorification of the invader has found expression in gigantic tumuli, such as those in the Valley

FIG. 11.—FORTS ON THE ARAN ISLANDS

of the Boyne. These tombs, like the Pyramids to which in essential details they bear a striking resemblance, are obviously the fruit of the fiat of autocrats who have enslaved the dwellers in large areas of territory. They tell us of a social order quite different from that which we envisage among the Halberd-Folk.

The latter formed amorphous groups of units, each established in its own self-centred village community, with its own head man to rule it and to direct its affairs. When one of these *roitelets* died, those who had served him during life, and now feared him all the more in that he had entered the number of the gods, of their own good will formed themselves into gangs of labourers, and erected a great tomb to honour him—and to shut him in. This tomb, whose coverless skeleton we call a dolmen, was a spontaneous expression of fear, reverence, honour, affection, or whatever other emotion the departed may have inspired in his own little domain.

But in contrast with the individualistic dolmens and their purely local interest, the social order, of which the great tumuli are the expression, is based on a centralized and widespread tyranny. They must have been made to order: not in the sense in which we use this expression in reference to a suit of clothes, which is paid for with an agreed sum of money: but in the manner of the Egyptian pyramids to which we have just compared them, made to the order of tyrannical Pharaohs. Such a monarch commandeers the available activities of a kingdom, and (except perhaps for just enough provision to keep his wretched serfs alive) he makes no return whatsoever. Without knowing how many labourers were actually employed, or the distance from which they were obliged to carry the material, it would be impossible to calculate exactly how much time the building of such a structure as the tumulus now called New Grange would occupy. I have made a very rough estimate that the weight of its materials may be about 50,000 tons; and when we recollect that when completed it was covered with a surface layer of blocks of quartz, the nearest natural source of which is about thirty miles away, we realize clearly that the tomb must have been a long time, perhaps many years, a-building, and must have been made under the auspices of its first owner; not hastily run up, like an ordinary dolmen-tumulus, which willing hands could readily erect in the few days intervening between the death and the interment.

Moreover, the builder of New Grange looked forward to leaving successors who would have an equal right with himself to interment inside it after death, and who were expected to have sufficient power during life to protect it from violation. Otherwise he would not have left it and its treasures with a vulnerable entrance passage. It was not, like the dolmen-tumuli, a single grave, made once for all for a single man: it was a common sepulchre, which was to hold the ashes of members of a special family or caste. Spontaneous loyalty to an individual is one thing: enforced loyalty to a caste or a dynasty is quite another, and the establishment of such a caste indicates, of absolute necessity, a complete change in social organization.

The sculptured stones contained within these chambers tell the same story. The more often these mounds are visited—and the present writer may fairly claim to have visited them more often than most people—the more does the conclusion appear inevitable that these stones were never intended for the place where they are now found. The sculpture was certainly executed before the building of the chambers, and with no reference to their decoration. We can find it built in, in places where it is almost completely hidden. There is no regularity, order, or rhythm in the arrangement of the designs inside the chambers. At least one of the decorated stones in New Grange has been broken to make it fit the place where the builders desired to set it—breaking the ornamental pattern also. This fact is sufficient to negative the explanation of these hidden sculptures which I was formerly inclined to give, namely, that they were magical in purpose, and might possibly have been expected to work their magic

THE MEN OF THE SWORD 61

all the better if they were unseen and so unlikely to be met by counteracting magic. A simpler explanation would be, want of forethought in correlating the work of a number of stone-cutters, each engaged in preparing decorated stones for the monument. But that explanation will not fit some cases where there is evidence of a change, not only of plan, but of technique, in the decoration; indicating that the stone had been used at different stages of artistic evolution, and therefore in different generations.

Nothing will satisfactorily fit these facts but the conclusion that the tyrant who, for his own glory and the glory of his heirs, forced the enslaved Halberd-Folk to build the sepulchre which was to be his eternal habitation, went so far as to compel his serfs to violate the tombs of their own fathers, and to appropriate as mere building-stone the memorial grave-marks upon which had been impressed their traditional religious symbols or totem-signs. In fact, we must conclude that the cemetery on which there now stands a number of small burial-mounds, and these three great royal mounds, was originally a forest of large memorial blocks of carven stones; and that these were all forcibly appropriated by the builders of New Grange and of the other great tumuli. It is possible, indeed probable, that from time to time symbols were added to the stones after they had been set in their new position and adapted to their new use. But we repeat—the vast majority of the sculpturings were never meant for the place where now we find them.

These chambered carns have been described so often that a brief general account of them is all that is here necessary.[5] As a rule (though not invariably) they are situated in elevated positions, where they are visible over a wide area. Doubtless this is intentional: like the hill-top shrines which are so conspicuous a feature of Palestinian scenery, they are placed as monuments to which honour can be paid from a long distance: as landmarks and as centres of local cult. The chambers (fig. 12) were built of large stones, closely set together on end, and roofed with slabs. Unlike the dolmen chambers of the earlier people, the roofs did not, as a rule, consist of one large slab only: there were several, overlapping each other after the fashion of the slates of a roof, though laid flat, not on a sloping base: or, to be more exact, propped up by smaller packing-stones to a slightly oblique position, sloping downward toward the outside of the chamber. Obviously the purpose of the slope was to carry away rainwater, and so to prevent it from flooding the chamber beneath. The entrance-passage was constructed in the same way—two parallel rows of stones on end, supporting a roof of flat slabs. The chambers having been built, the outline of the proposed carn was laid out with a ring of large boulders: and then stones were heaped up within the ring, till the entire structure was covered over. The opening at the outer end of the passage was closed with stones which could be removed when it was necessary to enter the chamber to deposit a fresh interment.

This entrance is usually low, and the passage, at least at its outer end, is often uncomfortable and awkward to penetrate. It widens inward; but usually the transition to the comparative spaciousness of the chamber itself is made abruptly, by an inner doorway and jambs. As a rule, the burial-chamber is of a roughly circular or oval plan, and around it there is ranged a series of recesses, no doubt intended for the reception of the buried dead themselves, and whatever deposits the survivors placed with them.

Cemeteries of such chambered carns exist on Carrowkeel Mountain, Co. Sligo, excavated by the Royal Irish Academy in 1911, already referred to in the previous chapter; at Lochcrew, Co. Meath (a series of about twenty-five such monuments, now much wrecked, and remarkable for the great series of carved slabs which have been incorporated in their structure); at *Brugh na Boinne* on the Boyne, about five miles from Drogheda; and individual specimens exist on Knocknarea Mountain (an enormous carn, dominating a wide area, and traditionally connected with Queen Medb), on several of the Dublin and Wicklow

FIG. 12.—INTERIOR OF A CHAMBERED CARN, SEEFIN MOUNTAIN, CO. WICKLOW

THE MEN OF THE SWORD 63

Mountains, and in some other places as well. It is suggestive that the majority of these monuments are situated in the region behind the vulnerable gap which faces Britain. It is also significant that while a number of the Carrowkeel series was found intact by the Royal Irish Academy excavators, there was among them one dolmen of the earlier type, and this had been wrecked by plunderers.[6]

The finds in the Carrowkeel carns were interesting but scanty. No metal was deposited with the dead. The bodies were normally burnt, and reduced to fine ash, but there were one or two groups of bones belonging to persons who had been buried. The ashes were in a few cases deposited in pottery vessels, all of them 'food-vessels', not the large cinerary urns; but as a rule they were merely placed upon flat stones of about the size of a child's school slate, which were piled up within the burial-recesses. A few beads and pendants of limestone and pins of bone, all intrinsically worthless, were the only gifts left for the dead, as well as the inevitable smooth quartz pebbles which, whatever they may mean, are a constant feature of bronze-age interments. Some sherds of the bowl-shaped vessels with impressed dots, characteristic of the Halberd-People, showed that the two civilizations overlapped at the time when these mounds were erected. This was also indicated by the long carn with horned ends, described above, page 44, evidently a reminiscence of the horned barrow of the Halberd-People. It was a late, degenerate example: the horns were badly built without regular shape, and there was no doorway in the portico which they formed. In all other respects the architecture and contents of its chamber conformed to that of the chambers in the circular mounds.

There is also one long mound, not yet investigated, in the series of burial tumuli in the cemetery called Brugh na Boinne, which includes New Grange. This important burial-place stands upon a tongue of land about three miles long and one mile across, formed by a long bend of the River Boyne. At its entrance, as we approach it from the mouth of the river, there is an enormous circular enclosure surrounded by a single earthen wall. This may be a fortification of some kind: but it is equally likely to be a sort of amphitheatre, the scene of the ceremonies which must certainly have taken place at the burial of important personages. It may further be suggested that *this* is the structure to which the name *Brugh na Bóinne*, ' Palace of the Boyne ', properly attaches. Such a name obviously is more suitable for a building of the kind than for either a cemetery or a burial-mound; but it is often applied indifferently to the whole group of burial-places in the area or, specifically, to New Grange, the largest mound in the series.

Once again, New Grange has been described so often that it is unnecessary to describe it again in detail. Let it suffice to say that it is a huge pile of stones, practically circular on plan, covering about an acre of ground, and something over 40 ft high. It is surrounded with a circle of large standing stones, which, if the intercolumniation was uniform throughout, must originally have been about thirty-five in number: but only twelve remain. Another standing stone was erected on the summit, and yet another inside the burial chamber; these were in existence down to the eighteenth century, but are no longer to be seen.

Round the foot of the mound there is a kerb of flat slabs, about 5 ft in breadth and 10 ft, more or less, in length. These are set up on their longer edges, touching one another end to end—or at least they were originally so set, but the pressure of the great weight of material behind them has thrown many of them out of plumb and out of alignment. There seem to be about 100 of these stones, most of which, at the moment of writing, are buried. A trench was run about half round the mound some years ago, and exposed such of these slabs as lay in its course.

Three of these slabs are very elaborately decorated— one at the entrance; one diametrically opposite to the entrance; and a third which, so far as can be determined at present, appears to have no relation to any interior structure. Of the rest, about one-half of the slabs, which were exposed in the excavation, were found to bear scribings of the simplest kind—on one stone a zigzag, on another a spiral, and so on. As a decoration of the great burial-mound nothing more pointless or undignified could be conceived; it would have been better to have left them in their unadorned simplicity. But we suggest that each of these may have once marked a grave, and that the zigzag or spiral would have told a contemporary passer-by all that he needed to know about the dead man underneath. So far as the present writer is concerned, the results of this partial and preliminary excavation strengthened him in the view that the stones were collected by the builders on the spot, from the graves of an earlier people. Indeed, there is actually one stone remaining, in a field close to New Grange, which escaped notice, and still appears to serve its original purpose as a gravemark; it is decorated with spirals and other geometrical patterns. We may however quite reasonably admit that it was the great elaboration of the carving on the stone at the entrance which led to its having been selected for the position which it now occupies.

The entrance to New Grange faces south-east (looking outward) and gives access to a passage about 3 ft wide and 62 ft long, formed of two rows of upright stones supporting horizontal slabs. This roof is very irregularly constructed, the height of the passage ranging at random between 4 ft 6 in. and 7 ft 10 in. according to Coffey's measurements. On both sides there are stones, some of which bear ornament; these are interspersed without any regularity among stones which are perfectly plain. It is evident that the builders have laboured to bring the stones to a true face by pocking over the whole surface: and here and there a stone can be found bearing faint traces of ornament, zigzags and the like, partly effaced by the pocking process—a further proof of the secondary use of the stones, and the obsolete nature of the ornament which they bear. The right-hand jamb of the entrance to the chamber itself has upon it a remarkable series of shallow horizontal grooves, which look as though they had been cut to deface some symbol offensive to the later builders. There is a similar grooved stone on the same side, about the middle of the passage.

Nothing new can here be said about the burial-chamber, with its three grave-recesses, and its ornamented stones scattered at random round the lower part of the walls. There is only one ornamented stone in the domed superstructure.

It may be noted that the sister mound of Dowth, a mile or so away, had also not improbably a ring of standing stones around it, which have been smashed up to provide building material for a little late mediaeval church in the immediate neighbourhood.

These tumuli are the monuments of the rulers. Only the highest aristocrats were in a position to have such grandiose tombs erected. The common people, Sword-Folk and Halberd-Folk, had to be content with lowlier obsequies. Simple burial was doubtless frequently resorted to, with or without associated grave-goods: but in the soil of Ireland such a burial could hardly have the smallest chance of preservation. Even the bones rot away to nothing in its humid climate. Cist-burials, where the enclosing stones keep the deposit from direct contact with the corroding earth, are more likely to retain some instructive material; and we may mention as of especial interest the cist found at Keenogue, Co. Meath, in which a flexed body with a food-vessel was discovered inside a massively built cist specially noteworthy for its 'crazy-paving' floor of irregularly shaped flat stones (fig. 13). This inhumation interment was part of a cemetery in which the majority of the bodies had been burnt, forming an 'Urn-field' that yielded some exceptionally fine pottery. Other 'Urn-fields' have been found at Ballon Hill, Co. Carlow, and at Drumnakilly in the neighbourhood of Omagh, Co. Tyrone; and doubtless there are many more awaiting an investigation which, it is to be hoped, will be more thorough and scientific than that accorded to the two places last named.[7] The Keenogue cemetery was carefully examined

FIG. 13.—BURIAL CIST AT KEENOGUE
NOW RECONSTRUCTED IN THE NATIONAL MUSEUM, DUBLIN

on behalf of the National Museum by Dr. Mahr, and the cist mentioned above, with its contents, has been reconstituted in the Museum.

A burial at Bunbrosna, Co. Westmeath, which was excavated by Miss Ruby Murray and the present writer, threw some light on bronze-age customs and manners in the presence of the mystery of death. The construction consisted of a well-built but very small cist in the heart of a low mound. There were two small food-vessels in the cist, lying on their sides, and evidently deposited empty; the bones of a single individual; and a couple of small beads of jet. The bones were not burnt, but they were all smashed into fragments, many of them not larger than a shilling: most of the fragments were inside the cist, but some of them were lying outside, covering the lowest of several large stones which were piled, one on top of the other, over the mouth of the cist. And on some of these bone fragments were bronze stains such as could have been produced only by long-continued contact between the bone and a bracelet: but the most careful search and sifting failed to reveal the slightest trace of such an ornament or of any other, with the exception of the two beads. There was certainly no bronze in the cist, and never had been.

The only explanation that seemed to fit the facts was as follows. The dead man must have received a temporary burial somewhere, the body being deposited wearing the ornaments which had decorated it during life: bronze bracelets, a jet necklace, and quite possibly gold adornments as well. It lay long enough for the flesh to decay and to mingle with the surrounding earth, and for the bones to rot. Then, for some reason, it was re-interred in the mound. The cist provided would have been too small to hold even a crouched infant's body: but it is big enough to hold the crushed fragments of rotted bones, carried from the first burial in sacks or baskets. Some animal bones, which happened to have been in the earth where the man was first buried, were accidentally transferred along with them: the animals could not possibly have made their way alive between the close-fitting stones of the cist, and even if they had done so, their skeletons would have remained entire. And further, the 'resurrection men' who transferred the bones must have appropriated the ornaments. They did not notice the two beads, which had slipped with the bone fragments into one of the sacks, nor yet the bronze stains, which remained for somewhere about three thousand years to testify against their act of sacrilege. That they realized that they were committing a dangerous crime against a vindictive ghost is suggested by the care which they took to close him in. Not one, but half a dozen large flag-stones were laid over the cist. After the first of these had been placed in position, a straggler arrived with another lot of bone fragments from the now-emptied grave. As the cist had already been closed, these were sprinkled over the stone cover, and then the other covers were laid down on top of them and the grave-mound closed in—till the day came for the revelation of guilty secrets! [8]

There are two chief classes of Megalithic monuments in Ireland: dolmens, and the various combinations of standing stones. The former we have assigned to the Halberd-People. Single standing stones may belong to any period whatsoever; they serve a variety of purposes, but have no distinguishing mark of date or of the racial connexions of those responsible for their erection. But groups of standing stones, especially those ranged in circles, have a specific character, and presumably belong to a specific stage of the history.

A circle of standing stones is a conspicuous adjunct to New Grange: and a very definite tradition of the use of these monuments lasted into historic times, a fact which suggests that they could hardly have had an origin in very remote prehistoric ages. Stone circles are not very conspicuous features of the Irish landscape: probability favours their ascription to invaders from South Britain, where this type of monument is frequent, where indeed some of the greatest examples in existence are to be found.

THE MEN OF THE SWORD 69

This involves the attribution of the Stone Circles to the Sword-Folk, not to the dolmen-building Halberd-Folk.

It is not, however, free from difficulty, inasmuch as, in England, the bronze-age sculptured symbols which in the preceding chapter we have assigned to the Halberd-Folk are found in association with stone circles: the Calder Stones near Liverpool, and the Penrith Circle ('Long Meg and her Daughters') are examples. But on the other hand the surface-pocking technique of stone-dressing links New Grange and Stonehenge closely together; and on the whole this view of the chronology is the simplest. It does not follow that *alignments* are necessarily to be ascribed to the later people: indeed it is not improbable that they are not, and that whatever (presumably religious) purpose was served for the Sword-Folk by stone circles was fulfilled for the earlier Halberd-Folk by the alignments. Both classes of monument are illustrated in fig. 14.

A stone circle is a structure which consists of (1) a ring of pillar-stones—the number of these is apparently immaterial—set on end and enclosing a circular space, and (2) a solitary stone outside the circle. Sometimes, but rarely, there is more than one outside stone: occasionally the stone is not outside but inside the circle. No rule can be discovered prescribing the distance of the outside stone from the circle, or its compass-bearings relative thereto.

A legend of St. Patrick appears to enshrine an authentic memory of the purpose of these monuments. The saint, in his peregrination through Ireland, came to the plain called *Mag Slecht*, 'the plain of prostrations', upon which stood what was described as 'the king-idol of Ireland'; whose personal name is variously given as 'Crom Cruaich' or 'Cenn Cruaich'. These names are most probably nicknames, given in scorn by the Christian writer: they long survived as 'Raw Head' and 'Bloody Bones'* in nursery folklore. The king-idol is described as being of gold,

---

* A mistranslation of *Crom* (which may mean 'maggot'), confused with *cnámh*, 'a bone'.

which we need not take literally, though it is quite within the bounds of possibility that it was gilded: and round it were twelve subordinate deities of stone—that is, not decorated with gilding, though they may have been painted. To this being human sacrifices were offered: and in holy zeal the saint destroyed the monument.[9] The constant tradition, told in Ireland as well as in England, of dances in connexion with these structures, seems to preserve a reminiscence of the rites which were there performed. We are told that the stones were originally persons, who were turned into stone because they danced a profane or improper dance, or because they danced upon a Sunday. The outer stone, in such tales, is identified with the piper who supplied the music.

There are not many Irish stone circles calling for special note in a general purview like the present. An extensive group of structures of this kind is to be found in the lands surrounding the lake called Loch Gur, some eight miles northward from Kilmallock, in Co. Limerick. Among them is one structure (here illustrated), not strictly a stone circle, but rather a circular space sunk in the summit of a mound, and having a number of stones lining its sides, with larger stones interspersed.* Such an enclosure might well have been an 'orchestra', in the Greek sense of the word—a place for ritual dances. The number of antiquities that have been found in the waters of Loch Gur strongly suggest that for some reason this little lake was sacred, and the recipient of votive gifts.[10]

Another stone circle of interest stands at Drumbeg, near Glandore, Co. Cork [11]; this has the peculiarity of being the only circle outside the Aberdeenshire area displaying the characteristic 'recumbent stone' of that region. The existence of this one specimen of a peculiar and very localized type of stone circle, far away from the region to which it is otherwise peculiar, cannot be without significance: but there is not yet sufficient knowledge of this

* It should be observed that this monument has undergone a certain amount of restoration, to what extent is not quite clear. See Sir Bertram Windle's paper, referred to in the notes.

FIG. 14A.—ALIGNMENT AT BARACHAURAN, NEAR DONOUGHMORE, CO. CORK

FIG. 14B.—CIRCULAR STRUCTURE BESIDE LOCH GUR, CO. LIMERICK

obscure period available to enable us to determine what that significance may be.

Whether the pentarchic division of the country was or was not established, in a rudimentary form, during the Halberd Period, it may be taken as certain that it was the basis of government during the Sword Period. The country was divided into five independent kingdoms, corresponding more or less to the provinces of Ulster, Connacht, Munster, and North and South Leinster. On the throne of each of these kingships there sat a despotic priest-king, whose godhead gave a superhuman sanction to the terrors which he impressed upon his subjects. Only thus could the kings of North Leinster summon a whole province to build their tremendous tomb-sanctuaries. These monarchs, who had established themselves at Tara, a sanctuary of unknown antiquity, appear to have assumed autocratic powers beyond their brethren : later, when attempts were made to bring the whole island under one king, it was the palace sanctuary of Tara which was the centre of ambition. The king reigned there as the incarnation of a storm-and-vegetation god, whose presence secured good harvests and equable weather : his breach of the tabus which hedged his divinity, his lack of acceptability for one reason or another to the gods, was followed by failure in the harvests of sea and land, storms, blights, and pestilences.

Thus, certain apparently insignificant facts, first observed by Walther Bremer—who, during the short nine months which Fate permitted him to control the National Collection of Irish Antiquities, made an indelible impression on the study of Irish Archaeology—acquire a momentous importance. There is a sudden halt, about the middle of the Bronze Age ; a dislocation in the continuity of civilization. After this, previous conditions are reversed. Ireland has been an exporter : now she becomes an importer. She no longer holds a dominating position in the development of North European culture : she becomes a learner, not a teacher. While possibly less importance may be attached now than formerly to the Montelius classification of bronze-age material into five more or less rigid pigeon-holes, it is a convenient method of stating the fact, that Montelius's Fourth Period has practically no independent existence in Ireland.

The more closely these facts are considered, the more clearly are they seen to be the straws which indicate the blowing, not of a wind but of a tornado. They speak of a destroying invasion by hosts from oversea—beyond all reasonable doubt from Britain—and a consequent destruction of the civilization, such as it was, of the Halberd-People.

The technical skill, which the Halberd-People had acquired during their domination of the country, was pressed into the service of their new masters, and applied to the manufacture of new types of objects, based upon foreign models. The socketed hatchet-head was certainly imported, for it shows no evidence of local evolution: so, unquestionably, were the spear-head, of which some beautiful examples have been found in the country, and the sword. The spear-head is a derivation from the dagger, and needs the intermediate tanged dagger of the type called by the name of 'Arreton Down' to explain its evolution: as this is not an Irish form, the evolution must have taken place outside the country. The socketed hatchet-head usually betrays its origin by having curved lines upon it, derived from the outlines of the flanges of the 'winged hatchet-head' out of which it has developed: as these are not found in Irish specimens, the development must have taken place elsewhere, and the Irish specimens must have been modelled upon importations which did not happen to display this characteristic. That the objects, once made, were imitated locally there can be no question: it is amply proved by the moulds in stone or in clay which have come to light in various places throughout the country.

Even in gold-work, which of all branches of industry might have been expected to preserve native traditions of craftsmanship, there is an abrupt introduction of a foreign technique—repoussé ornamentation. The gorgets,

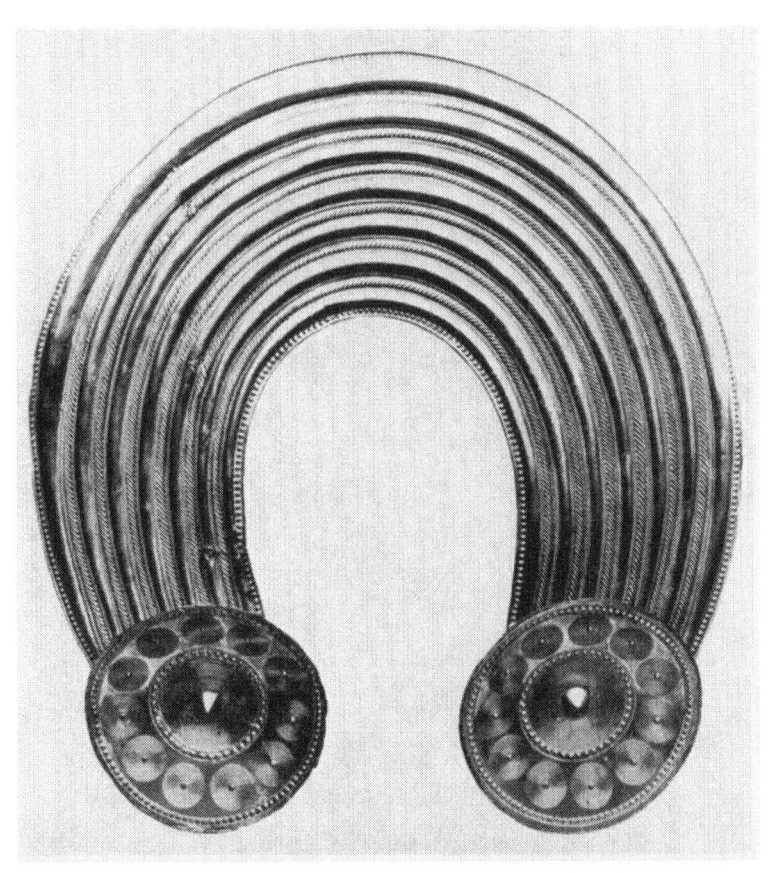

FIG. 15.—GORGET FROM GLENINSHEEN, CO. CLARE

with circular discs attached to their tips,* and the bowl, long ago lost, found on the Devil's Bit Mountain and once celebrated as an 'Ancient Irish Crown',[12] are not works executed in a native style, though the artificers who manufactured them may have been natives. Their ornamentation, wonderfully well-executed combinations of minute knobs, made by hammering sheet gold into the hollows of a mould, links them to the objects from the gold-find at Messingwerk in Germany. The actual forms are not Germanic; they are based on the native traditions of the lunula and the round-based pot, examples of which were doubtless common enough to serve as models. But the technique and the ornamentation are certainly foreign, and the usurpation of this important element in the native civilization is one more indication of the subjection of the country to foreign domination and influence.

Against these we cannot set a single export, except perhaps in one department only, where Ireland seems to have succeeded in maintaining a monopoly. The large curved bronze trumpets, belonging to the very end of the Bronze Age, which have been found over a wide area in Europe, appear to be of Irish manufacture. In Europe the finds are made singly—one trumpet here, one there. In Ireland, they are found in groups, apparently relics of the stocks-in-trade of artificers.[13] But apart from these objects, the thriving export trade, and the cultural domination which the Halberd-People had enjoyed, were destroyed.

The Sword-People had come with an invincible energy, and had subdued the land to themselves. They had established a complete social system, and had built their vast tumuli. But they reckoned without the climate. It was deteriorating annually during the whole time of their occupation, sapping their vitality, and reducing them to impotence. After building New Grange they never did anything else: their stone circles are trumpery affairs, in

* The fine specimen here illustrated (fig. 15), discovered in 1932, is especially remarkable for the delicate stitching with gold wire whereby the discs are secured to the body of the ornament.

comparison with those still extant in the land of their origin. The climate had not quite reached its worst when the Iron Men came in their turn : that was to happen somewhere about 150 years later. But it had already done its worst upon the Men of the Sword, and proud, savage, uncultured bullies though they were, they collapsed before the untainted blood of the small body of invaders who next appear on the stage.

CHAPTER IV

THE MEN OF IRON

ONCE again, the fatal curse of the gold-fields threw Ireland into confusion. The Men of the Sword had turned the world of the Halberd-Folk upside down, to compass their possession. But the doom of the Sword-Men had been writ one day, centuries before, in some far-off land; when a meteor fell, and when an unknown genius discovered that it contained a strange metal which, 'after much toil', as Homer expresses it, could be worked into serviceable weapons. Bronze swords could subdue the trumpery halberd: but bronze cannot stand against iron. 'Son of Ali', said an Arab chief to another, who dropped his useless lance before the cannon of Napoleon, 'dost *thou* yield to these infidels?' 'The Son of Ali cannot swim in Hell with a stick', said the other. Even so might the humbled tyrants of the Sword-People have expressed their resignation, as they fell before the flashing iron blades of the tall, fair-haired newcomers, who landed one fateful day in or about the fourth century B.C. And the 'sword of light', the possession which made the giants of the fairy-tales invincible, was added on that day of strife to the body of folklore which, in future years, Sword-Folk slaves were to teach to the children committed by their conquerors to their charge. For the giant, in spite of his brutality and cunning, is always defeated in the end: the hero, the little man, always succeeds in stealing the sword of light, and in cutting off its lawful owner's head. The children, pretty innocents, never dreamt that the slaves who fashioned for their amusement these delightful tales out of the common stock of folklore, were uttering dark parables

—outlets for the hopeless hatred of a slave. The ogre with the invincible sword was the omnipotent lord and master whom the children called 'father': the diminutive hero was the squat-figured slave's conception of himself, forced to tasks, which, if not so outrageously impossible as the stories represented, were no less galling and repugnant: while the princess whom the hero carried off in the end— she stood for the children themselves, over whom the slave gloated ghoulishly even as he bespelled them with his imaginings.

This invasion introduces us immediately to that nightmare of ethnology, archaeology, and, we may add, politics, the Celtic problem. Was this invasion a 'Celtic' invasion? And what is the meaning of this question?

The word 'Celtic' is derived from Greco-Latin literary sources, and presumably came to the writers who have recorded it, by some now irrecoverable channel, from certain of the people so designated. But we cannot read into it any more than a vague geographical significance. For the ancient writers it meant nothing more than the barbarians who lived in certain regions of Central and Northern Europe. The extraordinary contradictions between the statements about the Celts, made by different ancient writers, are enough to show the misty lack of science in their use of these and similar quasi-ethnic terms:[1] such words are void of scientific significance, and incapable of conveying any exact ethnological information.

In the regions which 'Celts' are said to have inhabited, linguistic survivals such as place-names show that languages of a certain clearly defined group were spoken, for which languages the name 'Celtic' may be appropriately used. They belong to the Indo-European family, and are distinguished from other branches of that family by certain peculiarities, notably the total rejection of the sound of P. This happens with the mechanical regularity of a typescript, executed on a machine in which that letter happens to be broken: and it may well have had a mechanical cause. Possibly the prehistoric people, among whom these languages first began to develop, mutilated their teeth (like

THE MEN OF IRON 77

the Aboriginal Australians) or their lips (like the Botocudos) in such a way as to render difficult or impossible the pronunciation of a voiceless labial sound. However that may be, one subdivision of the family afterwards recovered the sound of P, as an equivalent of the primitive Indo-European Q, while the other subdivision kept the Q; thereby introducing the further complication of P-Celts (Brythonic, Welsh) and Q-Celts (Goidelic, Irish).

No one *knows* where these languages originated. It has been conjectured that their cradle was somewhere between the head-waters of the Rhine and the Danube, which rivers have Celtic names (D'Arbois de Jubainville [2]); or further north, somewhere on the southern shore of the Baltic (Camille Jullien [3]). Nor can any one say what the ethnological relationships of the people who developed these languages may have been. One thing, however, is certain; that nowhere in the world can be found a better illustration of the independence of language and race. As many different racial types are found, in ancient and in modern times, among native 'Celtic' speakers as are to be found over all Europe, among speakers of other languages.

In short, there is no such thing as a recognizable 'Celt'. There is a group of languages; and there is a certain cultural complex associated with them. But these environmental marks of 'Celticity' have been imposed from without, during a long course of centuries, upon a number of ethnologically different communities: and they have not affected the racial character of those who are clothed in them. The Celticization of Northern Europe is due ultimately to a military expansion on the part of the tribe, whatever it was, among whom the characteristics of Celticity developed.

Their early history is obscured by their later developments. We may quote in this connexion the admirable statement of the facts by Georg Kraft.[4] 'The cradleland of the Teutons, southern Scandinavia, was never occupied by any foreign nation; in the case of the Celts no comparable nuclear region can be identified. Almost everywhere they have been expelled from their seats by the

Teutons. Even where they have succeeded in maintaining their purity, they occupy regions naturally designed as refuges, where they are probably mixed with older layers of exiles. Moreover, they only took possession of the major part of their territory, including northern France and Britain, in the centuries immediately preceding our era.'

The chief strongholds of the Celtic languages are now Great Britain and Ireland—the only strongholds indeed; for Breton, the last Celtic language to be spoken on the mainland of the Continent, is not a survival of the ancient Continental Celtic languages, but an importation, in historic times, from Great Britain. In spite of this, and although in the time of Julius Caesar South Britain, and probably most of Ireland, were inhabited by Celtic speakers, these islands and their inhabitants are *never* called 'Celtic' by ancient observers. To them they are the 'Pretannic' or 'Pictish' Islands; a word of which 'Britannic' or 'British' is a mere corruption. This being so, we must next ask, how and when were the 'Pictish' islands Celticized?

The problem is complicated by the Goidelic-Brythonic dichotomy. There is no unambiguous evidence for Goidelic in South Britain, other than what might have been introduced in historic times by colonists from Ireland. That country has certainly been the source of the Gaelicization of North Britain. Likewise there is no unambiguous evidence for Brythonic of non-British origin in Ireland—unless it be such a word as *Manapioi*, recorded in Ptolemy's map as the name of a people living on the East Coast. Till quite recently the problem seemed perfectly simple. The great invasion of the Beaker-People, from the Rhineland into Britain, at the beginning of the British Bronze Age, introduced the Celtic (Brythonic) speech along with the Bronze culture. Ireland remained Pictish-speaking till the iron-age invasion, which introduced the Goidelic speech from somewhere on the Continent, along with the iron culture of the Second La Tène Period.

External history seemed to favour this reading of the

indications. Those who developed the Celtic culture may have been receptive among their neighbours, and have been the first in Northern Europe to acquire a knowledge of the properties of iron. Indeed, it would appear that they somehow appropriated a monopoly of the art of the smith for Central Europe, as did the Philistines for Palestine: and that from the very beginning they realized the military advantage to be derived from this acquisition. We have no records by which we can follow their expansion step by step—but it is clear that no sooner had they mastered the art of making iron weapons, than they began a career of conquest almost comparable with that of Rome in later centuries. Almost; but not quite. They made no effort to weld their conquests into an empire; rather did they break into groups, each group dominating, and covering with the veneer of its language, religion, and civilization, the separate peoples and tribes whom they had subdued. Each of these, forcibly turned 'Celtic', retained an individuality, and maintained all their traditional hostilities, until the time came for the empire of Rome to devour them.

Some great movement must have taken place in the third and fourth centuries B.C. to disturb the strange amorphous Celtic world that was thus created. For we find them marching through Italy and sacking Rome. Shortly afterwards we find them pressing into Greece, and, after an abortive raid upon Delphi, establishing the Celtic colony of Galatia—the only Celtic community outside Europe in the ancient world. And about the same time, as an incident in the same course of events (according to the simple theory here stated), they first entered and occupied Ireland.

But the actual facts are by no means so simple as would be postulated by such a theory. It assumes an unbroken Bronze Age for Ireland: it also assumes the total absence from Ireland of the earlier iron-age phases, Hallstatt and La Tène I. But both assumptions are no longer admissible. We have seen in the preceding chapters that there is evidence for an abrupt break in the middle of the Irish Bronze Age: and a recent discovery in the North seems to be the cloudy semblance of a man's hand rising above the horizon, ultimately destined to tear away the second assumption.

The excavations at present (1934) in progress in the caves at Ballintoy, Co. Antrim, have yielded a quantity of early iron-age pottery of Hallstatt aspect, similar to those found in late Hallstatt sites in England. This at least proves cultural infiltration, if nothing else. Associated with this pottery, and of similar clay and technique, was the upper part of a roughly modelled female figure (fig. 16). The eyes and the mouth are indicated. Above the eye there is a hole, possibly a steam-vent, to prevent the clay from cracking when fired. The breasts are very conspicuous: the arms and the lower part of the body are broken away. This figure links in character with the mother-goddess figures found in Danubian sites, such as Vinča and Butmir; but it is surprising to find it in association with a late Hallstatt deposit. The cult doubtless lingered in outlying regions; the name of twin mountains called 'The Paps of Danu', *mater deorum hibernensium* according to the old glossator Cormac, seems to suggest that the personification of Ireland is no mere modern sentiment, but that her soil itself was regarded as being actually the body of the universal Mother.[5]

In the light of the Ballintoy discovery, the occasional Hallstatt objects which had already been recorded in Ireland take on a new aspect, and call for a revised consideration.[6] They have hitherto been looked upon as chance imports, having as little bearing upon the history of civilization in the country as a Chinese ornament, such as may be found in any modern house in Dublin. But they cannot now be dismissed so lightly. True, a sword, or a bracelet, or any object of metal, might be imported at any time. The East-Anglian disc-brooch, found at Togherstown on Uisnech Hill in Co. Westmeath, means no more than that a certain East Anglian happened to pass that way, and fell among thieves, or otherwise lost his property. But pottery has always a different story to tell. A metal object could travel from hand to hand between

FIG. 16.—POTTERY FIGURE FROM BALLINTOY, CO. ANTRIM

Spain and China. An impressive illustration of this would be presented by the two golden torque earrings, which certainly look more like Irish products than anything else, found by Sir Flinders Petrie in excavations near Gaza, Palestine, if we could find some way of surmounting the chronological perplexities presented by objects, made in Ireland about 1200–1000 B.C., travelling to Palestine, and becoming embedded in strata dated to 2000–1500 B.C.[7] But a pottery object would be practically certain to get broken on the way. No one imports common pottery; but the makers of a particular style of pottery can be imported, so that any peculiar form of pottery is always symptomatic of a colony of the people associated with that form.

Hence we cannot any longer deny the possibility of an indigenous Hallstatt occupation of the country. In fact, we have as yet such a scanty knowledge of the hidden things which await discovery beneath the soil of Ireland, that we are not entitled to make any categorical statement whatsoever about the early inhabitants of the country, without large reservations. And we are at present in that phase of scientific development where each new discovery increases our reservations rather than our knowledge. But for the sake of clearing our ideas, and to provide a starting-point for future research, we may venture to set down a tentative statement of the conclusions to which the new facts seem to point.

(i) At the beginning of the Bronze Age (say $2000 \pm x$ B.C.) Ireland and Cornwall were peopled by a Spanish colony (the Halberd-People); South Britain, excluding Cornwall, by a Rhineland colony (the Beaker-People). The former were not Celtic, nor yet Indo-European, in their speech: the latter, we may assume were Celtic. But were they Brythonic or Goidelic? The prevalence of the Brythonic dialect throughout South Britain would *a priori* incline us to the former alternative.

(ii) In the middle of the Bronze Age (say $1000 \pm x$ B.C.) the Sword-People subdued Ireland. As their greatest monuments, erected at their first entry and in their first energy, lie in the vulnerable region on the East Coast; as they appear to have been brachycephalic; the only reasonable view of their origin is that they were an invasion from South Britain, and if not actually identical with, at least cognate with the Beaker-People at a later stage of cultural development. This at once gets an enormous difficulty out of the way: why did the historians represent the *Tūatha Dē Danann*, who are beyond all possibility of question personifications of the Celtic pantheon, as being a race preceding, and *hostile* to, the 'Milesian' or iron-age 'Celtic' invasion? The two groups of invaders should have worked in partnership from the first, even if the gods had been euhemerized into men. It follows that it was they who introduced the Celtic speech into Ireland. But as the predominant Celtic speech of Ireland is, and always has been, Goidelic, we must revise our conclusions as to the Brythonism of the Bronze Age in South Britain; and attribute the later Brythonization of that country to the influence of the comparatively high culture of the Continental Belgae. This is perfectly reasonable, for even a slight superiority, in associated commercial or cultural advantages, is sufficient to tilt the scale in favour of one language as against another.

(iii) During the domination of the Sword-Folk, early iron-age culture filtered into Ireland as it had done into England, and early iron-age colonies established themselves here and there: but their history, extent, connexions, and influence are matters for future research, being at present quite outside our knowledge.

(iv) In the course of the La Tène II phase of the West European Iron Age, Ireland was again invaded, by the 'Men of Iron': and we must now consider who these were.

On the theory usually held, these were 'Celts'. But is that sound? Their tall stature and fair complexions would lead to the conclusion that in blood, at least, they were Teutonic. These racial elements remained uncontaminated for long enough to establish the tradition that they were the hall-marks of aristocracy. But so far as we can judge, in our as yet imperfect knowledge of Irish ethnology ancient and modern, the Teutonic *ensemble* of racial features is not conspicuously predominant in the country. All the races that have ever inhabited the land are now mingled together inextricably; the facts, as we have them, are quite consistent with the last invasion being that of a small military expedition, of pure Teutonic blood, who entered the country insufficiently provided with women; and who made up the deficiency by taking to themselves women of the conquered inhabitants, after they had completed their conquest.

The inevitable result followed. Whatever may have been the language of the invaders, the children grew up chattering the speech of their mothers and of the slaves who attended upon them; and so the speech of the conquered Sword-Folk persisted, and that of the conquerors was forgotten in a generation. So far as race is concerned, this so-called 'Celtic' invasion of Ireland was just as much Teutonic as the Saxon invasion of England. And it is quite possible to maintain that the invaders were actually Teutons in speech. If there be anything in the equation that has been suggested between *Fomorian* (the name traditionally given by the aborigines of Ireland to the raiders from oversea who harried them, mingling them inextricably with traditions of demons and wizards) and some form of the geographical term which we call *Pomerania*: if there be anything in another possible equation between the name of *Conaing*, a Fomorian leader, and some form of the old Teutonic *koninga*, 'a king'[8]: if we may interpret 'Heremon', the name given traditionally by Irish historians to the leader of the 'Celtic' invasion, as a corruption of some form of the Teutonic name *Herrmann*: we should be obliged to infer that so far from Ireland being naturally a Celtic country, it would really have been the first land of Western Europe to be Teutonized, if only the invaders had brought a sufficiency of women with them. Eremon was accompanied by his brother Eber, which is straightforward Teutonic for 'a boar'—compare the totemistic horse-names of the mythical invaders of England, Hengist and Horsa. Is this the explanation of the statement that these invaders of Ireland called or considered it *Muc-inis*, 'Pig-island'?

The absence of women is easily accounted for. The invaders must have come a long way—from somewhere east of the great 'Celtic' block which then occupied the north of the continental mass; but sufficiently near to its eastern border to have learned something of the art of iron working. The traditions of the immigration, enshrined in the *Book of Invasions*, give prominence to voyages of extravagant length. 'We shall have no rest', one of their 'druids' is made to say, 'till we shall reach Ireland, a place farther away than Scythia, three hundred years hence.' We can cut out the picturesque exaggeration, and still be left with the conception of a long voyage, in the tiny ships of the time, over trackless seas. On such an Odyssey there would be no room except for the warriors themselves, whose faces were fixed on the Land of their Golden Dreams, beneath the western horizon.

This reconstruction has many advantages over the earlier, simpler, but no longer sufficient explanation of the linguistic phenomena. If a Pre-Celtic language had been spoken throughout Ireland down to a date so late as the third or fourth century B.C., a very complete conquest would have been necessary to destroy it so thoroughly. It should have left many traces in the later speech, and especially in place-names. And such a conquest should also have its reflection in a very complete change of culture.

But there is, in fact, no such change. The persistence of bronze-age types, the extreme poverty of La Tène relics, show that in culture the intruders made very little change in the population—except possibly to depress them economically. We cannot safely argue from the particular to the general; but we can see a symbol of the change in the two contrasted cauldrons here depicted. The one (fig. 17) is the splendid late bronze-age specimen of 'Celtic' date but doubtless of aboriginal workmanship, for many years in private possession in Co. Tyrone, and now happily added to the National Collection. It is an unusually fine example of the remarkable type of objects,

FIG. 17.—BRONZE CAULDRON, CO. TYRONE

recently studied with thoroughness by Mr. E. T. Leeds.[9] The other (fig. 18) is a vessel of the same shape scooped out of a block of poplar-wood. It is obviously an attempt to copy the bronze type, made by some one who could not afford such a luxury; although (as is especially shown by the handles) he had a very considerable measure of technical facility.

Technical—but not artistic. He tried to decorate his handiwork, making a heroic but unsuccessful attempt to imitate a bit of La Tène ornament that had fallen under his notice.

Incidentally we may remark that the preservative quality of peat has prevented numerous wooden objects from falling into decay; and that we have in consequence a fuller insight into the domestic equipment of the folk than would otherwise be available. The carpentry is crude, on the whole. Vessels and other objects are hacked out of blocks of wood. There is little or no evidence of skill in joinery: even when a four-legged table was made, such as was found at Killygarvan, Co. Tyrone, in 1844, the whole is cut out, legs and all, from a single piece of firwood. True, the legs were only 6 in long, but this does not diminish the primitiveness of the technique.

These two cauldrons therefore show us just what the linguistic phenomena would lead us to expect; a population that had suffered misfortune, but had kept to its old culture and its old language. The archaeological evidence therefore shows us the population of Ireland in the following strata:

(1) A small body of Teutonic military conquerors, who have introduced iron, *but no art*; who have made themselves landlords, and marry native women, so that their descendants lose the environmental marks of Teutonism (religion, language, etc.).

(2) The Sword-Folk (Goidelic) now deprived of their independence, but speaking their Goidelic language, and maintaining their bronze-age culture with very little change.

(3) A few stray artists, here and there, presumably

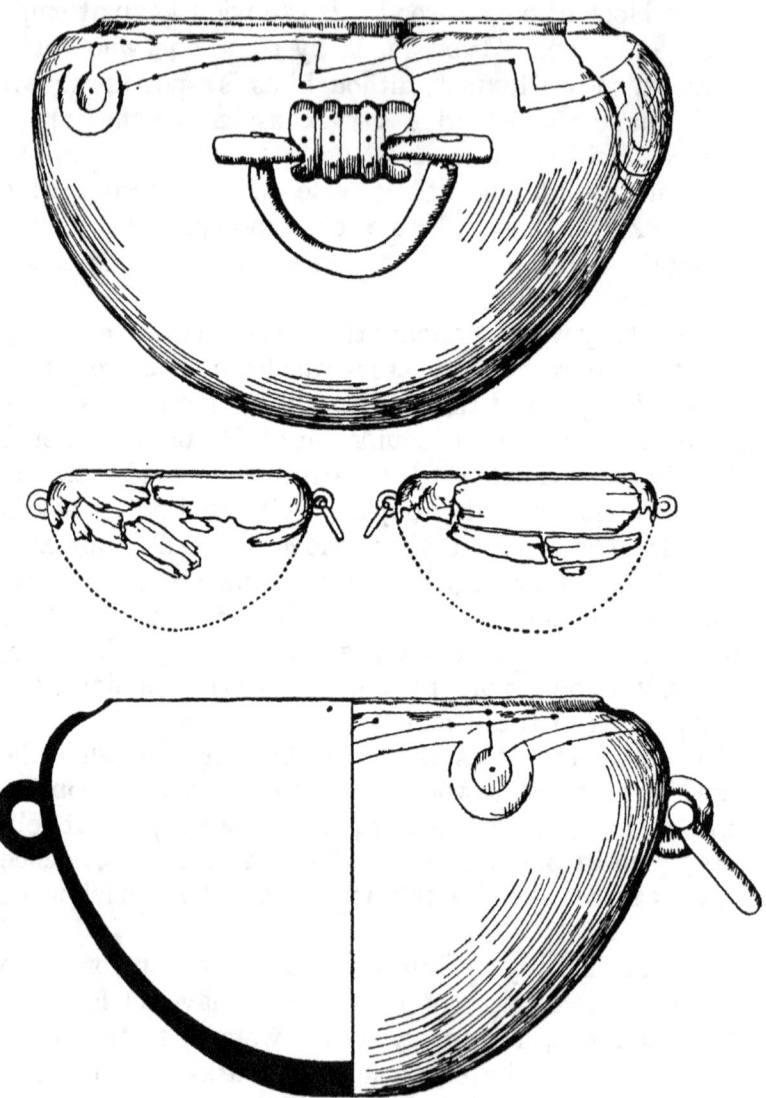

FIG. 18.—WOODEN CAULDRON, ALTARTATE, CO. MONAGHAN

coming out of Gaul or Britain, who ply their craft in the country (Turoe Stone, etc.) but who exercise singularly little influence on the local culture.

(4) The aboriginal Halberd-Folk (Pictish) serfs, and still deprived of all civil rights: perhaps still speaking their aboriginal language, which survived in the non-Gaelicized parts of Scotland. There are very few Pictish place-names surviving even in Scotland, a fact which has been used as an argument in favour of Pictish having been a Celtic tongue. But the real explanation is quite simple. To Gaelic and Norse speakers, Pictish (besides being the language of a despised people) was difficult both in construction and in pronunciation. Even the missionary Colum Cille was obliged to make his communications through an interpreter. Mark Twain's friends, on their tour in Palestine, substituted words adapted from their own speech for what they called the 'dreadful foreign names' of people and places which they found in possession. The English in Ireland, in the time of Charles II, did the same thing. And so did the colonists of Scotland.

Thus there are important differences between this iron-age invasion and that of the Sword-Folk. The latter was a colonization, starting from the country now called England: the former was a military expedition, starting from some eastern European source. But there are also certain notable analogies; both of them were mere single episodes in much more extensive shuffles of the pieces on the European chessboard.

The Iron invasion of Ireland coincides, as we have seen, with a great unrest among the Celtic peoples. Likewise, at the time of the incursion of the Sword-Men, we find Dorians and Achaeans in turn pressing down upon the bronze-age Pelasgians (we express no opinion as to where they came from, a point much in dispute, but here irrelevant): and extending their conquests into Asia Minor. The Trojan War is one of the incidents of this revolution, which utterly destroyed the ancient civilization of the near East, and left the stage clear for the glorious development of Classical Greece.

Roughly some eight centuries intervene between these two periods of unrest. Roughly again, another eight centuries forward sees once more a time of disturbance, when the Teutonic tribes began their complex wanderings over Europe; when the Roman Empire fell; when, once again, an ancient world was utterly destroyed and the stage left clear for its successor.

Can we trace these eight-hundred-year epochs further backward and forward? Perhaps we can. Going back eight hundred years behind the Men of the Sword, we come to somewhere about 2000 B.C., which cannot be far off from the beginning of the establishment of the Men of the Halberd.

Only the seaboard of the land available can set limits to the movements of peoples induced by some great upheaval —for it stands to reason that if tribe A crowds in upon the territory of tribe B, then tribe B will in its turn be forced to elbow out tribe C, and tribe C to treat tribe D in the same way—and so on, till the ocean stops all further advance and the impulse exhausts itself. All this takes time: and it is quite legitimate to regard the raid made by the Hittites upon Akkad, the invasion of Crete which brought to an end the early palaces of Knossos and of Phaestos, and the great swoop of the Hyksos, the (probably Arab) 'Shepherd Kings', upon Egypt, all of which events happened between 2000 and 1800 B.C., as being local aspects of a universal disturbance of Europe and of the neighbouring regions; and to treat the invasion of Ireland by the Men of the Halberd as one of the minor incidents of the same commotion.

If, on the other hand, we come forward to a time eight hundred years after the wanderings of the Teutonic Peoples, we arrive at the extraordinary outburst known as the Crusades. The ostensible religious inspiration of the Crusaders did no more than to give their actions an external form and orientation: in some shape the explosion would have taken place, even had there been no Holy Places, and no infidels to wrest them from. Social causes—an overcrowded Europe, desire for plunder, desire for new lands, desire for expansion, ambitions of barons thwarted by established kings—these less lovely motives lurked behind the religious fervour; and, as we trace the tragic story from the beginning to the end, we see them coming more and more unashamedly into prominence. In any case, critical history has cast the picturesque figure labelled 'Peter the Hermit' out of the realms of actuality into the dreamlands of folklore.[10]

If we come forward another eight hundred years, more or less, we find ourselves in the very middle of the contemporary chaos. These accumulated experiences teach us to anticipate that some time about 2700 A.D., the tidal wave of an Armageddon will sweep over the earth once more: once more to demolish the castles of sand, wherein poor puny children of men like ourselves; helpless, like ourselves, in the grip of the transcendent, ineffable forces around them; forgetful, as we were, that here we have no continuing city; shall have lodged, as we did, their treasures and their dreams.

This periodicity cannot be without a natural cause. It must be bound up with other periodicities, the existence of which has only in recent years begun to be suspected, and the causes of which are as yet unknown. There are weather or climatic periodicities, which at intervals produce long seasons of drought—notably on the plains of Turkistan, whose nomad inhabitants are forced by want, when their own pastures fail, to burst into the more favoured lands of their neighbours. Some one has said (and there is a great measure of truth in the arresting proposition), that if the Great Wall of China had never been built, Rome would never have fallen. For this wall prevented the eastward trek of the wanderers of Turkistan: these therefore pressed westward on the Goths, then dwellers on the shores of the Black Sea. The latter in their turn were forced still further to the west, with the disastrous consequences for the Roman Empire which are recorded in History. There are also population periodicities, and vegetation periodicities; and these are not necessarily synchronous. The failure of the potato in Ireland in

1846-7 coincided with an over-population far beyond the economic possibilities of the country : its history gives us what we may call a microcosmic picture of the immense world-movements, which these uncontrollable and incomprehensible pulsations automatically produce.[11]

In this and the preceding chapters we have ascribed the successive invasions of Ireland to gold-lust. This is certainly part of the story ; but not the whole. The invaders had to go somewhere. Forces which they could not see, of which they were not even aware, had driven them irresistibly out of their homes, wherever these may have been : and in choosing a new habitation, they naturally turned their faces in directions where they imagined that unexploited wealth awaited them.

Coming into Ireland, the Men of Iron carried out the same individualistic policy as characterized the 'Celtic' conquests. It is quite unnecessary to say that to make 'Ireland a Nation', out of the welter of kinglets that they found there before them, never so much as entered the heads of the invaders. On the contrary ; their own legends of their conquest tell us, that so soon as they had possessed themselves of the country, the two brothers who led the expedition quarrelled, and nothing would satisfy them but a partition of the land into two kingdoms. This may or may not have a basis in historic truth : in any case it is clear that the invaders adopted the fivefold kingdoms as they found them, and made them their own. This political division is well established when we get our first glimpse at actual history, divested of its garb of folklore : so well established, that it was never completely abolished except for one moment, at the beginning of the eleventh century, in the hands of the masterful usurper Brian. It is most likely that they also found ready to their hands, and adopted with little or no modification, the old *tūath*-communities, the political units of early Irish social life, and divided these among themselves. Each leader appropriated a *tūath*, ruled it, and established a family which thenceforth controlled it and pocketed its rents. The Norman Barons—who were of the same

THE MEN OF IRON 91

Teutonic blood as themselves—did precisely the same thing, when their turn came. They also took the old *tūath* lands, each one for himself, ruled them, and established a family which thenceforth controlled it and appropriated its rents. Thus it comes about that these aboriginal land-divisions, usually labelled with a Celtic or Celticized family name, remain on the map of Ireland under the generic term 'baronies'.

For be it remembered that none of these invasions were complete recolonizations. They were essentially acquisitive: the people as well as the country were captured and enslaved. The ancient curse of the Gibeonites fell upon the Halberd-Folk when the Sword-Folk conquerors seized their territories. The Sword-Folk lorded it over them—haughty tyrants, perhaps making even a terrifying claim of divinity. Then came the Men of Iron. They too seized the land, possibly at no such great cost of blood as in the earlier conquest. All that they had to do was to clear out the Sword-Folk aristocrats, and possess themselves of their palaces: the enslaved Halberd-People merely changed masters.

In Central Europe, during the Stone and Bronze Ages, those who had to protect themselves from their enemies established their dwellings on platforms supported by piles driven into lake-bottoms. Such are the famous lake-dwellings of Switzerland, our chief source of information on bronze-age civilization in Europe. In Switzerland this practice ceased with the Bronze Age—the settlement of La Tène, though on a Swiss lake-shore, is not a lake-dwelling—but it was maintained along the north coast of Europe, in Holland and Friesland, where the heaps of habitation debris called *Werfen* and *Terpen* survive, to tell of the semi-maritime existence of the Cauci, which has been described for us, from personal observation, by Pliny.[12] Cauci were also established on the eastern coast of Ireland, according to Ptolemy: it is possible that these people were the connecting link which brought the practice into Ireland.

At the beginning of the new regime, the climate was so extremely moist that most of the lakes were too deep for this kind of construction. We have no lake-dwellings from the beginning of the occupation of the Iron Men: the earliest is not older than about 100 B.C. and may be later. But as the Iron-Men landlords intensified their domination, they found in the contrivance of lake-dwellings a much-needed safeguard.

These were not pile-dwellings, as in Switzerland; they were houses, erected upon islands. The islands were formed artificially, if the lake did not happen to possess them by nature; they were made of earth and stones, heaped upon a wickerwork raft. This raft was at first set floating on the lake surface and gradually sank to the bottom, under the accumulation of material heaped upon it; there it made a footing, which prevented the material from sinking into the muddy bottom of the lake.[13]

Like the huge tumuli of the Sword-Folk, the lake-dwellings of the Men of Iron testify to the limitless slave labour available. To make a single house for one man and his family, many boatloads of earth and stones had to be ferried out to the selected site and cast overboard, till the heap rose high above the surface of the lake. It must have been galling for the Halberd-People to have been compelled to tear up their fathers' tombstones to make a grave-sanctuary for their Sword-Folk master: it must have been no less galling for a later generation of the same unhappy people to be compelled thus to construct a fortress which was intended to protect their master against themselves. For as their master's antitype and kinsman, the Norman baron who was to come in a later century, built a castle to keep his serfs at a safe distance, so the Man of Iron built for himself a stronghold, from behind which he issued the commands which must be obeyed. Here he lived, feasted, and listened to his bard chanting the tales of his ancestors. From here he sallied forth to battle, or to chase the wild boar whose tusks are among the most frequent objects found in excavating a lake-dwelling. Now, more than before, the contrast between the 'haves' and the 'have-nots' was deepened and intensified.

In these days of ours there is much talk about the

THE MEN OF IRON 93

desirability of establishing a Gaelic State. By all means let such a State be established: but let us know precisely what the expression means. To obtain that knowledge we must eschew the pretty but profitless books, which flatter the popular vanity by leaving out everything unpleasant. We must delve deep into those incomprehensible and forbidding documents, the Brehon law-tracts: and what do we find there ? A country divided up among a limited number of land-owners, whose possession of a retinue of tenants confers nobility upon them, and whose land is farmed by those tenants as cattle ranches. These tenants are serfs, to some extent different from their masters in speech and in religion. They are deprived of all civil rights. They pay an annual rental of 33⅓ per cent of the value of the farm stock which they administer—an extortion surely beyond that of any rack-renter of modern times; and there are methods of extorting that rent which would hardly be permissible in these latter days. Their masters—or, to speak more accurately, their owners—have an almost absolute judicial authority over them, and enjoy a practically complete control of all their actions. They have full right to conscript them for military service. In fact, as we read on—or, rather, as we excavate further, for the study of the Brehon law-tracts is much more of a slow and toilsome excavation than a perusal—we realise with astonishment that the social order which these documents contemplate and approve is nothing more or less than the social order which has been denounced from a thousand platforms as 'landlordism'.[14]

History records one great revolt of the serfs, which seems to have been accomplished with much bloodshed: but the details are hopelessly overlaid with folklore, though it is possible to gather that the serfs gained little or no advantage. For it was impressed upon their superstitious souls that the existing state of affairs was in accordance with the will of the gods, who punished with drought and pestilence the land that flouted them: and against the gods, who can fight ?

The iron-wielding invaders had need to exploit the lands

which they acquired : for in another direction they had met with cruel disillusion. Ireland's traditional wealth in gold had drawn them on : and when they arrived, the gold was no longer forthcoming. Reckless exploitation of the auriferous gravels, during the Bronze Age, had all but exhausted the supply. The Sword-Folk had used it with lavish improvidence. Most of the existing gold ornaments are of the late bronze-age cupped-bracelet form, which seem to have been turned out by the gross, and which were conceivably used as a medium of currency. By the time the Iron Men came the gold was all gone : the number of iron-age gold ' finds ' made in the country can be counted on the fingers of one hand. The contrast is most impressive.

It is possible to weaken its absolute character by theoretical considerations, which are quite plausible, but must remain in the realms of theory because it is utterly impossible to prove them. The bronze-age gold which we possess consists of pieces which had been lost (dropped into bog-holes or the like). The hypothetical iron-age gold remained above ground, passed from hand to hand, and ultimately gravitated to the treasuries of the monasteries. There it was remodelled into shrines and other articles of ecclesiastical furniture, until it was taken away by Scandinavian plunderers ; and if by any chance these overlooked anything, it was finally captured, at the dissolution of the monasteries, by the minions of Henry VIII. But for all this we have no authority : the hard fact remains, that there is next to no evidence in tangible actuality for the use of gold during the pagan Iron Age. True, gold ornaments are frequently mentioned in romances, which began to take shape about this time—but romance is not necessarily reality. It is much more impressive than the numerous crucibles for melting metals, which have been found in the lake-dwellings—the dwellings of the persons for whose delectation these stories were first told—prove on analysis to have been used for the manipulation of bronze, not of gold.[15]

The only really valuable find of gold ornaments, belonging to the Iron Age, that has as yet been made in the country, is the hoard from Broighter, near Limavady, found in a raised-beach site about 5,000 ft inland from the nearest point of Loch Foyle. It was discovered about the beginning of the present century in deep ploughing operations; it passed through several hands, and has at last found its resting-place in the National Museum in Dublin. The objects are of such a heterogeneous nature that the most satisfactory explanation of the cache is that it was the hoard of a thief. Some one wearing a handsome torque —the finest gold ornament of the La Tène style of decoration in existence—had, likely enough, been murdered; in any case, his collar was torn from him, breaking a piece from the joining of the two halves. Some one had made for some religious purpose (to this we shall return) a golden model of a ship. Some lady had worn round her neck a couple of chains of plaited golden wire, that may have come from distant Alexandria. Our bandit had possessed himself of these things. Elsewhere he had captured a couple of torques—constructed, not as in the Bronze Age by twisting the golden bar, but by engraving a twist upon its surface and neatly laying a golden wire into the engraved line. A little golden model of a suspended cauldron had also been appropriated. Having buried his loot, the thief set out in search of further plunder, and, we may presume, met the fate which he had merited. The decoration of the collar is *repoussé*, on a flat ribbon of metal afterwards rolled into a cylinder. The manipulative skill far surpasses that shown in the later products of the Christian period, if we exclude one or two outstanding works such as the Ardagh Cup. The collar was in two halves; one point of contact was secured by a projecting T-head, shaped like the handle of a stop-cock, on one side, which fitted into a slot in the other side, and which locked when the collar was turned into position on the neck. To take the collar off, one of the halves had to be rotated through a right angle on the ' stop-cock ' as centre, after which the T-head could be pulled out through the slot. How the other point of contact was secured it is impossible to say; there we see only the two ragged ends which testify to the violence with which the owner of the collar, dead or alive, was compelled to part with it.

The other ornaments have already been frequently described, and we need not repeat the description here, especially as it is not altogether certain that they are of Irish manufacture. The plaited chains assuredly are not. As for the collar itself, its Irish provenance has been doubted, apparently on the ground that it is of an order of merit too high to be produced in the country. In the presence of the Turoe stone, however, there can be no question that there were persons (native or foreign) resident in Ireland capable of achieving distinction in the beautiful art of La Tène. The collar might have been carried into the country from anywhere, but the importation of a very heavy block of granite is much less probable.[16]

La Tène decoration has a character which makes it easily recognizable wherever it may be found. It is primarily of classical origin, the borrowed motives being modified as they pass through the hands of the Celtic workman. The *anthemion* pattern which decorates, with a lavish—almost a monotonous—exuberance, the temples, theatres, and other buildings, the painted vases and other works of art, bequeathed to us by Ancient Greece, is taken to pieces; and is remodelled upon a geometrical basis, recalling the spirals of late bronze-age designs. It is on this principle that La Tène art patterns are founded. They are a kind of cross between phyllomorphic (vegetable) and geometrical devices: sometimes they incline to the one, sometimes to the other. Never do they become completely realistic, based on specifically recognizable vegetable forms; on the other hand, only rarely do they become so thoroughly geometrical as to lose all suggestion of their vegetable inspiration.[17]

This form of ornament is associated with the second phase of the European Iron Age, which takes its name from the type station of La Tène on Lake Neuchâtel, where it happened first to come to light. It is spread over Western Europe, and extends to southern Scotland and north-western Ireland. Most unfortunately, only one adequately furnished La Tène habitation-site has as yet come to light in Ireland; and this has suffered from having been made a private collector's happy hunting-ground. Our knowledge of it and of its stratification is in consequence practically nothing. It was a lake-dwelling at Lisnacrochera in Co. Antrim, and yielded, among its most striking products, a series of bronze sword-scabbards, richly engraved with characteristic ornament.[18] But until another site of the same date and importance shall have been found, and judiciously excavated, we must be content to know much less of this phase of Irish archaeology than we ought to know.

The most obvious and most frequent character of this ornament is the lobe-shaped leaf. It is an expansion, at the end of a spiral or otherwise meandering line, and is evidently the development of a single petal, plucked from a Greek anthemion. Two such lobes may hook into one another, forming rudimentary spirals: these can be placed at the eye of double spirals formed by the linear stems upon which they are mounted, or the lobe-shaped leaf may itself be wound into a spiral coil. The stems of two or more such coils often unite, and at the point of union there is usually a fanciful little leaf-pattern of perfect simplicity but great charm.

Besides the spiral and the lobed leaf with its graceful curves, the La Tène artists made great use of compass-drawn circles: and perhaps more than any others they succeeded in giving to these hard and mechanical forms an artistic significance. *Concentric* circles were carefully avoided: but by placing groups of circles with different dispositions of the centres in symmetrical relation to one another, patterns of great beauty and complexity were formed.

We say 'in symmetrical relation'; but anything like formal symmetry was avoided. A balanced rhythm there certainly was; but not a mechanical identity between the two sides of the pattern. Indeed, from this point of view the La Tène designers surpassed, in the pure artistry of their products, even the highest achievements of the Christian artists. Form ruled supreme in the latter school of decorative work : everything is as carefully balanced as in that Dutch garden of fable, in which the gardener, having locked up a boy in one of the summer-houses for stealing apples, was obliged to incarcerate another boy in the corresponding summer-house in order to maintain the symmetry. But a La Tène pattern climbs like a spray of ivy, at its own sweet will, over the surface which it adorns ; yet there is nothing chaotic about its formlessness. The Turoe stone is a very striking illustration of this fact ; it stands on one of the highest peaks to which Irish art, throughout the ages, ever attained. Its two rivals, the stone at Castle Strange, Co. Roscommon, and that at Killycluggin in Co. Cavan—so far as we can form any conception of the latter monument, which has quite clearly been iconoclastically broken—cannot rival it in the skill and grace with which the great master to whom we owe it, made it a thing of beauty.[19]

It is indeed strange that as yet so little survives to tell us of the La Tène Period in Ireland. The La Tène Period stood at the beginning of modern Ireland. It was the time when the Gaelic language was beginning to develop its literature. It was the time when history, as opposed to legend, begins to dawn. And yet very few remains coming down from this period are certainly known —extraordinary few, if the iron-age invasion was really a Celtic invasion.

One thing is, however, clear. This phase of art must have filtered into Ireland from the Continent or Great Britain *after* the invasion of the Men of Iron, if there is anything in our suggestion that these came from a Teutonic region of Eastern Europe. For the art is essentially a West European art, and has no certain analogies in the region from which we derive the invaders.

One of the most extraordinary facts in connexion with some of the sites of the pagan Iron Age is the total absence of pottery. In the two great enclosures excavated by the Archaeological Exploration Committee of the Royal Irish

Academy on the Hill of Uisnech, Co. Westmeath, the date of which may be roughly fixed about A.D. 150–200, not a single scrap of pottery was found from end to end: and that, although the profusion of bones of cattle testified to extensive feasting. From every point of view this fact is inexplicable. It is difficult to see how so elementary an art, freely practised during the Bronze Age, could have become lost: it is difficult to see how so convenient a technical process could have been abandoned: it is difficult to imagine what substitute could have been found to take the place of the pottery vessels for cooking and feeding. Doubtless wooden platters might be used for the latter purpose, and perhaps metal cauldrons for the former: but in a fire of any high degree of intensity, such as that which left an enormous bed of ashes on Uisnech Hill, and even burnt red the earth beneath its site to the depth of some inches, a bronze or copper cauldron would have melted.

But there the perplexing fact remains, that on these important sites no pottery was found: and a recent discovery, of which I must not anticipate the publication, would seem to suggest that the art had to be re-imported from abroad. There is no escape from the conclusion that this absence of pottery, more than anything else, makes it absolutely impossible to entertain the notion that the late Iron Age was a period of high civilization in Ireland.

The study of ancient agriculture in Ireland has hardly yet begun. Extensive air reconnaissances are necessary in order to discover traces of old field divisions. This has been carried out with wonderful success in the South of England, the chalky downs of which are especially suitable for this form of research. Sensational results are less likely from aerial photography in Ireland, but an air survey will be absolutely indispensable as an adjunct to the Archaeological Survey, whenever it is established.[20]

The literature does not encourage us to look for much evidence of extensive agriculture. The people were essentially meat-eaters, living on fish and on the flesh of cattle, sheep, swine (especially), and such chase-animals as the wild boar. Nuts and fruits supplied most of the vegetable diet—especially the former, which are so frequently referred to that they must have been a staple article of food. In descriptions of the famines that resulted from the accession of a king unfavourable to the gods, we read of the frequent storms, the failure of fish in the creeks (the fisher did not, apparently, like to venture into the open sea), and the scarcity of beech-mast and of nuts. To these is added sometimes that the corn had but one grain in the ear, and that there were similar deficiencies in other agricultural products. But on the whole we derive the impression that the cultivation of cereals was never a widespread industry. No remains of ancient wheat have yet been found in ancient habitation sites, such as have been yielded to the excavator in Great Britain.[21]

Rubbing stones for grinding grain are found, but not in very great abundance: down to the time of Christianity the saddle-quern, a more or less flat surface of stone upon which the grain was strewn, and a smaller stone to be rubbed backward and forward over it. The rotary quern apparently comes in early in the Christian era, and has continued in use till our own time. In the hagiographical and other literature, the task of grinding at the mill is always represented as being the dreariest of domestic duties. It is the labour of slaves: that enterprising etymologist Cormac gravely informs us that the word *cumal* ('a bondmaid') is derived from *cum mola* ('with a mill'), the quern being the chief instrument of her duties.

In the earliest times, digging-sticks and the foot-plough, the *cas-chrom* of the Scottish Highlands, probably represented the highest point attained by ploughing in Ireland. As we know, from rock sculptings elsewhere in Europe, as for instance in Scandinavia and in the valleys of the *maraviglie* near Ventimiglia, ploughing with yokes of oxen was already familiar in the Bronze Age: but when animals were used for ploughing purposes in Ireland even so late as the Christian period, they appear to have been used singly, not in pairs. Cattle were used exclusively; it is recorded as a miraculous exception that St. Ciaran was enabled to induce a horse to draw his plough. If the practice, recorded as late as the eighteenth century, of attaching the plough to the unfortunate animal's tail was in use, there is small wonder that the horses proved recalcitrant.

The grain was cut with small hand-sickles, some examples —but not very many—of which have been found both in bronze and in iron, as well as moulds with which the bronze specimens were manufactured.

So far as publication has gone up to the present—which is not sufficiently far to justify any unqualified dogmatism —there seems to be a total absence of traces of lynchet * cultivation in the country. And yet traditions would indicate that the existence and use of lynchets were recorded in the memories of the past. The Fir Bolg, 'men of the bags', were alleged to have been so called because, when they were under servitude to the 'king of Greece', they were compelled to carry earth in bags and to spread it over rocky mountain-sides, thereby making of them flowery plains. This form of industry persists still on the Aran Islands, which another tradition made one of the last refuges of the Fir Bolg, driven out by their successors in the occupation of the country. But nowhere have the terraces been recorded that speak of ancient cultivation.

We have spoken of the Hill of Uisnech : and the results of the excavation at this important site by the Archaeological Exploration Committee of the Royal Irish Academy call for a summary. It was the first of its kind to be examined from end to end : and though in some respects the results were disappointing, many valuable new facts were learnt from the investigation.[22]

Uisnech is frequently referred to in Irish literature; it seems to have been the site of an important cemetery, but

* Lynchets are artificial terraces, such as may be seen to this day on the hillsides in the Italian vineyard districts; there are remains of such constructions to be seen in many parts of Great Britain.

this was not confirmed by the excavation. Although the whole neighbourhood was carefully searched, nothing indicative of a cemetery was discovered. It was also the centre of great periodical assemblies, such as were convened at various places in Ireland at the critical seasons of the agricultural year, and, like the similar assembly place in the territory of the Gaulish tribe of the Carnutes, it was supposed to be the central point of the country which it served. This is so far true that, although not a hill of very great elevation, it commands an extraordinarily wide view: a beacon fire lit upon its summit could convey a message to numerous peaks upon its horizon, and from them could be relayed to the sea.

Many circular enclosures of earth or of stones exist on the slope of the hill and on the hills in the neighbourhood: and an ancient road leads upward to the important enclosure upon the summit. This enclosure is in two parts, a western and an eastern, with a sort of broad passage between them. The length (E.-W.) is about 365 ft, the breadth 285 ft. The excavation showed that the mound had been occupied during three periods, the principal remains of which (excluding some unintelligible fragments) are shown in fig. 19.

Of the first period the most important relic was a ditch, enclosing a circular space 156 ft in diameter, with a gap facing east. This ditch was independent of all the subsequent remains, and had been filled up and forgotten when they were built. Apparently a stone wall had run outside this ditch; fragments of it remained. Within the ditch there was a number of pits and post-holes, which seemed to be intended for the reception of wooden pillars like those of which the circle of Woodhenge was composed. Two large pits just inside the entrance might have been the foundations of a strong gateway, but it is difficult to see any very definite order in the remaining post-holes. A pin, with a simple La Tène pattern incised and inlaid with silver—the oldest known example of the use of this metal in Ireland—was found in the filling of the ditch: showing that the ditch must have been derelict and was gradually

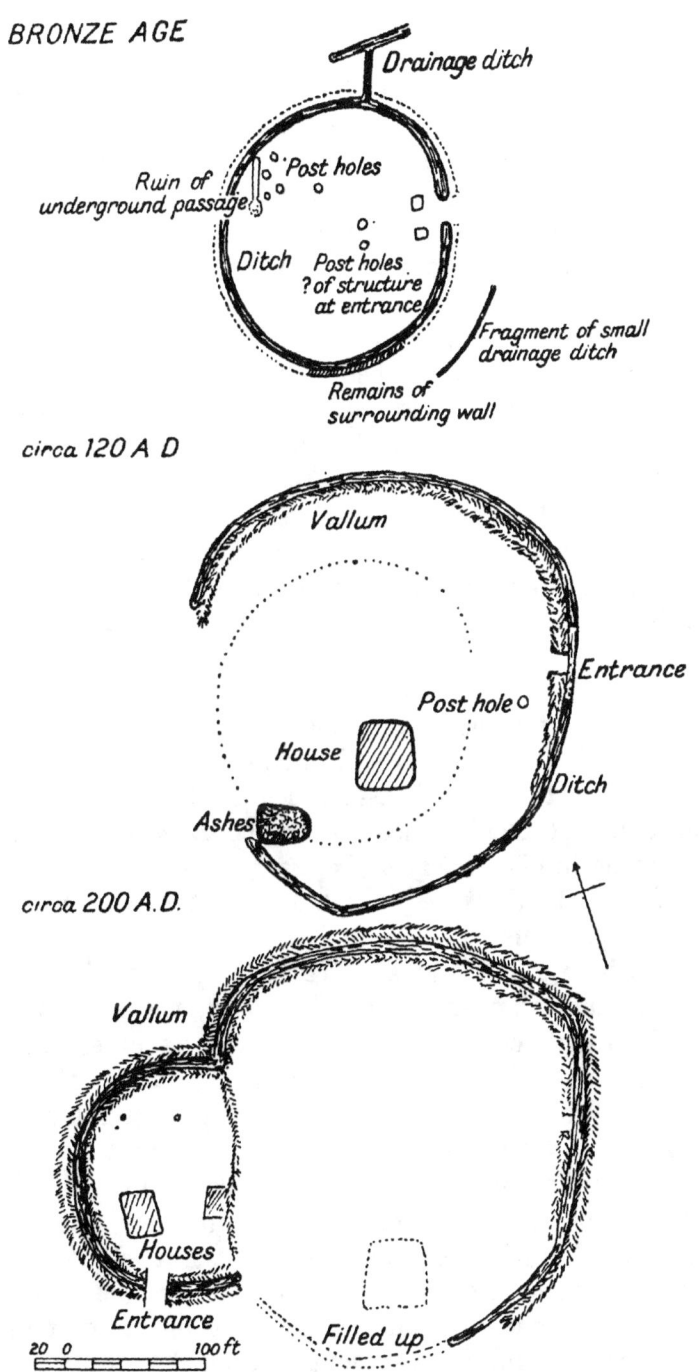

FIG. 19.—PLAN OF THE PRINCIPAL STRUCTURES REMAINING ON THE HILL OF UISNECH, FROM THE SUCCESSIVE PERIODS OF ITS HISTORY

becoming effaced during the La Tène period. It is therefore reasonable to assign these excavations to the Bronze Age. Outside the inner ditch there was an outer ditch, fragments of which remained, but which had been partly incorporated with the fosse surrounding the later structures.

During the La Tène period these bronze-age cuttings became filled up. But much use was made of the site. There were some fragmentary buildings, the purpose of which could not be determined; but the chief evidence was the enormous number of animal bones scattered through the soil, and the numerous iron knives of La Tène type which were found. As already said, there was a thick bed of ashes in one place, which must either have been the relic of a perpetual fire, or else (and more probably) of a great bonfire lit at intervals. Carcases of animals had been burnt in this fire, which was therefore of a sacrificial nature. Hither, then, people came to assemble for sacrificial rites, accompanied with barbaric feastings, in which the bones of the meal were cast promiscuously all over the ground. The Anti-Litter Society would have had to work overtime after one of the sacred assemblies of Uisnech! Vague traditions reported by the tract called *Dindshenchus*, and by Keating in his *History of Ireland*, connect Uisnech with great fires; the thick bed of ashes is the tangible record of these celebrations.

Somewhere about 150 A.D. Tuathal, king of Connacht, made an incursion across the Shannon, the river which had till then been his boundary, and he extended his dominion, over what we now know as the counties of Longford and Westmeath. In order to administer his new dominion he transferred his seat to Uisnech, and there reigned, as did the next four of his successors: the fifth seized the old royal palace of Meath at Tara, and there established himself. A king was as much a religious as a political functionary—more so, indeed—in the days of Tuathal: and the most natural place for his sacred person to be housed would be an ancient sanctuary. Accordingly, when we find, overlying the soil that contains its record of feasting-orgies, an extensive house (fig. 20) with no less than seven apartments, the scanty contents of which appear to be of about the date indicated, and a complicated system of ramparts fortifying the site, we may consider ourselves as near to certainty as the conditions permit, that we have the actual dwelling in which the monarch was

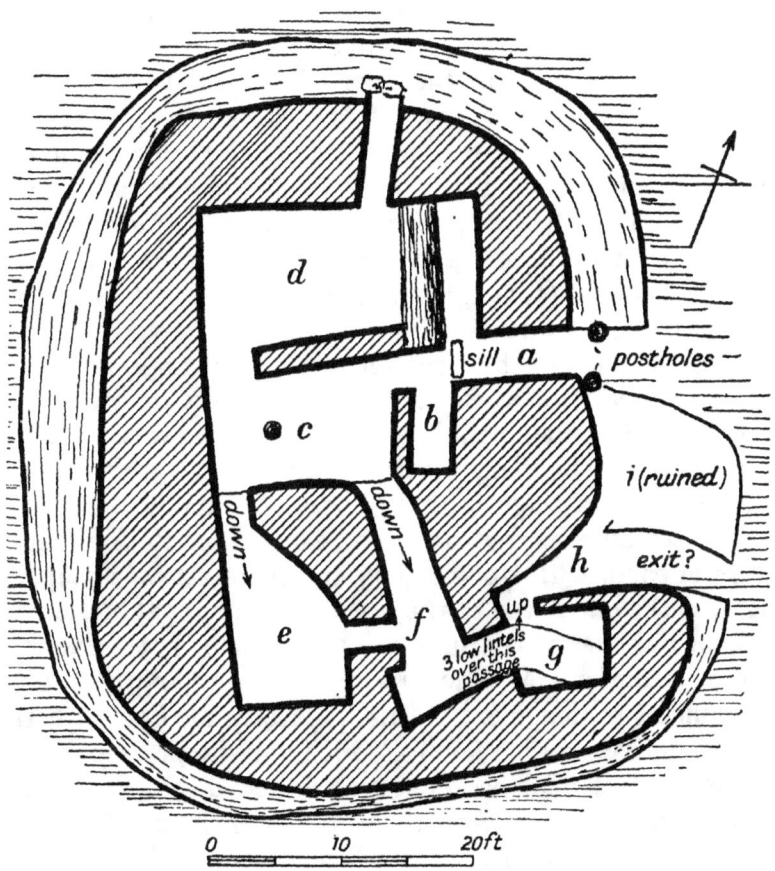

FIG. 20.—THE UISNECH HOUSE

housed. And there is no evidence of any later occupation on the spot. A casual penny of Henry II, which was the firstfruit of the excavation, might have dropped from the purse of any passing wayfarer.

Here then we have a royal house of the second century A.D. The entrance (*a*) faces east. It is flanked by a pair of post-holes which doubtless held the framework of the door. A passage through the thick wall leads to a sill at the inner end: on the left-hand side is a guard-chamber (*b*), beyond which is a more or less rectangular apartment (*c*). A similar apartment (*d*) opens off this to the north: it contains a sleeping recess (?) in the thickness of the wall; at its eastern end is a peculiar structure like a ridged grave mound, which was excavated without result. A post-hole in the floor of (*c*) perhaps held the wooden pillar which supported the tent-like conical roof. Two low doorways in the south side of the same chamber give admission to chambers (*e, f*) which also have a door of communication between them. These are possibly sleeping chambers. A low and narrow passage, doubtless a drain, runs from (*f*) to (*g*), out of which two small and very much ruined chambers (*h, i*) open: it was not possible to recover the plan of these completely: but it appeared that (*h*) had a back door, where the cesspit accumulations at the end of the drain could be emptied at intervals. When complete, the building seems to have been externally of the shape of a large carn or 'beehive' hut.

The structure was of stone and earth: the thicker walls were of earth with stone facing, and the earth was heaped against the outer face of the wall. Of this royal house we cannot in honesty say anything better than that a darker, more uncomfortable, and less sanitary dwelling it would be difficult to imagine. If this was really the Court where king Tuathal and his family gloried and drank deep, their mode of life cannot have been much above the level of an Eskimo in his *igloo*. And this is by far the most elaborate dwelling of the Iron Age that has yet been found in Ireland.

The western part of the enclosure showed less evidence of continuous occupation, and was probably a later addition: perhaps made by one of Tuathal's successors in the kingdom. But after the abandonment by the royal house the site fell into decay, was pillaged by generations of field-wall builders, and finally reduced to the few sorry mounds which is all that the visitor can see if he walks over the hill to-day.

Of the remaining mounds and enclosures of the site, one other has been excavated, and has yielded returns, if anything, yet more perplexing. For we cannot yet pretend to understand the archaeological records of Ireland. Much more intensive research is necessary, under competent scientific control, and with liberal subsidies. And we must resolutely wipe from our memories all popular ideas about prehistoric civilization in Ireland, such as have been made the theme of endless displays of oratorical and literary pyrotechnics. We must make a fresh start, right from the very beginning. We must come to the study with open minds, prepared to find, recognize, and reverence what is good, but equally ready to acknowledge what is crude, or savage, or ugly. After all, crudities, savageries, uglinesses existed in Crete, or Egypt, or Greece: they exist in contemporary Europe: how much more, then, may we expect them in an island at the remotest corner of the ancient world!

The second site on the Uisnech Hill (fig. 21), though smaller, was if anything more interesting than the site on the summit.[23] It was a structure or group of structures, not exactly circular, with an overall diameter ranging around 260 ft. The members of the construction, in order from outside inward, were:

1. A fosse between 6 and 8 ft deep, excavated in the intensely hard drift underlying the surface soil: material which a strong man armed with a modern pick could with difficulty penetrate.

2. A vallum, composed of the earth taken out of the fosse, revetted with stones.

3. A flat area, ranging in breadth, from 40 to 58 ft. This was divided into sections by radiating walls which, however, appeared to be of a later date than the main structure.

4. A second fosse, similar to the first, though of smaller size.

5. An inner vallum, similar to the outer vallum.

6. The inner area, about 125 ft in diameter. Admission was gained by a passage formed by leaving an undug space in the outer fosse, about 25 ft broad: a corresponding gap in the outer vallum; an undug space 21 ft broad in the

inner fosse: and a paved gap 8 ft broad in the inner vallum, which formed a 'grand entrance' to the central space.

This inner area was divided into a series of courts and

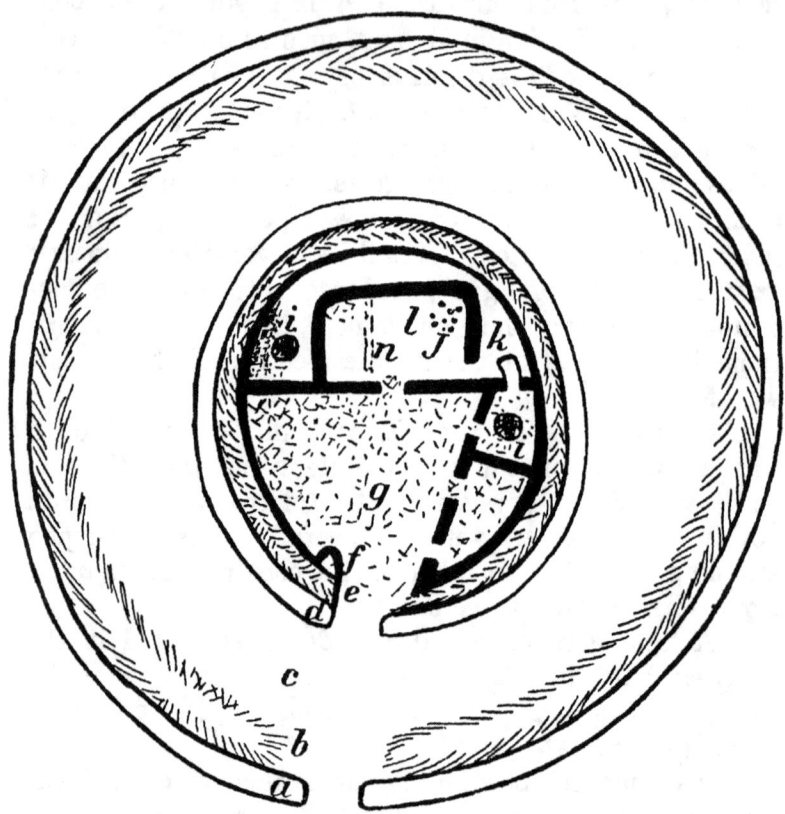

FIG. 21.—PLAN OF A STRUCTURE, POSSIBLY A SANCTUARY, AT TOGHERSTOWN, CO. WESTMEATH

a, Outer fosse : *b*, outer vallum : *c*, outer area : *d*, inner fosse : *e*, inner vallum : *f*, porter's lodge : *g*, paved court : *ii*, fire-pits : *j*, group of post-holes : *k*, entrance to underground chambers and passages : *l*, manhole of underground passage : *n*, ruined wall (doubtful).

chambers, roughly paved. In two of these chambers were pits, about 6 ft in diameter, in which great fires has been maintained—far more considerable than would have been needed for domestic purposes. There were also extensive underground passages beneath the floors, the purpose of which presented a host of problems which only further research will resolve. The conclusions as to the purpose of the construction arrived at by the Royal Irish Academy's Archaeological Exploration Committee may here be quoted, as they express the present state of the question very exactly.

'While the fires and other evidences of domestic use must not be forgotten, the indications that the enclosures were for the greater part not rooms but open courts, seem to militate against an explanation of this structure as a mere residential fortification. Other objections to this explanation are the width of the entrance gateway, which it would be difficult to defend, and the extensive paved court to which it gives access, and which looks like an area for the accommodation of a large assembly. The paucity of midden refuse is also against this explanation, as well as the extraordinary absence of organic matter over the greater part of the outer area. On the other hand, there is nothing pointing very conclusively in the direction of regarding the structure as a sanctuary, which is the alternative that naturally occurs to the mind, especially in view of the sacred character of the Hill of Uisnech in ancient times. More than this we do not feel justified in suggesting. So far as we are aware, the structure is of a type quite new, not only in Ireland, but also in Northern Europe. We must wait in patience till another of the same kind is discovered which, we hope, will be in a less dilapidated condition and will contain a greater number of instructive objects.'

There was a notable paucity of objects from the site. The most remarkable was the Saxon disc-brooch, referred to on a previous page—a form common in the eastern counties of England, but never found before in Ireland.

To some extent the site presented certain analogies with the temple of Lydney Park, Gloucestershire, excavated recently by Dr. Mortimer Wheeler.[24] The Lydney Temple is rectangular, the Togherstown site circular; but there is the same double enclosure, and the same row of three *cellae* at the inner end. These coincidences may not mean much, but they are worth noting. One of the Togherstown *cellae* seems to have been a sort of secret place, accessible only by a passage running behind the other two. It had a fire-pit, and the pavement had been laid with special care, and a certain approximation to art, in the use of an alternation of differently coloured stones.

We have seen how the Sword-Folk violated the sepulchres of the Halberd-Folk to get them building material for their own monuments. We now may see the sepulchres of the Sword-Folk going down before the Iron-Folk. This is especially clear in the cemetery of chambered tumuli which crowned the peaks of the Lochcrew Hills. These burial-mounds must have been broken open and looted early in the occupation of the Iron-People. They must have stood open and empty for a season: for at some time, still in the pagan Iron Age, a colony of metal-workers adapted them as dwelling-huts and took up their abode in them. That such an adaptation was possible once more indicates the very low grade of material civilization which was prevalent at the time: we must use of these dwellings superlatives of the adjectives which we applied to the palace of king Tuathal a few pages back. But there is no evasion of the facts. Excavation in modern times has revealed two groups of occupation relics: of a bronze-age burial occupation, and of an iron-age residential occupation. The yield of the former was exceedingly scanty—a few stone beads, odds and ends of bronze, and other objects of little or no intrinsic value: merely the stray leavings which the spoilers had cast aside as worthless, or neglected to notice. The chief yield of the latter was a large number of slips of bone, collected together for the purpose of serving as tablets, upon which the artificers could design the decorations to be transferred, when completed, to metal ornaments. It is likely that the second occupation was not of long duration, and that the squatters soon found that these rheumatism-breeding huts, on the top of a group of steep hills, were too much exposed and too inaccessible to be pleasant even to their undeveloped sense of luxury. This is indicated by the fact that the great majority of the bone slips had never been used for the purpose for which they had been so laboriously collected : only a few of them showed traces of the experimenting of the artists.

These, however, were quite sufficient to enable us to assign them to their proper chronological pigeon-hole : and the dating is confirmed by the numerous nails and other fragments of iron which were found in association with the bones. The ornamentation, composed, as it was very extensively, of compass-drawn curves, was certainly of the late iron-age period known by the name of La Tène.[25]

The reconstruction which has been set forth in this and the foregoing chapters seems to fit the facts of the case, as revealed by archaeological research, very fairly well. We begin with the Sword-Folk, whom we now assume to be Goidelic, with a Celtic language, worshipping Celtic gods, and submitting to the spiritual domination of Celtic Druids. They are gradually falling into degeneration owing to the deterioration of the climate : and their cultural decay is hastened by the Teutonic Iron-brandishers, who be-serf them, as they themselves had done to their Halberd-wielding predecessors. They are perhaps not pressed so low as the Halberd-People, who still remain at the bottom of society : through the intricate social scheme adumbrated in the Law Tracts we can see a tripartite division of society, which reminds us of the Spartiati, Perioeci, and Helots of ancient Sparta. But the initiative of the Sword-Folk was crushed, and their lives were henceforth devoted to ministering to their lords.

The lords themselves, in the next generation after the Conquest, were half-breeds, with all the energies that a mixture of blood enjoys. They were already forgetting the Teutonic speech of their fathers, and were substituting the Goidelic speech of their vassals. But they did little or nothing to check the cultural decay. The extraordinary poverty of the remains of the period immediately following the Iron invasion suggests that it was the time of lowest degradation since the Campignian or Asturian occupation, long before. The climate improved slightly, and temporarily, about 200 B.C., when a few individuals rose superior to the general squalor. Artificers may have been imported from Britain or from the Continent, to minister to these with works of art, in the shape of gold collars or fantastically carved tombstones; but the results of excavation do not suggest that there was the smallest appreciation of art among the vast majority of the inhabitants. There is an unhealthily small number of objects of any kind assignable to the La Tène Period, in proportion to the wonderful wealth that the Bronze Age has bequeathed to us.

The invaders, becoming assimilated in blood and in language to the inhabitants already in the land, though maintaining jealously their privileges of social rank, also conformed to the manner of the gods of the land, forgetting the Teutonic deities who presumably had accompanied them on their long voyage westward. They naturally seized on the numerous kingships in the country, and with them the magical duties and privileges associated therewith.

Now the king, especially he who reigned in the sanctuary of Tara, was the representative of the divinity charged with the cultivation and development of the generative or fertilizing power of Nature. On his accession to the kingship he renewed his powers by contact with a fetish-stone which was the central monument of the inauguration place.

With regard to this stone, I formerly expressed certain views,[26] which I have found myself forced to abandon as untenable. I am therefore bound to withdraw them, and (most reluctantly) to indicate the direction in which I am now compelled to seek its significance. It is called, in ancient MS. texts, *Lia Fáil*, the stone of 'Fāl'. What is this 'Fāl'?

Ancient authorities described the stone as *ferp cluiche*, which we may render into Latin as *uerpa lapidis*. Local tradition, as late as the time of Dr. Petrie, now about a hundred years ago, called it *Bod Fhearguis*, which again we may Latinize as *penis Fergusii*, whoever Fergus may have been. An amazing amount of pestilent rubbish has issued from the press on the subject of the forms of religious practice and belief indicated by such names; for this reason, and not from any motive of prudery (which is a sentiment that has no place in scientific work), it is a natural instinct to avoid dragging them in, unless the evidence is too strong to be overcome. I have done my best to escape from the conclusion that these names preserve a genuine tradition of the meaning of the stone. I sought in 'Fāl' the name of an aboriginal god; but was obliged to admit to myself that there is not a trace of any name resembling it to be found in the elaborate genealogies of the Tūatha Dē Danann, in which probably every god or goddess ever worshipped in Ireland finds a place. I sought over Europe for analogies—only to bring down upon myself the scornful double notes-of-exclamation of erudite German critics. And in the end I acknowledge defeat: the ancient authorities, and the modern recipients of old traditions, were right after all. This particular aspect of Nature-worship may have been made the theme of endless literary inanities, but we cannot on that account refuse to concede that it certainly existed in Europe, and that elsewhere it exists still. The Dionysiac rites of ancient Greece, much of the religion of modern India, can tell us that. Neither philology nor psychology can help us to resist the inevitable conclusion, which may be baldly stated: that the names 'Magh Fāil', 'Lia Fāil', involving the word *fāl*, genitive *fāil*, are not really ancient; much less 'mystical', whatever that may mean: that they are mere late scholastic inventions, fashioned by some one who had a knowledge of the facts, and who borrowed the Greco-Latin word *phallus* to express them: and that they mean 'Plain', 'Stone', of the organ and symbol of reproductive power.

Here we may find the explanation of a fact which would otherwise be perplexing. The Turoe stone shows exceptional skill both in the design and the execution of this difficult form of art. As a specimen of La Tène work, and merely as a piece of stone-cutting, it is beyond all praise. Whether the artificer was a native-born or a foreign craftsman does not matter: he was expert in his trade, and such expertness comes only from practice. He *must* have turned out dozens of stones of this kind: otherwise he could not have carved the Turoe stone. Where are all the rest?

The answer is easy. Broken up. Old bronze-age paganisms did not matter much. There was some superstitious reverence attaching to their antiquity, and it was regarded as vaguely unlucky to interfere with them. But here were a number of monuments, quite recent in date, with associations quite fresh in memory—associations which to Christianity would be hateful. Few ancient monuments are more obviously phallic than the Turoe stone: and it is not difficult to understand how a holy war against these symbols would be inaugurated in the first enthusiasm of a new-born Christian purity. How this one elaborate specimen escaped the crusade we cannot tell: perhaps a copse of trees hid it from the destroyers.

The same aspect of Nature-worship is illustrated by a figure found some time ago in a bog deposit at Ralaghan near Shercock, Co. Cavan (fig. 22). It is a statuette of yew, slightly over 3 ft 8½ in. high. The face is unusually well formed, but the arms are not, and never were, represented: there are not even sockets for the insertion of separate pieces to take their place. The legs, on the other hand, are carefully modelled, with a more than common attention to their anatomical configuration. The figure ends below in a tenon, to be stuck into a mortice, showing that it was not a complete monument, but only part of a larger *ensemble*. The closest parallel is presented by a model of a boat found at Holderness, Yorkshire, in 1836, and now in the Museum at Hull.[27] This boat has four figures, very similar to the Cavan specimen, morticed into it (fig. 23). The Holderness figures have arms, and one of them holds a round object which may be a shield, but is more probably a sun-disc. This difference, however, is balanced by the similar emphasis laid in all the figures on the pubic region, which was clearly the part of chief importance in the intention of the sculptor. A circular hole is drilled in the Irish as in the Holderness figures, evidently for the insertion of a phallus. This is a frequent

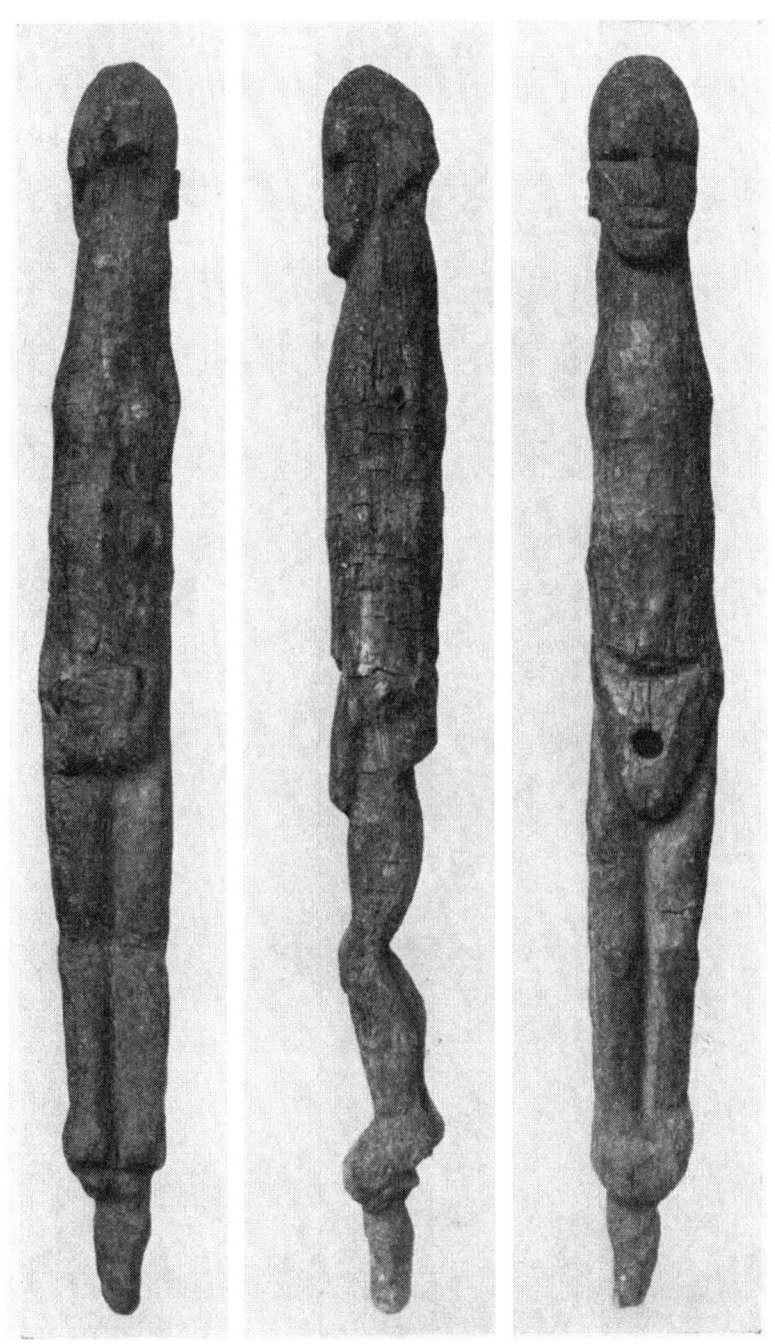

FIG. 22.—THE SHERCOCK FIGURE

THE MEN OF IRON

and prominent detail in the figures represented in the Scandinavian ship sculptures.

Now these ship figures *appear* to be representations of a certain form of fertility ceremonial. It may not be irrelevant to call to mind that a performance called 'The Building of the Ship' was traditional in some parts of Ireland, till its suppression by the clerical authorities, on account of its unduly frank character, a character which

FIG. 23.—THE HOLDERNESS BOAT

indicates it as having been originally a magical fertility drama. No full account of this ancient ceremony has been preserved, so far as I am aware: the late Mr. T. J. Westropp had acquired a few superficial traditions of it, and told me something about them, but I am not aware that he ever recorded what he happened to have learnt: I cannot find anything about it in the notebooks which he bequeathed to the Royal Irish Academy.

This raises a further interesting possibility, with regard to the numerous dug-out canoes which have been found sunk in bog-deposits. It is generally assumed that these were boats formerly used in lake navigation, which had been wrecked and ultimately embedded in the peat. But is this certain? Were all the bogs in which they are found actually lakes at the comparatively recent date to which the canoes seem to belong? Were these canoes sea-worthy? Some of them give me, at least, the impression that they would hardly float at all, if weighted by the full complement of a crew for which they appear to have been prepared.

The great mass of evidential material collected by Almgren, in his study of the significance of the ship-figures portrayed in Scandinavian rock-sculptures, sets us wondering whether these were not rather examples of a sort of carnival-ship, dragged over the land, on wheels or on skids, rather than launched on the surface water: but, at the end of the frolic, either sunk in a swamp or burnt. The sculptured figures associated with the ships in the Scandinavian carvings show us the close connexion of the associated rites with fertility cults, and the dances, prostrations, acrobatic performances and so forth with which the rites were accompanied. A canoe was found in Loch Erne with a number of holes drilled through it. This canoe, at least, could never have been floated for any length of time. But the fact is inconclusive, for as Dr. Mahr has suggested to me in conversation, the holes may have been mere drainage-scuppers, normally closed with wooden plugs. Such plugged holes are to be seen in some of the other canoes in the National Museum.

We may reasonably associate with these rites the ancient penalty of setting a culprit adrift on the sea, in a boat oarless and rudderless. He was, in fact, a *katharma*, sacrificed for the purification of the land and the propitiation of the vegetative powers: a prototype of the mock human sacrifice, annually performed at Rome, when the straw dolls called *argei* were cast into the Tiber. Analogous, though differing in that the sacrifice was by fire rather than by water, were the gigantic wicker puppets containing human victims which, we are told, were burnt by the Gauls. The purpose of the golden boat of Broighter may have been to serve as a votive offering in connexion with similar rites.

The East-European analogies presented by these ship-rites, if they be sound, give us a valuable link with the late Bronze Age of Scandinavia, and reinforce the probability that it was from somewhere in the South Baltic region that the invaders of the bronze-iron overlap originated.

We have said that at some time in the period of obscurity the Gaelic language began to develop a literature. It must have been at first under druidic auspices, as this caste of medicine-men were the only people who possessed a sufficient education. Their tentative efforts are all absorbed in later literature, and it is as impossible to isolate them as it would be to discover in the full-grown oak the acorn from which it sprang.

We have no direct evidence as to the script which they used ; but we may be able to make some deductions from the peculiar cypher with which the history of writing in Ireland begins, so far as the existing remains are concerned. This anomalous form of script is suitable only for very brief documents, and survives as the medium of expression of some three hundred short burial inscriptions.

The origin of this alphabet has been much discussed; many theories have been put forward to account for its peculiarities. The first and most obvious fact about it is that on account of its clumsiness, and of the room which its component characters take up, it could never have been used for literary documents of any length. The present writer has long been of the opinion that it was intended rather as a system of secret signs, made with the fingers in various combinations and held in various positions : and that its application to writing is secondary.*

The letters of this script are composed of combinations

---

* Such sign-communications can be developed with practice to a fine art. In the *Illustrated London News* for 25 August 1928 a case is described of a prisoner in Paris, actually communicating secretly at his trial with one of the witnesses by means of rapid motions of his fingers and eyes.

of strokes, in all but five of them parallel with one another. These strokes are from one to five in number, suggestive of the five fingers of the hand. The characters are twenty-five in number, divided into five groups of five letters each, the groups being differentiated by the position of the strokes with respect to a central stem-line. This line may be (*a*) vertical, or (*b*) horizontal; on the stones bearing these inscriptions, the angles usually take its place, as in the specimen illustrated (fig. 24), and the five groups are formed thus:

(1) Short strokes from one to five in number, at right angles to the stem-line and (*a*) to the right of (*b*) below it. These are the letters B,L,V,S,N.

(2) Short strokes from one to five in number, at right angles to the stem-line and (*a*) to the left of (*b*) above it. These are the letters H,D,T,C,Q.

(3) Strokes from one to five in number, running through the stem-line at an angle of about 60 degrees. These form the letters M,G,N_g,Z,R.

(4) Strokes from one to five in number, running through the stem-line at right angles. These form the vowels A,O,U,E,I.

(5) Combinations of straight and curved lines—five in number—in late times accorded a vowel or diphthong value, but originally consonants; and still used in a consonantal sense on some of the monuments.

That this alphabet cannot have had an independent origin is self-evident. A community cannot learn to spell with alphabetic finger-signs before it has evolved the art of spelling by means of written symbols. Therefore the alphabet must be founded upon some other. This cannot be the alphabet commonly used in Irish MSS., which is certainly of later introduction than the cryptical signs. The two alphabets do not coincide: for the 'Irish' alphabet has no symbol for V,Q,N_g,Z, which the cryptical (or, to call it by its native name, Ogham) possesses; while on the other hand the Irish alphabet has F, which is completely absent from the Ogham script, and P, which shares a character with a diphthong.

FIG. 24.—OGHAM STONE AT AGHASCRIBBAGH, CO. TYRONE

It might have been founded on the Roman alphabet, which we know to have been in use in Ireland, because one ancient inscription in that script is still extant in the country, formerly at Killeen Cormac, in Co. Kildare.* This is the opinion which I previously maintained, and which is usually received : but it is difficult to explain the principle upon which the Ogham letters were selected. Why did the inventor burden his system with Z, and omit F ? The one letter was not wanted ; the other would have been useful.

In view of this difficulty I have abandoned this Roman theory for another, which more completely accounts for the phenomena presented by the Ogham alphabet. It is to the effect that Ogham was invented, not as a script alphabet, but as a gesture alphabet : not in Ireland, not in Great Britain, but in Southern Gaul or Northern Italy, and by members of the druidic order. And that it was based upon a form of the Greek alphabet which had there been current in about the fifth and sixth centuries B.C., and which had presumably been borrowed for secular purposes and continued in use among the Gaulish men of learning.

This will at first sight seem fantastic. But it would be still more fantastic to suppose that two alphabets, *precisely identical in their selection of letters*—with one exception, easily explained—should have had nothing whatever to do with one another ; especially as the only five letters of the Ogham alphabet that possess any individuality are almost of the same shape as the corresponding five letters of the Greek alphabet.

The archaic Greek alphabet in question has been found scratched upon two vessels of pottery, one from Formello, the other from Caere in Etruria.[28] The first line of the following diagram represents the letters of this alphabet.

A B C D E F I ⊞ ⊕ I K L M M ⊞ O M ϙ P ξ T Υ + φ Ψ

a b g d e f z h t' i k l m n x o p(ng) qr st u ṣ pʰ kʰ

4 1 3 2 4 1 3 2 5 4 2 1 3 1 5 4 5 3 2 3 1 2 4 · 5 5

* Now in the National Museum, Dublin.

The letter **M** is a sibilant, rejected in the later developed standard Greek alphabet, though retained in the form ↑ as a numeral sign. The symbol ✛ was already moribund when these alphabets were scratched; a century later it would have disappeared altogether, and the last letter would probably have assumed its conventional form **X**. On the theory here set forth, it was just after these changes—which would point to the fifth century B.C., the alphabets of Formello and Caere belonging to the sixth—that this Greek alphabet was adopted by the druids for writing purposes, and subsequently made the basis of the finger cypher from which the Ogham script developed.

The sibilant **M**, a legacy from the Semites who had ultimately invented this alphabet, was needless beside the other sibilants, as the Greeks themselves afterwards realised. It was ultimately rejected by the Greeks: but by the druids was retained in the form ΓΓ, the conventional symbol used by the Greeks for the sound *ng*.

The figures underneath the characters in the above diagram are the numbers of the groups to which the corresponding Ogham letters belong. It will be seen that except for ✛ the two alphabets are absolutely coincident. This can hardly be an accident—especially in view of the similarity in form between the letters of the fifth group, and the Greek letters to which they correspond.

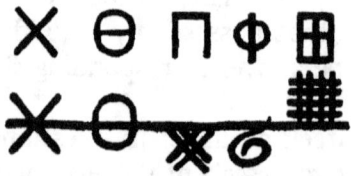

The Ogham letters are as near as possible to what would be produced in trying to make figures like the Greek letters on the fingers.* And the derivation is practically proved

---

* Notice especially that if the signaller tries to make a *Π* in the most natural way—opposing the tips of his outstretched thumbs to represent the horizontal stroke and protruding the first two fingers of each hand to represent the verticals—the slightest pressure of the thumbs will cause the protruded fingers to cross.

by the fact that although MSS. keys give the value of *diphthongs* to these signs, the second of them, in the only place where it is actually used, means SC or CS ($= \xi$); the third, in the few places where it appears, is invariably P ($= \pi$); and the fifth is almost invariably a guttural sound K or Ch ($= \chi$). The other two have never been found in practical use in Ireland, though the O-sign is used, with uncertain significance, in some of the Scottish Pictish inscriptions. In the alphabet, as it was finally developed, the letters were shifted about, probably on a phonetic basis; it is certainly not a coincidence that the vowels are *grouped by themselves*, in their proper phonetic (not alphabetic) order: that among the consonants letters representing cognate sounds (the stopped letters D-T; C-Q; G-Ng; and the continuatives L,V,S,N) are found side by side; and that among the extra letters, those which stand for aspirates (KH, TH, PH) come side by side.

What is the inference from these facts? That among the learned men of Continental Gaul, an early form of the Greek Alphabet was used for literary purposes (Caesar, in fact, tells us that they made use of Greek letters): that upon this alphabet they founded a sign-alphabet for secret communication: and that just at the end of the days of druidry, when secrets were being revealed or else forgotten, this alphabet was used for public inscriptions by those who held to the ancient ways. The degeneration into writing was gradual. At first the symbols were made by manipulating the fingers alone. Then it would occur to a druid, wishing to send a secret message to a colleague at a distance, to nick on the corners of a piece of wood the positions which his fingers would occupy if they were able to communicate face to face. When this habit became general, the secret would not remain a secret long.

Thus, strange though it may appear, we infer that the inscriptions in the Ogham character are the last relics, and the only record, of a means of symbol communication, invented somewhere in or near ancient Etruria, based on an alphabet of about the fifth century B.C. There is about them an odour of ancient sanctity. The forms of the language used upon them are consciously archaistic: it is as though Chaucerian or Wycliffite English had a religious or magical virtue, and was used for public and especially for memorial purposes even down to the days of the *argot* now current as colloquial English.

The contents of these inscriptions are meagre—little more than the name of a man and of his father. The Ogham script set invincible barriers on literary spaciousness, and the largest stone that could reasonably be used for monumental purposes did not afford room for much more than this minimum of information. Had it been otherwise, it is highly probable that the archaic form of the language used—much of which is mere Wardour Street, philologically indefensible—would have proved a serious difficulty in the way of interpreting them. We should have been as helpless as the scholars of Wales appear to be, in the presence of the early Welsh inscription at Towyn.

This fact is however of the deepest interest from another point of view. Why are these archaic or pseudo-archaic forms used? It certainly was not merely 'to puzzle posterity', as some one or other once suggested was the purpose of the Round Towers. Still less was it to puzzle contemporaries, though undoubtedly it would have done so if they had not the education to adjust themselves: for a bumpkin would be hopelessly perplexed if he could have contrived to spell out *CUNIGNI* and was given to understand that this referred to the great man whom he had known phonetically as 'Cunyeein'!

The key is in that word 'education'. The druids in Pre-Christian times were, as we learn from Caesar, educators of youth. They caused their pupils to learn by heart great numbers of verses, evidently a traditional body of hymns or the like compositions, the language of which soon became archaic in comparison with the colloquial speech of the untaught. This language became, and was, maintained as their medium of literary expression. It was not till Christianity was firmly established that the reduction of the vernacular speech to writing was attempted, and this was done with orthographical conventions totally different from those of the Ogham inscriptions. We have seen that the Irish alphabet and the Ogham alphabet are incompatible; whereas the Ogham alphabet and an early Greek alphabet are identical. The orthographical and linguistic conventions of the Ogham inscriptions were worked out in Greek letters on the Continent by Goidelic druids; the orthographical and linguistic conventions of later Irish literature were worked out in letters derived from a Roman cursive hand, by the missionaries who brought to the country a knowledge of the new faith, and by their native disciples.[29]

What was known in Ireland of the outer world, what did the outer world know of Ireland, during the pagan part of the Iron Age in the country? Not much; and little that is pleasant, so far as the population is concerned. Strabo and Diodorus Siculus, as is well known, accuse them of cannibalism. These passages can be explained away: but it is difficult to explain away the sober statement of the native Annals, that so late as in the great famine at the end of the seventh century 'man would eat man'. St. Jerome has a story that the Attecotti, whoever these may have been, were in the habit of cutting off and eating certain parts of the bodies of shepherds and shepherdesses. But shepherds and shepherdesses have no dietetic superiority to any one else, and such a practice would have the effect of depleting an indispensable industry. Nothing is clearer than that the story needs correction; it was the animals tended by these functionaries which the Attecotti ate. Why, then, does Jerome call such normal diet 'inhuman'? Apparently for the gruesome reason that, as in the Abyssinia of the eighteenth century, described by the traveller Bruce, the animals were eaten alive.[30] We hope that he was misinformed: in any case, as a resident in Palestine he could not avoid malaria, and was in consequence splenetic. But every ancient contemporary writer who mentions Ireland at all must have been splenetic also, for, one and all, they show a singular inability to see anything in the island but savagery!

The oldest contemporary document for Irish history is

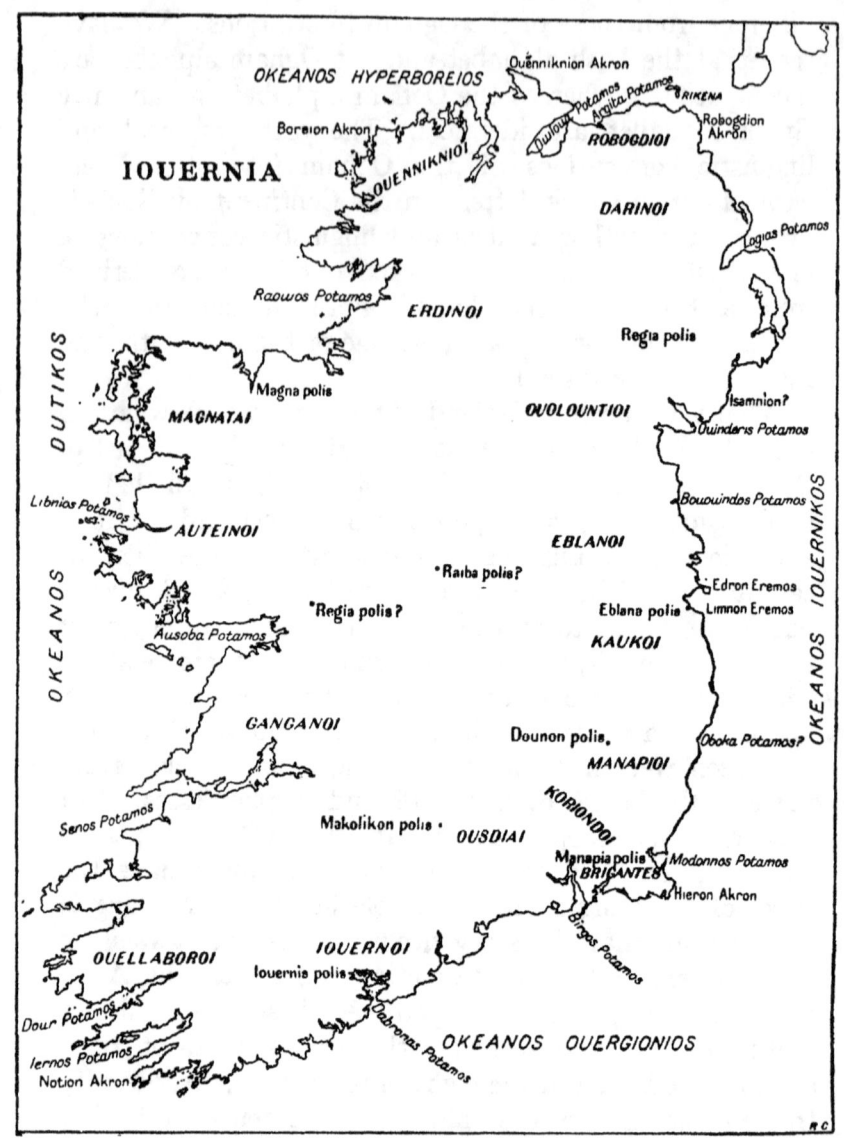

FIG. 26.—IRELAND AS KNOWN TO PTOLEMY

the section relating to the country in Claudius Ptolemaeus's map of the world (fig. 26). This is based upon information derived from mariners of Alexandria, the city where the geographer lived and worked: and while there are some errors and perplexities, it does seem to show that these sailors had an accurate knowledge of the main geographical features of the sea coast. It would be a grave mistake, however, to infer that merchants from Alexandria plied regularly to Irish ports. It is much more probable that they had at their disposal books of sailing directions, the result of a 'pooling' of information by these merchant adventurers for their mutual benefit. For what was there in Ireland to attract Egyptian merchants, and where can we point to the slightest evidence that such merchants even visited the country? There is the golden chain found at Broighter, which may possibly be of Mediterranean workmanship: but we know absolutely nothing of the history of the transmission of this isolated object, nor can we tell through how many hands it passed from its maker to its Irish grave. The interior of the country, in Ptolemy's map, is as blank as the interior of Africa on maps of a hundred years ago: except for an enigmatical 'town' *Raiba*, which may have something to do with the name of Loch Ree (Rib in Irish) but of which we know nothing whatever from native sources. Prominent islands, river estuaries, headlands, are named, with the populations that lived behind them. Several of the few names cannot be identified with security; a few mistakes are made, as when Howth (Edros = Beinn Edair) is treated as an island; and the latitudes and longitudes leave something to be desired. The map is no more than a list of the landmarks for which an anxious sailor might with advantage keep watch, as he sailed on his way along an unlighted, more or less uncharted, and extremely dangerous coast, perhaps to the amber-lands of the Baltic, or to dealings with the Roman colonists in Britain.[31] But there is nothing to suggest that the sailor ever landed.

CHAPTER V

SHADOW-SCENES

THE student of Irish antiquity has an advantage which in many other archaeological centres is not available. Time has left to him the fragments of an extensive body of literature, written and oral, transmitting a memory of the life of the people who wielded the weapons and the implements which he can handle. From this point of view, oral ' literature ' is less trustworthy than that which has a long manuscript tradition : it is liable to become impressed with the changing conditions of life in successive centuries, and to be delivered to the collector in a form as much modified as the material used in the children's game called ' Russian Scandal '. Even manuscript materials require to be treated scientifically before they can be used to any good purpose. The large volumes of O'Curry are still valuable as repertories of illustrations ; but they are melancholy examples of the loss involved in failing to pass the ore through a crucible, and thus accepting the precious metal still contaminated with its attendant dross.

We shall take three ancient tales and endeavour to see what they mean. We have here nothing whatever to do with any literary value that they may possess : to the scientific student, the literary aspect of folk-stories is a nuisance, and their literary manipulation anathema. Nor have we here anything to do with philological problems, or with the interpretation of difficult passages : our only concern is with the contents of the tales in their most general form.

We begin with the story, or, rather, sheaf of independent and imperfectly united stories, called *The Cattle Raid of*

Cūalnge. This narrative does not possess the literary pre-eminence of the Homeric epics; but from the point of view of cultural history it is hardly less important. The Homeric epics illuminate for us a period of the history of the Aegean Sea and the coasts around it, upon which we have no other light from literary sources. *The Cattle Raid of Cūalnge* illuminates for us, in a way that no other document does, the manners and thought of Europe in the later La Tène Period. It shows us men and women living the life of the time, using the cultural apparatus of the time : and if it occasionally introduces supernatural events which we cannot accept as literal history, it shows us what they believed to be possible.[1]

Can we accept the testimony of this document? Is it really an accurate picture? In the form in which the story has come down to us it is much later than the time which it professes to describe. The oldest manuscript containing it is of the beginning of the twelfth century. Doubtless it has been copied from earlier sources, now lost : but for philological reasons we cannot date its text to a century earlier than about the sixth. This is still as far removed from the alleged events described as we are from the reign of King John. Mere oral tradition could not possibly convey accurate details across that long and varied stretch of time. Is the gap to be bridged in any other way?

The answer must be in the affirmative. The tradition can be corroborated from other sources. The archaeology is remarkably accurate : the people use the weapons and the implements which they should have used at the time indicated. The testimony of Poseidonius, Caesar, and other contemporary writers, so far as it goes, gives us a picture quite consistent with that drawn for us by the Irish story. We can make allowances for changes here and there, due to the changed outlook of the Christianized compilers; but on the whole the story is an authentic record of life and belief, even though we may not take it as an authentic record of prosaic history.[2]

The *name* of the piece introduces us at once to a matter of importance. It is one of a series of stories which have, for their subject, cattle-forays. Where cattle is the chief wealth of a community, raids on the cattle by acquisitive neighbours become matters of commonplace: both in Ireland and in the Scottish Highlands they formed a traditional industry. These stories all bear the name *Tāin Bō* —— ' The Cattle-Raid of ——', with a name of owner or of locality filling the blank.

The story thus belongs to a specific class. Now, in the *Book of Leinster* there is a list of stories which the men of learning were expected to be able to recite upon great occasions. These stories are said to have been 350 in all, though only a comparatively small number has come down to our time. They were grouped into twelve categories, namely—

togla (*destructions*).	uatha (*caves*).	forbaisi (*sieges*).
tāna (*cattle-raids*).	imrama (*navigations*).	echtrada (*adventures*).
tochmarca (*courtships*).	aideda (*tragedies*).	aitheid (*elopements*).
catha (*battles*).	fessa (*feasts*).	airgne (*plunders*).

—a list which, for all its baldness, is itself a picture of life, as it shows the types of incident which were matter for intellectual interest.[3]

It is not to be supposed that the recitation of these stories was a mere act of amusement. If it were, the narrators would have been encouraged to fashion new tales —or at least, seeing that such a feat is probably impossible, to re-group the stock incidents into new and surprising combinations. It was much more like a religious ceremony. These 350 stories formed a sort of sacred canon. Just as the sacred books of the Hebrews are practically the history of the nation; just as the histories of Homer became practically sacred books to the Greeks: so the sacred books of the Irish were tales of the adventures of notable people, carefully committed to memory by those whose business it was to recite them at the periodical festivals. Thus the story before us is essentially a sacred book. It stands first in the list of cattle-raids, as befits its importance. It relates the raid not of a cow (*bō*), but of the *bull* (*tarb*) of Cūalnge; but the formula of the title is conventional, and the slight solecism is of no importance. Cūalnge is the name of a district between Dundalk Bay and Carlingford Loch, now represented by the parish of Cooley in Co. Louth.

The political background of the story, so far as it can be recovered from the narrative, is as follows. The country is a Pentarchy, each kingdom being governed by its own king. Each king is independent of the rest. There is no effective trace of a ' High King ' having real or theoretical authority over the country, either in Tara or anywhere else : and occasional references to this functionary are later anachronisms. So far as the story has historical importance, it is the record of the beginning of an aggression, on the part of the rulers of Connacht, upon the adjacent kingdom of the Ulaid, whose name, though not the exact delimitation of their territory, survives in the modern province of Ulster.

The scene opens with a dispute between Medb, queen of Connacht, and her insignificant husband Ailill. It is not unimportant to make a differentiation between this ancient queen's name and the euphonious modern adaptation thereof: the latter should be spelt ' Maeve ', and pronounced to rhyme with ' *save* '; the former should be spelt ' Medb ', and pronounced something like ' *my-eye-w* ', in one syllable. For this word appears to mean ' mead-(drunken) ', old Celtic *medva* : compare the Cymric *meddw*. In such a name there would at the time be no disgrace. Many ancient classical authorities speak of the Celtic disposition to inebriation,[4] and their testimony is confirmed by the native literature. We read of even an admired hero like Fer Diad, the friend and combatant of Cu Chulaind,[*] drinking himself drunk.[5] In one of the lives of St Brigid contained in a manuscript (Rawl. B. 512) in the Bodleian Library, we may find what to our ears is an utterly hateful story [6] to the effect that ' Bishop Mēl, by

[*] Who, however, is dismissed by Prof. Zimmer as a mere borrowing from Scandinavian literature : Berlin *Sitzungsberichte*, 1910, p. 1057.

the Grace of God being drunken', knew not what he was singing in his book, and so, when placing the veil on St Brigid, he inadvertently conferred episcopal orders upon her.* We might read without surprise such a tale in some blasphemy issuing from modern Russia: to find it in a composition seriously intended to do honour to the saint and to her spiritual adviser, is truly disconcerting! Even if we take *inebriatus* in a figurative sense ('drunken with the Grace of God'), which is the only interpretation that can make the incident tolerable,† it is astonishing that the writer used such a metaphor at all, and, using it, did not realise and guard against the obvious ambiguity of his words. Such an oversight could not possibly happen except in a community where no stigma was attached to inebriation: where, indeed, as among the ancient Aztecs, a drunken man was regarded as being in a special state of spiritual exaltation, so that to injure or even to mock at him was a deadly sin.

However that may be, it is hard to believe that any one would care to be a full namesake of that horrible woman, too politely described by Sir Samuel Ferguson as 'the Helen and Semiramis of Irish romance', whose unspeakable personality towers gigantic in some of the most ancient records of the country.

The dispute between Medb and her husband begins with Ailill's uttering the platitude that 'a rich man's wife is a lucky woman'—which is just the sort of thing that we expect to hear from him. Medb agrees, but suspiciously asks him why he thinks so: and Ailill, to her indignation, points to the advantages which she has gained from marry-

* 'Ibi episcopus, Dei gratia inebriatus, non cognouit quid in libro cantauit, in gradum enim episcopi ordinauit Brigitam.'

† But it does not altogether reconcile us to the story. Other versions say nothing of the bishop's *ebrietas*, but tell us that he saw flames of fire issuing from the saint's head. We cannot help wondering what would be thought of a modern bishop who attempted to explain his commission of an extremely serious liturgical error by such a story of hallucination! As a mystic he might be all that could be desired, but he would be a very bad bishop.

ing himself. Medb tells him that she had been just as well off before ever he saw her—

My father was high-king of Ireland, Eochu Fedlech, and he had six daughters, of whom I was the best and noblest, in grace and largesse, in battle and combat. I had 1500 royal hirelings of the sons of foreigners, and 1500 of the sons of freemen of this land. Each hireling had ten men in his troop; each ten had nine; each nine had eight—

and so on till we reach 'each one had one: and that was my standing'.

If Queen Medb really said this, I am afraid we must accuse her majesty of over-statement; for the retinue specified amounts to 40,478,703,000 persons, if I have not made an arithmetical error; or rather more than three times the whole population of modern Dublin crowded upon every single square mile in Ireland. This is a mere indiscretion: the rest of the speech is of more importance from a sociological point of view. We mark that women take their place in battle along with men, and recall the familiar narratives of the British queens Boudicca and Cartimandua, who have much in common with Medb. Not till long years afterwards, when Adamnan brought about the passage of a law of emancipation, were women relieved from this obligation.

The reference to the 'high kingship' of Medb's father is, as we have seen, anachronistic.

'And that is why my father gave me one of the provinces of Ireland—that of Cruachu (in Connacht), so that I am called Medb of Cruachu. Folk came from Find son of Ross the Red, king of Leinster, to seek me—and I refused. They came from Cairpre Nia Fer son of Ross the Red, king of Tara: they came from Conchobar son of Fachtna Fathach, king of Ulidia: they came from Eochu the Little (king of Munster): and I went not. For it was I who demanded an unwonted bride-price, such as woman had never demanded before of man among the men of Ireland: a husband void of greed, void of fear, void of jealousy.

'Were he greedful, the husband whose I should be, it were not fitting that we should be together. For I am good in grace and largesse, and it were shame for my husband that I should excel him in grace, and shame to my husband that folk should say that

I exceed him in treasures or in wealth. But it were no shame were we alike—be they both good together.

'Were my husband fearful, no more would it be fitting that we live together. I break battles and fights and combats single-handed, and it were disgrace to my husband that his wife should be more quick than he, and no disgrace that they were quick alike—be they both quick together.

'Were he jealous, the husband whose I should be, there could be no agreement between us: for I never was without one leman on the heels of another.

'Now I found that man—thyself, to wit, Ailill son of Ross the Red of the Leinstermen. Thou wast void of greed, of jealousy, of sloth. I gave thee the contract and the bride-price, a thing that of right cometh to the bride: twelve men's raiment of clothing, a chariot worth thrice seven bondmaids, the width of thy face in ruddy gold, the weight of thy left forearm in bronze. Whoso should inflict shame or sorrow or madness upon thee, no fine or compensation is due to thee more than is due to me; for it is I who have the compensation,' said Medb; 'for thou art a man living on a woman's patrimony.'

'Not so was I,' said Ailill. 'I have brethren twain, one over Tara, one over Leinster—Find over Leinster and Cairpre over Tara. I left them the kingship, forwhy they were my elders, not forwhy they excelled me in grace and largesse. Never heard I of a province of Ireland being a woman's patrimony save this province only. So I came and took kingdom here, as successor of my mother; for she was Mata of Muresc, daughter of Mago. And what better wife could I have than thee, seeing that thou art daughter of a High King of Ériu?'

'Still,' said Medb, 'my goods are more than thy goods.'

'A wonder!' said Ailill. 'No man surpasseth me in riches or in treasure or in wealth: of that I am assured!'

The right of women to inheritance and to hold property was recognized by the ancient legal codes of Ireland, and the property was not alienated by marriage. One of the classes, into which *Senchas Mōr*, the chief law-tract, divides wedded couples is 'A man living on his wife's property': and although the sense of the passage is less clear than we should wish, it appears that in such a case the man took second place in the establishment.

Here is to be seen a survival of the ancient form of social organization known as *Matriarchate*. The matriarchal system precedes the patriarchal, and is always symptomatic of low civilization. In a hunting community, where the adult males are absent on the hunting-fields for almost the whole time, it is natural that the children and the scanty property of the family should fall under the control of the women. Indeed, the fathers might hardly know anything about their children. When the pastoral and agricultural life develops, the father remains at home : and when he does so, he is sure, sooner or later, to claim the commanding place to which his superior strength and initiative entitle him. But survivals of the early stages of social development come to the surface at surprisingly late phases of social evolution : Medb's freedom of choice of her husband, her demand of complete freedom in her dealings with her favourites, and her final claim that she had married Ailill, not *vice versa*, are all thoroughly ' matriarchal ' in principle.

In fact, society in Ireland was not yet fully reconstituted. The early bronze-age traditions were still dominant over the majority of the population ; the scene is set in a time of transition. Ailill's answer to Medb's statements of her position emphasizes this. No one, he asserts, ever heard of a province of Ireland being under the rule of a woman. He was as good as his two brothers who were in sovereignty, the one in North Leinster or Meath, the other in South Leinster. He had left their kingdom and had come to Connacht, to which he claims a hereditary right through his mother : thereby giving away his case completely. Medb would in her own interest revive the matripotestal and matrilocal elements of the principle of Mother-right. Ailill rejects these, which do not suit his purpose, but holds firm by the matrilinear succession.

They then proceed to compare their several properties. The inventory is interesting, as showing what a wealthy house of the time might be expected to possess—buckets and cauldrons, iron vessels, jugs, tubs, pitchers : garments, checked and striped, of seven different colours, which are enumerated : golden rings, bracelets, thumb-rings, and other ornaments : flocks and herds, sheep, horses, swine, cattle, each group headed by a notable animal of the standard value of a bondmaid. And, at the last, Medb's property is found to be deficient by one bull called *Findbennach*, or 'White-horn', which had once been hers, but having the intelligence to regard it as disgraceful to be under a woman's domination, had joined himself to the herd of Ailill.

Of course this was no common bull. Findbennach and the Bull of Cūalnge started in the same cradle. A wild tale, prefixed to the main epic, tells us that they were rebirths of swineherds in the service of the *sīd* or fairy-folk of Munster and Connacht respectively, by name Friuch(t) and Riucht. Such jingling names are suggestive of Dioscuric worship, the objects of which are a pair of twin deities. In the course of this preliminary tale, which we cannot find room here to summarize at length, these swineherds pass through a bewildering series of transformations, of which the last takes the shape of the two bulls. If the swineherds were gods, the bulls were also gods. We are here face to face with the crude primitive worship of an animal divinity, incarnate in an actual bull kept at the palace sanctuary; first, under a matriarchate, ministered to by queen-priestesses, and then, with a change of regime, transferred to the domination of a king-priest. Thus what appears at first sight to be a childish piece of silliness becomes full of meaning and of historical worth. The bulls are the *palladia* of the provinces where they are respectively kept.

The Cūalnge bull is now the incarnation of the Ultonian god. Connacht seeks to seize the bull, and thereby to seize the province.

Medb first sends a messenger to Daire son of Fiachna, owner (or rather custodian) of the Cūalnge bull, offering him rich rewards, and certain personal privileges regarding herself which need not be specified, if he will lend her the bull. The scene now shifts to Daire's house. The messengers arrive; Daire is so transported with delight at the offer that he bursts the seams of his feather-bed by bounding about on it, and he promises to send the bull whether the *Ulidians like it or not*. He has in fact no right to send it. He is its custodian, its priest; and it will be an act of treason to his province to accept the unprincipled queen's offer.

Then comes an interesting snapshot of the feast wherewith Daire entertains the messengers. The floor is spread with fresh straw and rushes. Choice food and drink is set before them—especially drink, for one at least of the guests becomes a little too free with his tongue. We can supplement the sketch with Poseidonius's description of the feast with which he was entertained during his wanderings in Gaul. The guests sat on a carpet of rushes, or upon the hides of dogs or wolves, near the pots and spits of the fireplace. They had small tables, one to each, on which the bread was set out in baskets. There was plentiful store of meat, roast and boiled, which the guests ate 'after the manner of lions': each, receiving the joint into his hands, gnawed off a piece and passed it to his neighbour.[7] We recall the episode of a certain bishop who was sailing on the sea, and was incommoded by a storm coming on at dinner-time. He *happened to have the joint in his hands at the moment*, so he went on deck with it and waved it in the direction of the wind—presumably to show to whatever Aeolus had sent the wind that he had chosen an unsporting time for his frivolity—at the same time invoking the aid of St Senan. Aeolus, prompted by the saint, took the hint, and the storm ceased forthwith.[8] The guests—returning to Poseidonius—drank abundantly of beer and mead. They sat according to precedence, but all alike had their full share: for if there should be a quarrel about the helping of the food, or the right of precedence, it was fought out to the death.

And such a quarrel broke forth at this feast in Cūalnge. One of the guests began a sort of maudlin eulogy of Daire, praising his generosity for giving up the bull. Another, who was in the combative stage of intoxication, cursed the speaker, and said that if Daire had not given the bull they would have taken it by force. Unfortunately at this moment the steward came into the house with a further supply of provisions, overheard the remark, and went to report it to his master. Here we notice a point of etiquette.

Daire is too great a man to dine with his guests: he goes so far as to entertain them in a separate house. Even royal messengers must keep at a distance from the priest of a sacred bull. Daire, on hearing the report, was naturally furious. He swore ' by the gods whom he worshipped '—the scruples of the Christian redactor, unfortunately, did not permit him to set down their names—that neither by fair means nor by foul would the messengers get the bull.

On the morrow the messengers, now sober, prepared to depart, and respectfully asked of Daire deliverance of the bull. Daire replied sharply that if it had been his custom to deal amiss with heralds—even in this wild society the herald is inviolable—not one of them would have departed alive. Crestfallen they returned to Medb, who promptly determined to seize the bull by force: and thus the great war began.

The troops were summoned. They were separated *racially*, into companies with close-cropped black hair (aborigines) and flowing fair hair. The first carried long shields, the second round shields: this is apparently a slip, for archaeology suggests that the contrary would more probably have been the case. Another error is the mention of silver among the equipments of the hosts, for there is no evidence of the ornamental use of silver at this early date.[9] Next we learn the very interesting fact that for lack of a favourable omen ' the druids and the poets ' kept the host inactive at the Connacht palace for a fortnight. So in Gaul, no one would embark on any enterprise without first consulting a soothsayer and obtaining an augury of success. Medb herself, according to another document, had the whole course of the coming year foretold regularly every Samain-day. This incident enables us to correct an error of Diodorus Siculus (or of the source from which he borrowed), who tells us that where two Gaulish armies are ready for the fight, their poets rush in between them and cause them to lay down their arms. Even among those barbarians, it seems, the war-god yields to the muses.[10] Nothing of the kind: the warriors are not troubling their heads about the muses; the poets have discovered at the last moment that there is something wrong with the auspices, and rush in merely to postpone the fight till a more favourable occasion.

At the end of the fortnight Medb sought an augury of her druid. 'There are many', she said, 'parting from their homes and their friends, and if they come not safe home again curses will fall on me'—and will be much more real in their effect than mere impotent imprecations would be, in these sceptical days of ours. 'But', she added characteristically, 'for any of those who are now setting forth we have no greater affection than the affection we have for ourselves: therefore tell us whether *we* shall return.' The druid reassured her: whoever may or may not return, *she* will come safely through. So Medb departed from the druid, and the driver of her chariot, for the sake of a good omen—or, as a modern gambler might say, 'for luck '—wheeled the vehicle round right-hand-wise.

This is a good example of the sunwise turn of which we hear frequently, and not in Celtic literature only. According to Plutarch, Marcellus, leading his army against the Gauls, rode a horse which in its terror at the shouts of the enemy forcibly turned back. Marcellus, fearing lest his soldiers should look on the incident as an evil omen, with great presence of mind made an act of reverence to the sun, as though he had intended the movement: for, says Plutarch, the Romans always turn round when they worship the gods. Other instances might be multiplied indefinitely.[11]

As the chariot turned, Medb espied another chariot in which there was a young woman standing on the pole— an athletic feat which Roman observers admired in British charioteers.[12] It is one of the indications of the cultural authenticity of this story that the warriors fight from chariots. War-chariots were used in Gaul before the days of Julius Caesar, and the Gaulish warrior was buried in his war-chariot, as the Viking sea-lord was buried in his ship. But on the continent this custom had been abandoned by Caesar's time, though it survived, to the Roman embarrassment, in Britain. After the period to which this story refers war-chariots were abandoned in the islands also. The maiden was a sort of war-spellwinder, like the Valkyries of Northern mythology; she was engaged in weaving a fringe, using a sword as a bordering-rod. Medb spoke to her: she proved to be Fedelm of the *sīd*-folk of Cruachu, and in her eagerness for a vision of the future Medb asked her for an augury. It is a pity that modern perversions of speech import an ambiguity into the fairy-lady's response, ' I see red ' ! Medb protested. This cannot be. The periodical pains had seized upon the Ultonian heroes one and all, and therefore Medb anticipated an easy victory. But Fedelm persisted in seeing red, and ended her discouraging prophecy with a long description and eulogy of the Ultonian champion Cu Chulaind, who was destined to destroy the Connacht host.

The ' pains ', which play an important part in the subsequent story, were a hereditary curse that had been pronounced upon the men of the Ulaid. An Ultonian farmer, by name Crundchu, had lost his wife. A mysterious lady named Macha entered his house, and took on herself all the wifely duties. Assuredly she was not of common clay, but was of the kin of the swan-maiden, a stock figure in folk-romance. At a subsequent feast the horses of the king were successful in a race: the poets praised them, and said that there was nothing in Ireland faster than they. Crundchu, forgetful that this was mere courtly sycophancy of the usual kind, indignantly blurted out that his wife could run faster; thereby, as analogous stories make us understand, breaking some tabu which the lady must have imposed upon him. The king, in rage, ordered that she should prove the words of her husband. She begged for a respite, on the grounds of prospective motherhood, but the petition was unheeded; the race was run; she was the victor, but at the end of it she fell with a scream, and died in the act of giving birth to twin children. With her last breath she cursed the Ultonians: for nine generations let them be subjected to such pains as were at the moment afflicting herself, and thus let them be incapacitated in times of stress.[13] This strange story is bound up with beliefs of a very primitive nature, though I am personally not convinced that it has anything to do with the custom called *couvade*.

Notwithstanding Fedelm's vision of red, Medb, reassured by her druid of her own personal safety, gave the order to set forth. Two interesting illustrations of the localized patriotism of the time may be here noted. At the first bivouac Medb made a circuit of the host, and found that the Gailioin, a pre-Celtic community of Leinster, who must have been proverbial for their martial qualities, were a stage before every other unit in their preparations. She reported this to Ailill, who as a (more or less) good Leinsterman expressed his satisfaction. Medb however refused to let them go any further, and indeed wanted them all put to death, apparently in a jealous fear lest these foreigners should take from Connacht the glory of the expected victory. A heated discussion followed between the leaders of the army: the result being that the lives of these too-efficient warriors were spared, and they were allowed to proceed, but the troop was broken up and distributed through the rest of the army.

Fergus mac Roig,* the exiled king of Ulidia, had been seventeen years with the people of Connacht. Being familiar with the topography of his native province, he was sent to spy out the land. But once on Ultonian soil he turned Ultonian again: he sent warning messages to the Ultonian braves, and at the same time led the Connacht host by devious ways, hoping thus to gain time for the Ultonians to recover from their sickness. This neatly illustrates a precaution set forth in the ancient law-tracts. A king should have a bodyguard of men whom he had rescued from death, and who were thus tied to him by bonds of gratitude. But men whose lives he had spared in battle were ineligible: their allegiance would necessarily

* It seems unnecessarily pedantic in the present context to mark all the long vowels: we have indicated a few, but have allowed Crúachu, Crundchú, Cú Chulaind, Róig, Láeg, and some other names to stand unmarked.

be divided between their actual master and their native *tūath* or province.[14]

Once more the scene shifts, from the Connacht host to Ard Cuilenn, a place somewhere near Mullaghmast in southern Kildare, where Cu Chulaind and his father Sualtam are keeping solitary watch. These two persons, whatever their origin, were not native Ultonians: they were therefore exempt from the curse of Macha. They stand one on each side of a pillar-stone—doubtless a sacred fetish-stone of some sort. It is noteworthy how often stones of this kind are referred to in the story. The Connacht host is espied, and Cu Chulaind directs his father to give notice to the Ultonians. He himself has a private engagement—a tryst with the daughter of the King of Ulidia. Sualtam expresses a very proper disapproval of such frivolity at such a time, but Cu Chulaind insists on keeping his appointment. He takes steps, however, to check the Ultonians by magic. He goes to the wood and tears up an oak-sapling. Using one foot, one hand, and one eye only, he weaves the sapling into a ring, and forces it down upon the thickest part of the pillar stone. Then upon the ring he carves Ogham. We learn afterwards what this Ogham says : ' Let no man pass here by, till he can cast a ring like this. Fergus does not count.' Fergus, as the champion knew, could do the trick, so he was excluded from the competition. But if Cu Chulaind cut all that in the ordinary Ogham, his woven ring must have been of very considerable size !

First, he chose an oak—the especially sacred tree, whose close association with the sky-god and the thunder-god is a commonplace of comparative mythology. Then he used one foot, one hand, one eye in manipulating it. In other words, he personated one of those strange demons, the *Fomorians,* whose raids on the early settlers in Ireland are so conspicuous in the compilations of the synthetic historians. These demons of darkness are described as having single feet, single hands, and single eyes, and we have more than one example of spell-weavers endeavouring to put themselves temporarily into the same condition: pretending to be devils in order to exercise the magical omnipotence of devils. Then he presses his wreath upon the stone, to absorb its sanctity and to secure the protection of whatever supernatural being was present within it. Finally he carved his warning in the secret script of druidry. After such a plethora of precautions, who can blame him for seeking a little spell of relaxation?

But penitence comes on the following day. The Connacht host is stopped by the stone: but they turn aside, and cross the frontier at another place. An intervening forest they cut down with their swords. In real life they would hardly have put these valuable weapons to such rough usage, but the story presupposes what would have been the fact, that they had not mere bronze blades, but the strong iron swords of the La Tène Period. Cu Chulaind returns in his chariot to the defence of the frontier on the morrow, and when he finds that the host has turned aside and crossed the border, it repents him that he kept the tryst. His charioteer Laeg, who acts throughout as confidant and adviser to his master, 'rubs it in'. However Cu Chulaind pulls himself together and returns to his duty. He sets Laeg the task of estimating the number of the enemy host from the tracks in the snow which had fallen in the night and now covers the ground. Laeg is unequal to the problem, which is then undertaken and, after a long time, solved by Cu Chulaind himself.

This is an interesting passage, showing us—what we know from other sources—that the tracking and interpreting of the evidence of footmarks was a fine art, as it is still among peoples in much the same level of civilization—the aborigines of North America, the Bedawin, and others. There is exaggeration in the idea of estimating the number of an army from its tracks, but only in degree. To a trained eye, footprints have as much individuality as faces; native trackers can often name the person whose footprints they observe in the ground. In Wales it was regarded as sufficient evidence of complicity in a theft if the tracks of a thief led to a house and no further: at least, it put on the owner of the house the obligation to prove that the thief had gone beyond it. The detectives, as we may call them, declined to entertain the possibility that any further track could escape their notice.[16]

Cu Chulaind next proceeded to a ford near Knowth on the Boyne called *Ath Gabla*, no longer to be identified. Here once more he had recourse to the magic of the Ogham, and cast into the stream a rod with four prongs, in such wise that no chariot could cross the ford on either side of it. As he was doing this he was attacked by two Connacht youths, eager to behead him ; but he did the same to them and to their charioteers, and let the horses go back to the host dragging with them the chariots containing the headless bodies. The Connacians imagined that these rushing chariots were the leaders of an attacking Ultonian force : they sent out spies, who found the rod in the river, now decorated with the four heads, and with an Ogham which said, ' One man cast this fork with a single hand (another illustration of the " Fomorian " assumption in magic). None may pass till one of you can do the like. Fergus does not count.' In this case there was no sacred stone —though the ' fork ' had been thrown with so much force that it had passed through a flagstone—but undoubtedly the barrier was under the aegis of the goddess of the river. Its magic prevented the passage of the Connacht troop. This I myself can well believe, having seen something similar among the Arab peasants of Palestine. Eight strong men carrying a corpse for burial to the village cemetery—an area of ground entirely unfenced—started backwards with one accord the moment the feet of the leaders touched the known but unmarked limits of the enclosure. This they did several times, approaching the cemetery from all sides. The idea apparently was that the spirit of the dead sought to prevent the disposal of the corpse in the cemetery. I, watching the tragi-comedy, saw nothing : but the action was so perfect that I could well believe that for them imagination had conjured up the spirit in actual visible form, barring their way. Not till the village sheikh had called upon Allah to make the way plain before them, could the burial ceremony proceed.

Ailill, the Pantaloon of the comedy, wondered who had planted the fork. He made several fatuous guesses, but was told it was Cu Chulaind. Medb spoke scornfully of this 'beardless implet' only seventeen years of age—the age of a marriageable girl. (From other sources there is confirmation that seventeen was the usual age for marriage.) Fergus however set her right in this contemptuous estimate of the Ultonian David: and here follows an episode, interrupting the course of the tale, in which Fergus relates to Medb and her companions the story of the youthful exploits of Cu Chulaind.

This we can pass over. There is not much of value in it for our present purpose. We hear something of the rough horseplay games of the boys, and their use of slings, hurleys, and toy spears—rods with pointed and charred ends. Once more we read of a stone with a magic Ogham, and learn some topographical facts of interest, but not of present importance.

When the story of Cu Chulaind's youthful exploits had been told, the army proceeded. Once more Cu Chulaind stopped them with a magic Ogham—this time upon an oak over which they must needs leap. Fraech, a kinsman of Medb, went forward in search of Cu Chulaind, and found him bathing. He entered the water in front of him and the two wrestled: Fraech was drowned. The body was brought to the camp: but suddenly a number of women in green made their appearance and conveyed it into a fairy mound.

This is evidently one of the occasional apparitions of the ancient corn spirits, undoubtedly among the oldest supernatural beings venerated in Europe—the almost impersonal groups of sprites, indefinite both in number and in individuality, who haunted the fields and the cattle-byres of the Neolithic husbandman, and rewarded his labour or thwarted it according as he propitiated them or neglected to do so. Side by side with the mighty gods of Celtdom and Teutondom, side by side with the gods of Rome, the conquering destroyer, they lived on, and under the names of Matres, Matronae, Campestres, they received votive altars in the very latest days of European paganism. All these upstart deities they outlived. Side by side with the saints of Christendom they have endured even to our own time; though their existence has at last become precarious, and in another generation or two they will have flickered out, like the fire-flies and wills-of-the-wisp which gave them birth, who shall say how many thousands of years ago?

Passing over one or two episodes in which certain individual warriors go out to fight, unsuccessfully, with Cu Chulaind, but which do not contain matter of moment, we come to a visit of people called *Crutti Cāinbili*, ' the Fair-lucky Harps ', to make music for Ailill and Medb. But inasmuch as they came from the Ulidian side, the Connacians took them for spies, and chased them away, so that they escaped in the guise of deer to the standing-stone at Liic Mōr, wherever that may be. For though they were called ' the Fair-lucky Harps ' they were men, who had knowledge and prophecy and wizardry in abundance.

We cannot dissociate this episode from the strange tale of Patrick's escape from the ambush set by King Loiguire, in which an ' invisible cloak ' came upon him and his companions so that they passed their enemies unrecognized, in the guise of deer. They chanted the famous Lorica, beginning *Atomriug indiu niūrt trēn* (' St Patrick's Breastplate ') and thus were delivered.[16]

What do these tales mean? What are we to understand by them? It needs no very robust scepticism to refuse to believe that the saints could have transformed themselves into deer: or that they would have done anything so undignified even if they could; or that even magical deer possess the mental or bodily apparatus necessary to enable them to sing hymns; or that in the circumstances they would have done so. A singing deer has very little chance of escaping notice! The story reads, once more, like mere childish silliness.

Are we then to explain it in this unsympathetic way? Far from it. The story is one of quite exceptional interest, and of enormous value for the history of culture in Northern

Europe. Once more we look far over the sea, round to the other side of the world, and when our telescope rests on the island of New Britain in the Bismarck Archipelago, we find there its complete and only reasonable explanation. Among the natives of that island there exists a dreaded secret society called *Duk-duk*. Its members, dressed in grotesque masks and robes, counterfeiting the snouts and pelts of animals, hold wild revel with dances and songs, and terrorize the common people with the magical powers attributed to them (fig. 27). The college of 'Fair-lucky Harps' (not 'harpers': they were not the originators of their magical music, but the instruments through which some higher power expressed himself) these, credited likewise with supernatural gifts, must have formed just such an infernal freemasonry as the guild of the Duk-duk. They were in the direct line of descent from the sorcerer whose painted effigy, tricked out with stags' horns attached to his head, has been posturing for ages of ages on the wall of the wonderful prehistoric picture-gallery called *Caverne des Trois Frères* in Ariège.[17] In their deer-disguise, these mysterious personages might be expected to come to sing spells for the victory of a host to whose interests they were favourable.

Such a masquerade, however, gives an opportunity to an impostor. Admittedly it might be as difficult for a non-initiate to pose as a member of this society as it would be for a member of the public to pose undetected as a policeman in a city street. But on occasion a bold spirit might try the risky experiment and 'pull it off'. And the two most probable motives for such a venture would be espionage and escape.

The Connacht host were shrewd enough to notice that their disguised visitors did not come from the direction of the eldritch place Assaroe, which was apparently the headquarters of the order, but from the direction of Ulidia. They were therefore impostors, come to spy out the disposition of the host. And the summary flight of the Brotherhood showed that the diagnosis was correct. It required much courage to attack a body of visitors ostensibly belonging to this mysterious Brotherhood: the Connacht folk must have been fairly sure of themselves before they did so. The masqueraders were lucky to escape with their lives, if indeed they did escape; we are told that the pursuit went as far as the pillar-stone of Liic Mōr, but we do not learn what happened there.

No one would with full knowledge dream of accusing St Patrick and his companions of evading their enemies in a disguise so cowardly, ridiculous, and heathenish. This must be said as clearly and emphatically as possible, to avoid the least chance of misunderstanding. His ancient biographers have told us, almost in so many words, that they did so; but that is a very different matter. These people knew not what they said: that must be their condonation. When they wrote, this college of deer-dancers, its members and their antics, belonged to the dead and forgotten past. But here and there, in a literature now lost to us, they found how this one or that escaped from a tight corner in a 'cloak of concealment' and in the form of a deer. The original writers knew what this meant: their later readers did not: and, not realizing its implications, they thought that it would be a picturesque incident to adapt to their own purpose. It would have been especially appropriate in the Patrick story, for the song said to have been chanted by the saint bears the name *Fāed Fiada*; and whatever the real meaning of these mysterious words may be, they can be understood as signifying 'The Cry of the Deer'.

But it was a true instinct that made them call the disguise *dīcheltair*, 'a cloak of concealment', like the *Tarnkappe* or invisible cap of fairy-tales. The king's crown, the chancellor's robe, the mayoral chain, the medicine-man's dance mask, what are these but cloaks of invisibility, blotting out the mere man whose duty or privilege it is to wear them, and concentrating attention upon the abstract authority which he wields, and of which these things are the outward symbols?

After this interlude we are given a remarkable picture of the Bull, the objective of the expedition, led out with

FIG. 27.—DUK-DUK DANCERS

fifty heifers to grass. As he paws up the earth, The Morrigu, daughter of Ernmas, one of the three war-furies of Irish tradition, appears to him in bird-form. The analogy of the divine bull with three cranes, depicted on one of the famous Paris altars under the name *Tarvos Trigaranos*, is obvious and is probably sound, though the birds in the Irish story are not cranes. The Fury perches on yet another standing stone, and utters one of those odd abrupt ecstatic 'poems' in which magical prophecies are expressed. The text is in places unintelligible, and has become even more so by scribal corruptions: it may have been translated without clear understanding, from a traditional spell in an archaic form of the language. Anyhow, the prophecy foretells the death of the bull and the great battles that shall take place on its account. Then follows a list of its magical virtues, all showing clearly that we have to deal with a supernatural being, not a common bull. Fifty youths would play draughts or leap-frog on its back: but this represents a misunderstanding on the part of the literary story-teller, or of some gloss-writing wiseacre, after the fashion of his kind. The painted walls of the palace of Minos enable us to correct him. These 'fifty youths' were bull-fighters, and the statement is a precious record which tells us that here in Ireland also ceremonial bull-fights took place periodically. No goblin or other spirit would come into the same cantred with the bull: and as it returned to its byre its lowing was a delightful music.

Once more we pass over a number of episodes in all of which Cu Chulaind does much damage to the Connacht host. Medb at last resolves to send a herald to treat with him. Mac Roth, in spite of his unsuccessful negotiations with the custodian of the bull at the beginning of the story, is the messenger chosen. He bears a staff of white hazel, and a one-edged sword with ivory hilt-fittings. These are the tokens of a herald: the one-edged sword is an indication of Teutonic influence. No one-edged swords have been found in Ireland: but Montelius figures a specimen from Öland in Sweden, which he ascribes to some time between 150 and 1 B.C., in other words to just about the time to which this story is to be assigned.[18] The ivory mounting is also suggestive of the products of a seafaring people : it can hardly have been anything but walrus or narwhal ivory.

Mac Roth comes up with Laeg and asks him his name. 'I am the servant of yonder youth,' is the reply. He comes to Cu Chulaind, and asks his name. 'I am the servant of Conchobor.' 'Hast thou no other name?' 'That will suffice.' This is a supremely interesting example of the name-tabu. Among many primitive peoples it is the height of rudeness to ask a person for his name. The name is a part of the personality : indeed is *the* personality. To leave a child unnamed is to leave it unsouled; that is the meaning of the curse of Arianrhod in the Mabinogi of Math of Mathonwy. To put a name into the keeping of another, like giving him a portrait, is to put the owner of the name, or the original of the portrait, into the other's power for good or for ill. Not to repeat examples already published in accessible books, I give another Palestinian reminiscence of my own. Hearing a man passing my tent one night, I called out, 'Who is there'? 'I,' said the man. 'Who is "I"'? said I. 'A certain person,' was the reply. 'And who is that "certain person"'?—this obliged him to name himself without an evasion, which was quite unnecessary from the first, for he was well known to me. It merely proceeded from an inborn hereditary caution.[19]

Fergus now goes to parley with Cu Chulaind. They make arrangements for the series of duels, which culminates in the fight of Fer Diad. The decision of disputes by ordeal of duel is an old Indo-European custom. We find it in Homer, in early Roman history (Horatii and Curiatii) and in Teutonic mythology. It is not a Semitic custom : but it appears once in the Old Testament, on an occasion where the Hebrews meet in battle with a people of European origin, the Philistines. There the victory is decided by the combat of two champions, David and Goliath.

An overbearing youth, by name Etarcumul, accompanies

Fergus, and offers to be the first champion. Cu Chulaind endeavours to dissuade him; he is under the protection of Fergus and should therefore be inviolate. Etarcumul will not hearken, so Cu Chulaind knocks him down by cutting away the earth from under him (thus he avoids touching him). Etarcumul is still obstinate, and Cu Chulaind cuts off all his hair with a stroke of his sword (thus coming nearer to but still avoiding a direct assault). Even this is not sufficient for Etarcumul, so Cu Chulaind with a vertical stroke splits him to the waist, and with a cross stroke cuts him into three pieces. This is greatly resented by the Connacht host, till they learn that Etarcumul had brought his troubles upon himself. His body is dragged behind a chariot in a way that reminds us of the treatment of the body of Hector at Troy.

The next champion sent against Cu Chulaind is Nath-Crantail who, despising him and trusting to his own gigantic strength, will attack him with nothing but holly-stakes. So our story-teller says, once more misunderstanding the original tradition. In fact, Nath-Crantail was taking no risks. Holly, with its evergreen leaves and red berries, is a most powerful binder of spells. Cu Chulaind himself does not disdain to use it on the very special occasion when he has occasion to meet Fer Baeth, whom he dreads, because his training had been equal to his own. The use of holly-sticks in fighting is obscurely alluded to in a gloss in the law-tract known as *Bretha Comaithchesa* [20]: and outside the limits of Irish literature it is familiar as in the following passage from the lay of *Sir Gawayne and the Green Knight* (ed. R. Morris, p. 7).

> Weþer hade he no helme ne hawbergh nauþer,
> Ne no pysan, ne no plate þat pented to armes,
> Ne no schafte, ne no schelde, to schwne ne to smyte,
> Bot in his on honde he hade a holyn bobbe,
> Þat is grattest in grene, when greueʒ are bare,
> And an ax in his oþer, a hoge and vnmete . . . *

---

* He had neither helm nor hauberk, nor gorget nor plate appertaining to armour, no shaft nor shield to protect or to smite; but in his one hand he had a holly-bough, greatest in green when groves are bare, and an axe in the other, huge and immense.

—where however the tradition is fading, for this holly-bough makes no further appearance in the story as we have it. To this day cattle-drovers prefer the hard wood of holly for their stakes.

After losing many more of her champions Medb attempts to parley with Cu Chulaind once again, and seeks to bribe him with the offer of her daughter. Cu Chulaind, however, is guilty of the unpardonable rudeness of cutting off the young lady's hair and pinning her to the ground by planting a pillar-stone through her flowing robe ; and even commits the further solecism of killing her escort and planting a second pillar-stone through his body. These two pillar-stones were still extant when the story as we have it was written. Doubtless the story is a bit of droll folklore which attached itself to them : most likely they originally represented twin gods, like Cu and Cethen, and Blocc and Bluicne, who were represented by similar pairs at Tara (and incidentally, who appear among the transformations intervening between the swineherds and the bulls).

Another strange episode, intensely primitive, follows. The Morrigu appears to Cu Chulaind, and makes offers of love, which he rejects. In anger she threatens to take successively the forms of an eel, a wolf, and a heifer and so to embarrass him that he will fail in his combats. She fulfils her threats, and he is sore wounded ; but he gives as good as he gets, and wounds the war-fury. No one— not even a supernatural being—could recover from a wound inflicted by Cu Chulaind unless he himself blessed the wounded person. The Morrigu assumes the form of a hag, blind and lame, milking a cow. Cu Chulaind, mad with thirst after his combat, begged for a drink, which The Morrigu gives him, whereupon he pronounced upon her ' the blessing of gods and un-gods '. A glossator has here interpolated the explanation ' their folk of craft were gods, their folk of husbandry were un-gods '—meaning that there were deities of various departments of nature and of human life, and in addition the heterogeneous mob of corn-spirits and the like, worshipful, but not considered as gods in the strict sense of the term. Search from end to end the islands of the Southern Ocean, and a more archaic expression of the relation of man to the world of the unseen will not be discovered. Other primitive features follow: Cu Chulaind's own healing at the hands of the god Lug, of whom he is a rebirth, and who appears to him as he stands on a grave-mound, a fit place for a theophany: his assumption of an artificial beard of bewitched grass, because one of his opponents, Loch, objects to fighting with a beardless youth: his attack on the Connacht host with an invisible cloak, riding in a chariot with sharp blades attached to it which cuts a way through the host. This last seems to be the only extant Irish reference to the famous scythed chariot, invented (according to a Greek and Roman tradition reported by Xenophon and Livy) in Persia, and attributed by Lucian to the Galatians and by Pomponius Mela to the Britons.[21]

A certain Connacht exile, by name Ferchu, hearing that Cu Chulaind was thus holding up the men of Connacht at the Ford, resolves to slay him and so, by currying favour with Ailill and Medb, to secure his restoration to his patrimony. He goes, with twelve followers, each of whom throws a javelin at Cu Chulaind. The javelin sticks in Cu Chulaind's shield and weighs it down, whereupon Cu Chulaind hacks the shaft through with his sword and releases it. (Certain La Tène spear-heads were fitted with long iron sockets in order to forestall this very manoeuvre.) Cu Chulaind, of course, kills them all, and then sets up twelve pillar-stones and fastens their heads upon them, one on each. This is perhaps a corrupt bit of folklore such as is commonly told about stone circles being transformed men; or perhaps it is a reference to the practice, which disgusted Poseidonius until he became accustomed to it, of having the heads of conquered enemies as a decoration of the dwellings of successful warriors. The same practice is remembered in certain folk-stories which tell of the hero seeking the bride, ringed around with a fence of impossible tasks which must be accomplished before she is won. The parental castle usually has a circle of spikes, each bearing the head of an unsuccessful candidate: the hero generally finds that one empty spike awaits, in grim suggestiveness. One touch of nature makes the whole world kin: Cu Chulaind is of one flesh with the Dyak or Formosan head-hunters on the one side, and on the other, with the authorities who decorated Temple Bar in a like fashion, not more than a couple of centuries ago.

We must pass rapidly over the remaining part of the epic. An Ultonian champion, Cethen, comes to attack the Connacians—for the Ulstermen have now recovered from their periodical sickness. Ailill, as usual a poltroon, puts his cloak and other equipments upon one of the pillar-stones with which the story bristles—Cethen, who is mad from the many wounds that he has received, rushes at the pillar-stone and drives his sword through it and his fist after it. This is evidently a fragment of folklore that has grown up to explain a holed-stone, a pillar-stone with a hole through it, one of the numerous perplexities which the Bronze Age has bequeathed to us.

Toward the end of the story, in the later version, wheeled turrets used as siege engines are mentioned. These are most likely borrowed from some Greek or Roman source: they are noted in the text as being foreign.[22]

In the long run the enterprise is successful, the Bull of Ulidia is captured and carried to Connacht. There he meets his rival, the Findbennach of Connacht. A great fight follows, continuing and completing the rivalry, begun long before, of the twin swineherds. Findbennach is killed—thus far the Ultonian story. But Connacht has tacked on an appendix. The Ultonian bull seizes the Connacht bull on his horns, and rushes left-hand wise—the ill-omened *sinistrorsum*—around all Ireland, shaking him to pieces in his course. Wherever a fragment falls, after that fragment the place ever afterwards takes name. Thus is Ireland girded round with fruits of Connacht planting: and thus, in spite of a temporary Ultonian victory, did a Connacht dynasty assert its rights of domination over all the land.

The second tale which we shall analyse is known universally in ancient authority as the *Exile of the Sons of Usnech*.[23] This is one of the best-known of ancient Irish romances: but it is altogether misrepresented in modern adaptations. The personality of 'Deirdre of the Sorrows' has elbowed herself forward, and in these days of aesthetic sentimentalism has become the centre of interest. In the ancient story she is merely the pawn, the *fons et origo mali*, and the story-tellers were not interested either in herself or her 'sorrows'.

The Ultonians were at a drinking-feast in the hall of Feidlimid, the story-teller of the provincial king Conchobor. An unborn child of Feidlimid's wife uttered a scream. Cathub the druid explained the portent as signifying that the child would be of great beauty, but would bring much ill-luck. The child was born, and in reference to her antenatal performance, was named Derdriu, or in the later form, Deirdre. The Ultonians, having regard to the sinister prophecy, would have had her killed, but Conchobor interfered. Let her be reared apart, and when the time came he himself would take her to wife. Doubtless he flattered himself that his royal divinity would be powerful enough to withstand the ill-luck foretold by the croaking druid: and why waste a good-looking girl? So Derdriu was put in charge of one Leborcham, and kept in seclusion till the time should come for her to enter the royal harem.

But one snowy day she saw a calf being killed for her dinner, and a raven drinking the blood: and she expressed a desire to have a husband with hair black like the raven, skin white like the snow, cheeks red like the blood: a not uncommon motive in folk-tales. Leborcham, who had many shortcomings as a chaperon, told Derdriu that Nōisi son of Usnech fulfilled the specification.

So one day as Nōisi was passing by, out went Derdriu, primly pretending to be walking past unconscious of his presence. And Nōisi said, we regret to record, 'What a pretty heifer!' To which Derdriu answered, 'It is usual for heifers to go where the bulls are.' 'You have a bull already,' said Nōisi, 'the king of Ulster.' 'You don't suppose I would have anything to do with him, when I could get a bullikin like you,' said Derdriu, in effect. 'None of that,' began Nōisi. But Derdriu jumped up on him, and seized him by the ears, and said, 'Ears of sorrow and shame shall these be, unless you go off with me.' And the poor man had to do it.

After reading the page of the *Book of Leinster*, upon which this pleasing incident is related, we cease altogether to believe in the anaemic, drooping-lily, mid-Victorian bore, beloved of literary sentimentality. If (to our grave disadvantage) Derdriu had embellished these days of ours, she would have thoroughly lived up to her name, which may be interpreted, with no more than legitimate freedom, as 'The Rampageous'.

What spell did Derdriu bind upon Nōisi to compel him to yield to her importunities? This is a difficult question, which presents itself once more in the story of the *Chase of Diarmait and Grāinne*. Indeed, the latter is merely another version of the same romance, with different personages and different incidental details. Find mac Cumaill was betrothed to Grāinne, daughter of king Cormac mac Airt. She objected to marrying a man older than her father, not, we may concede, without some reason; and having put all the guests at the wedding banquet to sleep with a potion, invited Find's handsome young lieutenant Diarmait to elope with her. For reasons both of loyalty and of prudence Diarmait declined, even as Nōisi had done: whereupon Grāinne put upon him 'taboos of the climax of druidry' to do her will. And once more he had to do it, though he foresaw that ill-luck and death would be the inevitable result.[24] Before the vengeance of the insulted betrothed, neither Nōisi nor Diarmait ever had in life a moment's peace again. And we ask in wonder why those two nincompoops did not give their respective vampires the sound box on the ears which they most righteously and richly deserved, and go their way without bestowing upon them a second thought? Public opinion, at the time, would not have been unduly perturbed.

Unless the reason be nothing more than that if they had

shown this modicum of common sense the story-teller would have had no story to tell, we must conclude that there was some sort of magic involved. They must have been bespelled. And when we recall how 'St Patrick's Breastplate' invokes the protection of the Almighty against 'the spells of women, smiths, and druids', we realize that the supernatural power, which somehow, and for some reason that certainly does not lie on the surface, may have been credited to persons like Derdriu, would have added a new terror to life in ancient Ireland.

We need not follow out the details of the story, which have been told a hundred times, in as many different ways. How Nōisi and his brethren fled to Scotland: how they entered the service of the king of Scotland, who with native canniness found no difficulty in resisting the temptation of knocking the brothers on the head and appropriating the damsel, which in ordinary circumstances would have been the obvious thing to do: how Conchobor, at the advice of Eogan mac Durthacht, King of Fernmag (Farney in the present Co. Monaghan), sent treacherous messengers to the brethren, and inveigled them back: and how, when he had got them into his dominions once more, he caused them to be slain and took Derdriu to himself—these incidents are too familiar to need re-telling.

But we must expend a paragraph upon the *dénouement*. Derdriu sulked for a whole year in the palace. ' She was a year', says the narrator, ' and never displayed a smile of laughter, nor ate sufficiency of food, nor slept her fill, nor raised her head from her knee.' At the end of this year, Conchobor asked her whom she hated most. 'Thee', said she, 'and Eogan mac Durthacht.' 'Good,' said the king, ' to Eogan mac Durthacht shalt thou go for a year. Thou shalt be a sheep between us two rams ' (the zoological metaphors of the story are a little mixed). So she was put in a chariot and posted off to Eogan. On the way she contrived to jump out: it is not made clear that she actually contemplated suicide, but, as the events turned out, her head struck on a stone, and she was killed. Though the ancient narrator does not actually write the words 'and a good riddance too', we have a feeling that some such sentiment was at the back of his mind, and we heartily concur.

Why did Conchobor send her to Eogan? Probably less to spite her, than to injure him. They had been at enmity; but when Eogan gave his advice in the matter of the sons of Usnech, they had patched up a peace. Such a peace would hardly be enduring. Conchobor was not sorry to kill two birds with one stone—to rid himself of an incubus, and to unload this unattractive and disagreeable young person, along with her cargo of ill-luck, upon his rival.

The third story which we have chosen to illustrate life in pagan Ireland is the very important tale of the *Feast of Bricriu*.[25] Bricriu of the Venomous Tongue prepared a great feast for Conchobor and his followers. He built a special house for the purpose, with a chamber set apart for himself: he knew only too well that his guests, while partaking of his hospitality, would never allow him and his poisonous tongue into their company at the feast. Then he proffered his invitation, which was received with modified enthusiasm: 'If we go, our dead will be more than our living, after Bricriu has incited us to strife,' said some. But at last these prudent counsels were overborne, and they went to the feast. As in most primitive communities, the duty of hospitality was incumbent upon those in authority. A king persistently inhospitable might be deposed. So Dr. Rivers found that a chief of Eddystone Island with whom he had to do, one Rembo, was called 'Kikere' or 'bad' by his subjects, not because he was tyrannical or cruel, but because his feasts were few in number and poor in quality.[26]

But Bricriu had an *arrière pensée*. The prudent spirits among the Ultonians were right. He meant to set them by the ears and to bring about a carnage: why, we are not told—apparently for no reason more specific than because he was that sort of person.

So he secretly told three of the braves individually to expect the 'champion's morsel' as his due. In the banquet-hall of Tara every man had his place according to his rank; and every man had his special part of the meat according to his rank. As Agamemnon set aside the choicest of the meat as the honourable portion for Aias: as Samuel set aside the choicest of the meat for Saul; as the feasters of Gaul set aside for their chief warrior, *teste* Poseidonius, the choicest portion, his right to which he would defend to the death,[27] so Bricriu set aside the chiefest of the dainties—and promised them to three separate persons. And of course a fight took place on the floor of the palace so soon as they put in their claims.

Meanwhile the ladies of the court had been drinking far more than was good for them, and they deemed it advisable to come out for a little fresh air. Bricriu went to them, and made three of these inebriated queens believe that whichever of them first returned to the hall should become queen over the whole province. So they began to return, at first slowly; but when they realized that they had competitors, they went with increasing swiftness, at the last raising their vesture up to their waists so as not to be impeded in the mad rush; and such a noise did they make that those within thought that the house was beset by enemies. For self-protection they slammed the door in the faces of these drunken furies, who promptly began a wild 'word-battle', each of them reeling off long rolling strings of verses extolling herself and her lord. Two of the husbands broke a hole in the wall of the house to admit their own wives: but Cu Chulaind tilted the whole house over against his bed, admitting Emer his wife and her women, and then slammed it down again so that it sank seven feet into the earth. The shock threw Bricriu and his wife out of their private apartment, and they fell into the filth of the palace courtyard. All bespattered, recognizable only by his voice, he came into the palace, and protested at the way in which the house had been treated. (When we remember that the house was absolutely new, having been specially built for the purpose of the feast, we realize that this incident throws a flash of lurid light upon the contemporary theory and practice of sanitation.) Cu Chulaind was seized with one of his epileptic fits, but when he recovered from it he put the house straight, and they set them down once more to the feast in a comparative tranquillity. But not for long. The quarrel broke forth again, and the feast came to an end in confusion. The braves went forth in search of adventures whereby each could prove his claim to the champion's morsel. Adventures came, in an amorphous medley which we cannot stop to analyse: it would involve printing the whole story.

Doubtless this part of the tale has grown like the tube of a caddis-worm, built up of all manner of odds and ends collected from anywhere that might supply the story-teller with material. In the end the champion's morsel was adjudged to Cu Chulaind: and another story tells us how the mischievous Bricriu was gored to death in watching the fight between the two great bulls, with which the curtain fell upon the first of our three 'shadow-scenes'.[28]

Long ago, in the early dawn of Gaelic enthusiasm, a speaker committed himself to the assertion that there was more of educational value in Gaelic literature than in all the Classics. He has for many a year passed from the things of time: in the words of the traditional Irish periphrasis, which confounds a well-known theory of Plato by marvellously blending poetic beauty with profound philosophy, he is On the Road of Truth—and there we may safely leave him. But were he alive, and a citizen of the ideal state of our dreams, he would of a surety be prosecuted under the Act for Restraining People from Talking Nonsense, which would be the chief corner-stone of that favoured country's constitution: and on conviction he would be sentenced to solitary confinement, until he had learnt enough Greek to read with appreciation some overwhelming masterpiece such as *Oedipus at Colonus*. A defending counsel might, however, get him off on the plea that he was referring to the education of anthropologists: in honesty the jury would be obliged to admit that neither individually nor collectively could Homer, Pindar, Vergil, and all the rest of them, draw from inside knowledge so complete a picture of the thoughts, manners, and customs of primitive man, as the nameless tellers of these tales have done, in the words which they have been speaking to us, out of the murk of long-forgotten days.

CHAPTER VI

THE MEN OF THE CROSS

OFTEN do great matters spring from beginnings so small that they pass unheeded. Often, when we seek to trace the history of some movement, institution, or what not, we are baffled by the lack of records upon which to base our opening chapter. No one notices the faint ripple of a lake-surface: only when the forces of which it is the premonition increase to a hurricane does the chronicler take up his pen.

So was it with the conversion of Ireland to Christianity. It was no spectacular transformation-scene; it was the outcome of a slow and tentative process, extending in its operation over several centuries. It had already begun in the fourth century, if not earlier; it was not completed by the eighth.

Though Ireland never came under direct Roman control, the people of Ireland were not cut off from intercourse with the neighbouring portions of the Roman Empire—Britain, Gaul, Spain. We have already seen that a geographer in Alexandria was well informed as to the maritime features of the country, presumably deriving his information from trading sailors. We can, if we please, fill the abhorrent vacuum by guesswork, so long as we remember that it is only guesswork, and therefore scientifically worthless. Christian merchants, travellers, slaves—these may have come into the country from time to time, and some of them may have carried on at least an amateur missionary activity. Or perhaps a few of the weaker spirits in Christian communities within the Empire, unable to brave the fire of persecution—always smouldering, and periodically bursting into conflagration—had sought asylum in a country where the Roman emperor would not take the trouble to follow them : and, deterred by the scorn with which their brethren would have greeted such defaulters, had there settled permanently, seeking to spread whatever knowledge they themselves had of Christian truth, and thus to salve their consciences for their cowardice. Or for this flight of fancy we may substitute another : we may tell ourselves that inasmuch as we have no authentic record of the movements of more than three or four of the earliest Apostles, it is not beyond the limits of the conceivable that one of the uncelebrated residue may have found his way to Ireland and there laboured for a time. And the end of all such guessing will be to leave us precisely where we were at the beginning : there is absolutely no evidence to show how Christianity first found a footing in the country, and even if we guess aright we have no means of assuring ourselves that we have done so.

There is a story—late in the form in which we have it, but who shall say that it is not founded upon older and more trustworthy materials ?—to the effect that the enterprising king Cormac of Tara, in the middle of the third century, had assimilated enough of Christianity to make him chary of burial in a pagan cemetery, even though it had been the traditional repository of the ashes of kings.[1] The story may be mere romance, but it is not against the laws of nature. This particular king seems to have had a mind open to new ideas ; it is not impossible that there is a germ of truth at the heart of the fable. The miraculous consequences of Cormac's decision, which have found literary expression in Ferguson's fine poem, we naturally brush aside. Humanity likes a good tale, and having invented or adapted impossible wonders, will father them upon any one who attracts attention, from Alexander the Great to the village idiot. But in any case, it is to be feared that this king mingled his full share of original sin with whatever religious tenets he may have inherited from his ancestors, or adopted of his own accord !

The evidence for third-century Christianity in Ireland

rests therefore on the very shaky foundation of this story of king Cormac. For fourth-century Christianity we are on firmer ground, though the direct evidence is contained in one sentence only, and actually refers to slightly later times. This one sentence is perhaps the most frequently quoted of all historical statements having reference to Ireland. It is the assertion of Prosper Tiro, that Palladius was sent by pope Celestine to be the ' first bishop of the Scots (= Irish) that believed in Christ '. With this we may couple the record of Muirchu maccu Machtheni, to the effect that ' the wild and ungentle people ' of Ireland would not hear the doctrine of Palladius ; that he had no desire to spend his time in a land not his own ; and that in consequence he returned to him by whom he had been sent.[2]

Prosper tells us that Palladius was sent to be ' first bishop ' of the believing Scots. This has been interpreted as meaning ' first canonical bishop ' ; but Prosper himself does not say so, and the explanation would open, as a curious subject for investigation (or rather speculation), the origin and history of the implied *un*canonical bishops of the pre-Palladian Christians. It is admittedly quite possible that Prosper thought that this would be so obviously the sense of his words that it was needless to emphasize it. But we have no access to Prosper's inner consciousness ; once we begin on conjectures like that, we embark on an ocean illimitable, with neither star nor compass to guide us. Cold science demands that we assume that when Prosper said ' first bishop ' he meant ' first bishop ' ; and that we accept the only legitimate implication of the words, that before Palladius came there were no bishops at all in the country ; until some solid impregnable fact comes into view, which proves that we were wrong.[3]

Muirchu, as we shall see presently, is not a trustworthy historian : but in connexion with his account of the rejection of Palladius, the fate of the churches founded by the missionary bishop is suggestive. These were three in number. One of them, *Cell Fhine*, is now utterly unknown. The second, *Domhnach Arda*, was presumably at Donard in Co. Wicklow, but there is no trace there remaining of any very ancient ecclesiastical foundation. The third bore the name *Teach na Romānach*, ' the house of the Romans ', which yet survives in the corrupted form *Tigroney* : a name in which, with no straining of probability, we may see a touch of that impatience of the foreign intruder that found its expression in the outbreak of hostility recorded by Muirchu.

Was it in this obscure independent colony of Christianity, outside the Empire, and in consequence out of touch with the central authorities of the Christian Faith, thrown back on themselves and on their own intellectual resources, that the doctrines of Pelagius were conceived ? Certainly their chief exponent, next to the titular leader himself, was an Irishman ; whose name, whatever it may have been, is latinized *Caelestius* by the controversialists and historians who have preserved for us the records of his person and his teaching. It is against Caelestius, not Pelagius, that Jerome's oft-quoted taunt about ' Scotic porridge ' is directed. Certainly even orthodox Irish Christianity was deeply impressed with the teachings and by the writings of Pelagius, as no one can doubt who has studied carefully the imposing mass of material laboriously accumulated by Prof. Zimmer.[4] Both of these men, Pelagius and Caelestius, in the words of Harnack (here quoted in abbreviated form), were ' enthusiasts for virtue, and possessed by the idea of summoning Christendom to monachist perfection ; familiar with the Fathers, and above all following that Stoic and Aristotelian popular philosophy which numbered so many adherents among cultured Christians of the west '. They were joined by Julian from Eclanum, a town about fifty miles earth-north-east from Naples, who is described by the same scholar as an ' early widowed bishop, more active and aggressive than the reserved and prudent Pelagius, more circumspect than Caelestius the agitator, and more cultured than either '. ' Certainly ', adds Harnack, ' no dramatist could have better invented types of contrasted conceptions of life than those furnished by Augustine on the one hand and Pelagius and

Caelestius and the daring worldly bishop Julian on the other.'

This present book is not a treatise on history: still less is it a treatise on the history of theology. Any attempt to follow out the complex story of the Pelagian controversy, which shook the Church almost to its foundations in the latter half of the fourth century (even if the writer had the necessary competence for the task), would be wholly out of place. Indeed, to do so adequately would more than fill a book the size of this. Its only relevance to our present subject is the fact that it puts beyond doubt the establishment of bodies of Christians in both islands, during the fourth century, able and ready to think for themselves—a primary fact not affected by the lines on which their cogitations proceeded, or by the desirability or otherwise of the conclusions to which these led the thinkers and the world at large. Representatives of these bodies could be received and could find a hearing, even in Rome and in Jerusalem. When their teachings were found unorthodox, the most prominent theologians of the time could not afford to treat them as negligible cranks, as *gobemouche* amateurs from the backwoods of barbarous and distant islands: they were obliged to take them very seriously.

In a few words, the teaching of Pelagius may be summed up thus: God is a God of goodness and justice; the existence of righteousness is in itself a proof of the existence of God. Therefore everything created by God is good—both in the beginning and now. Therefore the now-born creature is naturally good. Nature, and human nature, were created good, and indestructibly good: they cannot be perverted except by active sin, which is a wilful act against righteousness. Evil may thus come to pervade an individual; so that every sin is mortal, in its effect on the individual sinner. But it cannot pervert human nature as a whole, nor can it be inherited; so that there is no 'original sin' inherited as the result of the guilt of Adam's transgression. Sin has come to prevail among the individual inhabitants of the world, but its apparent

THE MEN OF THE CROSS 165

universality is due entirely to children, born innocent, having acquired its taint from their environs. The grace of God through Christ can enable a man to resist the tendency to sin; and even in this life he must strive, and may actually attain, to a literal fulfilment of the command of Christ, *Estote ergo uos perfecti, sicut et Pater uester coelestis perfectus est.* The fatal oversight of these eager enthusiasts for righteousness, in the midst of a wicked world, was their failure to give due prominence to the doctrines of redemption, repentance, forgiveness : thus was the crystal of their pure souls, to which even their opponents bore ungrudging testimony, flawed to the core, and thus in the end it broke asunder.

A relic of the obscure Christians of pre-Patrician days may perhaps be found in the small cemeteries, called *ceall*, or *ceallūrach*, which exist, especially in South and West Munster. These enclosures are viewed traditionally with dislike. No one is buried in them except suicides, and children who die unbaptized. And yet there are occasionally to be seen within them ancient stones inscribed with small rude crosses : a sign that some one was there interred at some time under the Christian hope. Why then are they now degraded and deconsecrated? Surely the most reasonable explanation is that they carry a traditional taint of ancient heresy.

In 432 A.D., the year after Palladius arrived and departed, Patrick landed to begin his great mission.[5] The few recorded, and still fewer certainly authentic, details of his long and arduous life have been told and re-told, till there is nothing left to say about them : certainly nothing that is not familiar to every one likely to read this book. His father and grandfather were in ecclesiastical orders : but these seem to have been assumed, probably late in life, in order to escape from the burdensome duties of the office of *decurio*, which fell upon them in their capacity of land-owners ; rather than from any spiritual call to divine service. The homes of such ecclesiastical camp-followers were not necessarily godly ; Patrick himself had lived a life of youthful carelessness—his own words, doubtless expressed with the exaggeration of sensitive penitence, are *Deum uiuum non credebam, neque ex infantia mea*—and on one occasion he fell into an act of youthful sin. His dwelling-place, wherever it was, was in Britain, and was accessible from the sea. He was captured in his fifteenth year by plundering raiders from Ireland, carried thither, and there sold as a slave. Here he learnt the difficult language of the country, and acquired a knowledge of its complex social structure. Here he found the Lord—there is every reason to believe, through the offices of a certain Victoricus, presumably one of the 'Scots believing in Christ': who befriended the unhappy exile, and to whom in after years his protégé must have referred as 'his guardian angel'—for 'the angel Victor' is a stock character in the later apocryphal lives of the saint. How he escaped in a trading-ship: how he landed at Bordeaux, and went with his shipmates for a trek across a region recently devastated by the passage of the Vandals: how the timely capture of a herd of swine saved him and his companions from death by famine: how, after his long experience of semi-starvation as a slave, his digestion was unequal to a surfeit of pork, with the consequence, normal in such cases, of a terrific nightmare, which made a lasting impression upon him: how after many vicissitudes he succeeded in finding his way to his old home, where he was welcomed with rejoicing, and settled down in the hope that he would never again depart: how this hope was frustrated, when he was driven forth once again by a vision of the night in which his friend Victoricus, like another 'Man of Macedonia',[6] summoned him to come over and help the Irish whom he had hoped to have left behind for ever: how he was not disobedient to the heavenly vision—all these things have been narrated scores of times, nowhere so vividly as in the wonderful *Apologia* which has come down to us from his own pen. Judged as the world judges literature, by grace of style, logical coherence, and even attention to the elementary rules of grammar, this book is as remote from any normal standards of composition as the Apocalypse. Judged as the self-revelation of a personal spiritual experience, only the Apocalypse excels it in sublimity.

The mission of Palladius to Ireland was primarily to counter Pelagianism. For the same purpose, Patrick was sent in the year following his predecessor's departure. Palladius was sent by the Pope: Patrick does not appear to have had a personal papal mandate, but it would be a mere quibble to assume that the two missions had any essential difference. Palladius was sent by the ecclesiastical authorities to oppose the doctrines of Pelagius, and to be the first bishop of the Irish Christians. Patrick was sent by the ecclesiastical authorities to oppose the doctrines of Pelagius, and to be the second bishop of the Irish Christians.

But was he? The doubt arises even as we pen the words. A historian must be sure of his ground. He must take into account every scrap of the extremely scanty evidence available, whatever bearing these may have upon his interpretation of history. And there are two fragments of contemporary, or nearly contemporary evidence, patent for every one to see, and it is extremely difficult to imagine how they can be made to fit in with this easy solution of the Patrick problem.

A certain Columba—perhaps, but not certainly, the expert scribe and evangelist of Scotland more accurately known as Colum Cille—spent twelve days in transcribing for his own use a good copy of the Vulgate translation of the Gospels. This book has gone the way of most ancient books: but before it finally disappeared it fell into the hands of an artist, who based upon its text the admirable illuminated manuscript which we call the *Book of Durrow*. Our artist, high though his special talents may have been, was not otherwise a man of practical intelligence, for he conscientiously but illogically copied into the book, which he himself was preparing, the personal note with which Columba had signed his own handiwork. This note prayed for the intercession of Patrick, that whosoever should take the gospel-volume into his hands should remember the writer (in prayer). Whether this Columba was or was not the great Colum Cille, he certainly lived much nearer to Patrick's time than we do, and presumably knew a great deal more about him than we can ever hope to know: and he addresses him as *Sancte praesbiter Patrici*—' holy *presbyter* Patrick '. If Patrick was in episcopal orders, Columba ignores the fact. This is all the more pointed, in that Columba is at the moment petitioning him for a favour.

In perplexity we turn to the *Confessio*, the Saint's own autobiography. And there we meet with the second fragment of evidence, and this bewilders us yet further. In § 32 (in White's edition, published by the Royal Irish Academy), we read how one whom he had cherished as a dear friend, but whose name we never hear, had told him that episcopal orders were to be conferred upon him: of which (he characteristically adds) *non eram dignus*. But when the question of his advancement to the episcopate was finally decided, this Judas, although he had stood up as Patrick's champion on previous occasions, now suddenly and inexplicably came forward as his opponent; publicly divulging the secret of the saint's early lapse, which had been confided to him. The revelation turned the scale against Patrick's ordination: *reprobatus sum*, he writes, under the smart of a wound still painful after a lapse of years, and he could hardly make use of a stronger expression. But in the following night he had a vision. He saw his own name, with no mark of honour over against it, and he seemed to hear a divine Voice that spake thus: ' We have been grieved to see the face of one denoted, with a name emptied [of honour] ' (*Male uidimus faciem designati nudato nomine*). The phrase is difficult to translate neatly, but the sense is obvious: the Almighty was grieved by the slight which had been put upon His chosen vessel. And in the following paragraphs the Saint adds in effect: I give thanks to Him who comforted me in all things and hindered me not from the journey on which I was resolved. My conscience troubles me in nothing. I grieve for my good friend that I should have had to say this of him, but I have said enough: I dare not hide the gift of God.

We cannot apply normal standards of criticism to the

strange tangle of reminiscences that lie upon the surface of this wonderful book, or to the allusions, intelligible perhaps to contemporaries but certainly not to us, all of which we must penetrate before we reach its divine soul. But if we were to read in any ordinary autobiography, written when the writer thought himself near to death, ' I was told that I was to be made a bishop; my friend betrayed me; *reprobatus sum*; I pray God that it not be reckoned to them as sin; a vision from the Almighty comforted me ' —without the faintest hint or suggestion that the ' reprobation ' was ever reversed, or that an ordination ever actually took place, we should certainly understand that the writer had *not* been ordained as bishop. If we had reason from other sources to believe that the wrong had been righted, and the ordination actually conferred, we should not unjustly accuse the writer of a peevish fretfulness, for harping on his injury: and this is a quality utterly remote from Patrick's character.

These facts are, as I have said, patent for all to see. They call for explanation: and there is no other light from contemporary sources to cast upon them, and to illuminate their obscurity. We dare not trust later tradition in a question of history—we have only to read some of the late biographical homilies, after coming fresh from a perusal of the *Confessio*, to realize the illimitable nonsense of which tradition is capable. In fact we may lay it down, as a sound working principle, to believe nothing whatever about St Patrick which he does not tell us himself. Taking these isolated facts as they stand, they indicate that the saint's episcopal ordination, withheld from him as the result of a shameful act of treachery, was not conferred upon him by the laying on of human hands; but that in his heart of hearts, with all the firmness of which his great soul was capable, he believed himself to have received it from the Eternal Father Himself, as a mandate that admitted of no disobedience. In the *Letter to Coroticus* he begins: I assert (*fateor*) that I have been appointed a bishop in Ireland. *From God I am most confident that I have received that which I am.* Like one of the Hebrew prophets, whose writings he had assiduously studied, he had received a special call: the door, which intrigue had slammed in his face, had been opened by supernatural intervention.

But his mighty work in time met with recognition, for in the year 441 he was 'approved' at headquarters, as we learn from *The Annals of Ulster*. Long ages ago the writer of Deuteronomy formulated a test for the genuineness of a prophet's mission: later, it was applied on a momentous occasion by Gamaliel [7]: and it set a seal upon the mission of Patrick. It follows that the *Confessio* must be of an earlier date. Patrick was then 57 years of age, and might have supposed himself nearer to death than actually was the case. Some such exceptional dircumstances are required to explain this 'approval'.

This interpretation also explains what is otherwise not altogether easy to understand—the purpose for which the *Confession* was written. It is the Saint's *Apologia* for having, in this technically irregular way, assumed episcopal functions,[8] not yet regularized when he wrote it.

Such a procedure as is here suggested would have been in accordance with Patrick's temperament. He was unduly sensitive to dreams and omens. Were it not that in this he was a child of his own time, it would be difficult to withhold the harsh word 'superstition' from the attention which he paid to them. It is not a little pathetic to see his anxious gropings after the meaning of the trivial coincidence that he awoke from his nightmare in the wilderness with a cry of 'Heliam Heliam!' to find the sun (*helios*) shining upon him.*

Now, if a person who had such a mental bias saw a vision of the night, in which he was commanded to go to Ireland and there to live and act as a bishop among those

---

* *Dum clamarem Heliam Heliam.* This should not be translated 'While I was calling Helias': in the report of a speech, *clamarem* would not induce the accusative. Obviously what really happened was that in the agony of the nightmare he woke himself up in the middle of the unconscious effort to cry out the words of Christ on the Cross, *Eli, Eli, lama sabachthani.*

bishopless Christians, he would undoubtedly have been as obedient to the call, as he had been to the summons that came to him through the mouth of the phantasm of Victoricus. This view of the case is further corroborated by the indications that he went at his own charges, and paid his own way. There is not the least hint that he derived money from any organization : he definitely assures us that he refused fees and gifts : but yet, on his own showing, he was able to disburse considerable sums on various occasions. There may be relevant facts which he has not seen fit to record, but these hypothetical possibilities apart, the only available interpretation of the evidence is that he retained an interest in the family property, and drew from it a revenue sufficient for his needs.

Muirchu, it is true, tells us that he was ordained bishop by Amathorex (otherwise Amatus) bishop of Auxerre.[9] But Muirchu cannot be trusted further than we can test him; for even when he narrates incidents that Patrick himself narrates, he shows what it is not too harsh to call an unconquerable bias toward inaccuracy. A good illustration of this is his version of the story of the swine, which appeared so opportunely in the wilderness. Wild honey also was found, not necessarily on the same occasion, and Muirchu tells us that Patrick refused to eat either of the honey or of the swine, because they had been offered to idols ; and that in compensation he received some vaguely specified miraculous sustenance. Patrick himself reports his abstinence from the honey only ; and it is easy to see how this could have come about. The rough sailors found the dainty, and one of them, wishing to secure Patrick's share for himself, performed some mumbo-jumbo over it which would call into action the scruples of the Christian captive. But the swine were a very different matter. The sailors were kindly enough, even if not unduly amiable : they would hardly have suffered their protégé, escaped slave though he was, to starve : and Patrick himself would hardly have abstained from a provision which he believed to have been sent as a direct and providential answer to his own prayer. That he partook heartily of the indigestible food is sufficiently proved by his subsequent, and consequent, nightmare: surely a supernatural sustenance (of which he does not give us the remotest hint) would not have produced an effect so unpleasant! Thus Muirchu turns a simple and natural narrative into nonsense: and we must with regret conclude that whatever he chooses to tell us is not evidence, unless it can be confirmed from other sources. But we cannot confirm from other sources his assertion about Patrick's ordination, for other sources teach us that Bishop Amatus had died some fourteen years before Patrick's mission began. Admittedly Muirchu may have inadvertently named the wrong bishop. But a historian guilty of such an inadvertence cannot claim any right to be taken seriously; and in this case also we have no access to the arcana of his mind. To base any superstructure on guesses as to what we might possibly find there would not be the way to erect a *monumentum aere perennius*.

However irregular the procedure may have been, when measured by the standards of later ecclesiastical developments, it is not for a moment to be supposed that Patrick had any idea of founding in Ireland an ecclesiastical body differing from that to which in youth he had nominally belonged, and to which he owed what little education he had enjoyed. This *a priori* probability is put beyond doubt by a detached sentence attributed to his authorship, and recorded for us in the *Book of Armagh*. From it we may deduce the fact that in addition to the *Confessio* and the *Letter to Coroticus*, there was once in existence a third tract from his pen, and that this would have been historically more precious than the other two put together. The sentence runs thus: 'Church of the Scots—nay, rather, of the Romans—that ye may be Christians as well as Romans * ye ought to sing at every hour of prayer that

---

* *Ut Christiani ita ut Romani sitis.* Doubtless what he means is *Ut Romani ita ut Christiani sitis*: the inversion is in accordance with Patrick's difficulty in literary self-expression, and is an argument in favour of the authenticity of the fragment, which has been impugned by Bury, *Life*, pp. 228 ff.

THE MEN OF THE CROSS 173

praiseworthy hymn, *Kyrie eleison*. Let every church that followeth me sing, *Kyrie eleison*.' The use of *Kyrie eleison* had shortly before been introduced at Rome, but not as yet into Gaul; this explains the sentence, which otherwise would have neither point nor meaning. It must be the opening words of a manifesto, addressed to the pre-Patrician Christians, enumerating their liturgical and other shortcomings as measured by contemporary Roman standards, and directing them how they should act, in order to conform to the church which Patrick had come to establish among them: at the same time giving liturgical and doctrinal instruction to the churches of his own foundation. The use of *Kyrie eleison* happened to be the first item in the list: the rest of the catalogue was, to our grave loss, suppressed; presumably because by the time the *Book of Armagh* was written the absorption of the pre-Patrician into the Patrician Church was so far complete that the document was no longer of any practical importance. Indeed, it may have been considered inadvisable to perpetuate what from the standpoint of that time would have been regarded as a catalogue of heresies.

The Apostle's chief foes were those to whom he should have most naturally looked for support. His ecclesiastical superiors were never sympathetic. The familiar friend to whom he confided the story of his early lapse—what it may have been we do not know, have no right to know, and should not wish to know—was not the only one who gave him pain. *Is it nothing to you, all ye that pass by*, might have been set as a text at the beginning of the book, which for all his ardent reliance on Divine support, is dominated throughout by intense sadness. Why does he find it necessary to set forth so minutely all the conversions which he has made, all the injuries which he has experienced, all the gifts which he has refused?

The answer is obvious: he was looked at askance, for if he had a mandate, he had gone beyond it. What was wanted in Ireland was not a missionary, but a substitute for Palladius; whose business had been not the conversion of heathens, but controversy with Christians. This follows inevitably from Patrick's own report of his critics. ' Behind my back they kept on telling and talking (*narrabant et dicebant*)—That fellow, why does he put himself into danger among enemies who have not known God?' (*Conf.* § 46). In sober truth, the missionary enthusiasm of the Apostolic Age had for the moment exhausted itself, and needed re-kindling at the hands of just such men as Patrick and Colum Cille. But though carpers might rail, and friends might prove faithless, Patrick faithfully carried out the mandate given him, whether by man or by a direct inspiration from his Lord, in a slower but in the end more effective way than his critics could have contrived. He had before him, as an object-lesson, the fate of the tactless Palladius: had he attempted to follow the same methods he would have fallen likewise, and shared the obscurity of his predecessor. His natural power of organization, his insight into the hearts and souls of men, saved him from such an error. He set himself to build up a rampart of the Church, whose sphere he had come to extend, formed, not of the ' Scots believing in Christ ' but of converted heathens. These latter, he hoped and believed, would in time grow, and would embrace and absorb the descendants of the native Christians, to whom, for all their heresies, he was himself under such profound obligations. Though the process lasted through several centuries, the result justified his foresight. Nevertheless, in the early days of the monastery at Tallaght, three hundred years later, there still lingered in that neighbourhood certain ' old churches ', the communities and ministering officers of which were looked on by the orthodox with suspicion and dislike.[10]

As there is no exception to the law of gravitation, so there is no exception to the law of evolution. Even ecclesiastical discipline, order, and doctrine, inasmuch as their threads are woven through the web of life in the material universe, must be subject to that law. The teachings of the physical sciences, of anthropology, of literary and historical criticism, and so forth, are divine revelations to Man no less than the teachings of prophets and apostles in days of old: they are indeed the channels through which his knowledge of the works and ways of the Creator is ever renewed and enlarged: so that it is his duty to hearken to their message. If (to take a single illustration) these sciences oblige us to regard the old Hebrew allegory of the Fall of Man as something other than literal history, then the Pauline doctrine of original sin (to which we have already had occasion to refer), in so far as its statement presupposes the literal historicity of that narrative, must needs be re-stated in terms free from such a presupposition. And we need not be surprised if in disciplinary matters we find less rigidity in the fifth century than in, say, the thirteenth. It would indeed have been impossible, considering the chaotic condition of Europe between the first tottering of the Roman empire and the rise of Charlemagne: a chaos which even our experience of contemporary unrest does not qualify us so much as to imagine.

Nor can we set any mechanical limitations on the work of the Spirit of God. We can trace His influence in a Socrates, nay, even in any nameless African medicine-man who in his darkness imposes on his people a tabu of real moral or sanitary value: all the more in a Patrick, by whatever gate he may enter the divine Service. If we admit that the Lord of Nature is free to suspend the laws of Nature at His pleasure, in the performance or sanctioning of miracle, we must also admit that the Lord of a Church is free to suspend at His pleasure the laws of His Church. If we admit that a divine Power on earth was pleased to give sight to a man born blind, and afterwards, when he had been cast out by the Church of his day, to seek him out and enlist him in His own service, we must admit that the same Power could at his pleasure give sight to a man born in the blindness of illiteracy, and reared in the squalor of servitude; and afterwards, when he had been rejected by the Church of his day, could seek him out and promote him to high honour in His Service.

There I leave the much-disputed questions relating to the origins of Irish Christianity. All they who ransack, for controversial ammunition, the few faded, tattered documents which happen to have fluttered down to us out of the wreckage of time, take out of them precisely what they put into them, and convince no one but those who are already convinced. No doubt future discoveries may bring us unexpected revelations. But for the present there is no authority on earth that can settle the disputes to the satisfaction of every one. I have conscientiously set forth the views toward which I have found myself impelled: but controversy may pursue its dreary circling till the end of all things, and I have no intention of taking a stand upon that profitless treadmill.

Anyhow, Patrick came to a country predominantly Pagan, and he left it with its face stedfastly set toward the light. Yet withal the ghosts of the mighty dead ceased not to haunt the mounds wherein they had been laid; they haunt them still. The nameless, unindividualized 'spirits of the corn and the wild' ceased not to haunt the fields and the cattle byres, ceased not to dance in the moonlight—under their new name of 'fairies' they linger still, loth to desert the old ring-walled farmsteadings to whose long-vanished indwellers they were wont to bring good luck or ill according to their whims: loth to quit the ancient meads and the woodlands wherein they had held high festival ever since the days of the Stone Age.

The Bronze Age in Ireland is illustrated by a rich store of relics which have come to light; and doubtless many more remain to be discovered. The pagan Iron Period is less well 'documented', but still has left a fair number of traces. But when we cross the borderline into the time of Christianity we are met at first by a rebuff. So far as tangible monuments go, an almost death-like silence shrouds the first centuries of Christianity in Ireland. We read in the Annals of the lively activities of saints and sinners between the fourth and the seventh centuries. We hear of the establishment of churches and monasteries, of schools of art and of learning: but we seek in vain for actual evidences of their existence. No recognizable monument marks the graves of Cormac, Loiguire mac Neill, Patrick,

Diarmait mac Cerbhaill, Ciaran, or any other of the men who made history during this time. We possess a considerable number of Ogham inscriptions, coming down from these centuries of obscurity: we may presume that most of them commemorate persons of some local repute: but we can easily count on the fingers of one hand those that record persons who have earned even a passing mention in any book of Annals. So far as art is concerned, the country might have been depopulated. Future discovery may fill the gap; we have no idea of what may or may not be underground, to be revealed when funds for the search are available. But for the present there is a notable hiatus in Irish archaeology, between the pagan Iron Age and the high tide of Christian Art.

During this obscure time a new learning was evolved. Latin (with a *soupçon* of Greek, and even what chemical analysts call 'traces' of Hebrew) was imported with Christianity; as well as the knowledge of how to prepare books from vellum, and to record thoughts and facts upon their pages with ink and pen. Among the busy scholars, there were brethren with artistic instincts, who experimented in imitations of the quaint frets and twists which Byzantine art had made current over Europe; and who sought to reproduce them in vellum, embroidery, metal, carven wood, and perhaps, though at this stage less probably, carven stone.

No one is likely to maintain that the perfection which we find in the greatest works of Christian Celtic art was attained at a stroke. Everything, human endeavour included, is a matter of evolution, sometimes very slow, calling for infinite patience, and liable to retardation or to a partial or complete interruption by such external accidents as wars or famines. We are often able to retrace the steps of the development—a most instructive exercise —by bringing together products of different stages and comparing them; but in the case of the art of Christian 'Celtic' Ireland this is impossible, for two reasons: the loss of the earliest relics, and the difficulty of arranging the surviving remnants chronologically.

Destruction has removed from our reach practically all the examples of the early stages. The sentiment of preserving an ancient relic, merely because it is ancient, is entirely modern, and is not always effective even in modern times. In these days people will sell the jewellery that had been worn and treasured by their own mothers, for the sake of a few paltry shillings' worth of gold: in like manner, obsolete works of art, in any of the precious metals, would in former days have been melted down and remodelled without a qualm—the more so, because they did not then possess the antiquity that might have hallowed them for us. As for books, they would be worn and thumbed out of existence, like any modern school or story-book: and the thumbs were usually grimy. Even in these days very few people know how to treat a book, as any librarian will tell us. If the book had been the property of some notable saint, its chances of survival—contrary to what we might have expected—would be diminished to evanescence. As the sorry fragments of the *Gospels of Clones** show only too clearly, such a book would be ruined without remorse by people cutting snippets from it to make amulets, or pouring water over it to make healing draughts for sick cattle.

Thus, for the present, we have no preliminary studies to help us to discern the beginnings of the art which, in the ninth and tenth centuries, so abundantly enriched the Christian life of Ireland. But we are not entitled to jump to the conclusion that such preliminary studies did not exist, and that Ireland had no share in the development from La Tène art to, let us say, the art of the ninth century. There is undoubtedly a hiatus, a very disconcerting hiatus, between the two periods: but it is a hiatus in our knowledge, not in the ordered sequence of evolution. Until all the possible fruits of excavation have been garnered, we cannot dogmatize on what may or may not have been the course of artistic evolution.

There is actually one transitional monument in exist-

* In the Royal Irish Academy Library: erroneously called ' St Patrick's Gospels ' or ' The Domhnach Airgid MS.'.

ence: the stele of Mullaghmast (fig. 28). This most important stone, now in the National Museum, is a small pillar, roughly triangular in horizontal section, and bearing decoration over its whole surface. There is no trace of an inscription. The decoration has strong La Tène reminiscences: indeed, in the first published description of its designs, it was coupled with the La Tène stones at Turoe House and at Castle Strange.[11] But we have only to see them together to realize immediately that it represents an art that has travelled far from the La Tène standard. It reaches forward to the formal diapers of spirals, linked by C-shaped curves, which we find in especial profusion in the earlier works of Celtic Christian art.

As yet the Mullaghmast stone is unique. Nowhere else, in Ireland or out of it, is there such a perfect example of a transitional stage between the two styles. Where there is one, there ought to be more, still awaiting discovery: but in the meantime the Mullaghmast stone is fatal to theories which would deprive Ireland of a share in the development of the early Christian art of the North. To claim the *whole* credit would naturally be ridiculous; indeed, to claim the whole credit for *any* country or region would be ridiculous. Evolution was working all the time, over the entire area involved, and was producing local developments which, as they grew to maturity, met, intermingled, and to some extent pooled their new resources. But concurrently with this development, a ceaseless destruction was also in progress—wear and tear, superannuation of antiquated forms and fashions, the attentions of raiders, all took their toll; and naturally the older and least developed works suffered the most. Wood, textiles, parchment, all these decay; metal can be stolen and melted down. Stone is enduring: but stone sculpture does not appear to have been much practised in the early beginnings of Christian art; and we have only to visit any old and ill-kept cemetery to see how obsolete tombstones become defaced, broken, and appropriated to other uses. A friend of my own found part of a tombstone inscription on the

FIG. 28.—DIAGRAM OF THE ORNAMENTATION REMAINING UPON THE MULLAGHMAST STONE

back of a marble chimney-piece, during some repairs in his house.

The remains of early Irish Christianity are partly architectural, partly monumental, partly artistic.

The architectural remains are almost entirely ecclesiastical, though not exclusively church buildings. There is a ruined dwelling-house with Romanesque detail at Kilmalkedar, Co. Kerry, locally called 'The Priest's House',[12]—a name which may or may not enshrine authentic tradition. The three-storey stone building at Kells commonly called 'St Columba's House' is presumably the residence house of an early monastic establishment. The gatehouse of the monastic enclosure at Glendaloch is still preserved in part. But most of the residential portions of the primitive monasteries were made of wood, or (when established on an island like High Island [13] or the Skellig Rock, where no wood was available) were crude beehive huts. All the architectural powers of the workers in stone were concentrated on the church, and, later, on its associated belfry-tower.

It is unnecessary to recapitulate the story of the derivation of the primitive stone churches from wooden prototypes, and of the traces of the wooden constructions which they present. The process has already been described in the author's *Archaeology of Ireland*, at p. 248; but the statement there made that the ridge-piece of the roof was laid in the fork of crossing gable-principals must be corrected. My friend Mr. H. G. Leask, the Superintendent of Ancient Monuments for the Irish Free State, has confirmed the doubts of the possibility of this construction which had begun to present themselves to myself. The ridge-piece must have been secured in some other way, of the nature of which we have no evidence.

The most important of the facts regarding primitive church Architecture in Ireland will be found summarized briefly in a later chapter. One point of ritual rather than of architecture may here be mentioned, as it may have some bearing on the reason for the multiplication of very small churches, practically incapable of accommodating more than the officiating clergy.

If we take the well-known description of the church of Kildare in Cogitosus' *Life of Brigid*, as a specification, and endeavour to draw a plan to correspond with it, we shall find ourselves obliged to place a screen in front of and hiding the altar (fig. 29). Such a screen corresponds to the iconostasis of the Oriental Churches; and there is a possibility that it was a portion of the fittings of the early churches in Ireland. In the church of the monastery of Tallaght there was what was called the *clais tarsna* [14] in front of the altar. This word might mean 'transverse choir', as it is translated in the printed edition, but that

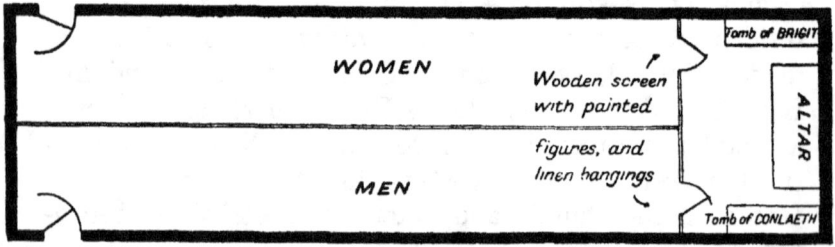

FIG. 29.—THE CHURCH OF KILDARE FROM THE DESCRIPTION OF COGITOSUS

does not seem to correspond to any liturgical actuality. We must take the word *clais* in its other sense, as 'groove', into which a movable screen could be or had been fitted. This makes intelligible the passage in which the expression occurs. It is on record that any one who passed between the altar and the *clais tarsna* incurred penance: in other words, no one might walk between the altar and the iconostasis. This is avoided, in the Kildare church, by providing a doorway at each end of the screen.

If then the altar was normally screened from view, we can understand better why the oratories were so small that the laity could not find accommodation within them, and remained in the open air during the performance of the various ceremonies. The whole church was in such a case the sanctuary, corresponding to the part of Cogitosus' church behind the iconostasis.

THE MEN OF THE CROSS 183

The monumental remains are the simple memorial pillars and slabs which imperfectly perpetuate the memory of individual Christians, clerical or lay. Imperfectly, because only in an insignificant modicum of cases do they present indications to enable us to identify the owner of the monument. More than half of them have no inscription at all —just a cross, sometimes of the plainest kind, but more frequently treated decoratively. The decoration is quite simple: nothing more than the development into triangles, spirals, and other devices of the ends of the arms of the cross, or the addition of round hollows or other embellishments to the spaces in the four quarters. Rarely does the stone bear any device other than the cross. Even when there is an inscription present it does not leave us much the wiser. It begs for 'a prayer for Cellach' or 'for Ruarcan' or for some one else, but the personalities whom these names once denoted have vanished like last year's snows. Sometimes it adds the father's name, and this narrows our search: we occasionally find a similar combination of names in the Annals, and are correspondingly thankful to find such a chronological datum. Yet more rarely does the inscription specify the office of the deceased—king, bishop, priest, wright, or what not: and even then we are liable to disappointment. Thus, at Clonmacnois there is a slab commemorating a certain 'Bishop Dathal': but who this prelate may have been is absolutely unknown—no collection of secular or ecclesiastical *fasti* records his name.[15]

The earliest memorial slabs at Clonmacnois show us that the series of cross-inscribed monuments begins with those in which the four arms of the cross are of equal length— the Greek cross: and it is possible that this fact, united with the evidence for an iconostasis in the churches, may indicate an oriental influence in the ecclesiastical art of Ireland, of which further evidence is not lacking in the details of monumental sculptures in the crosses and early church buildings.

Probably the most important of the inscribed monuments in the country is the pillar-stone at Kilnasaggart,

Co. Armagh. On one face this monument shows a series of circular discs, in relief, each bearing an equal-armed cross with spiral ends to the arms. This spiral end is probably a development of the ancient *Chi-rho* symbol, the single 'rho' having been multiplied by the influence of a desire for symmetry (fig. 30). Underneath, there is a large series of tool-marks, made in the process of sharpening the ill-tempered tool with which the sculptor executed his work. These discs are ten in number, and it is evident that ten, and no more, were required, for they are disposed symmetrically till the last example, which upsets the balance (fig. 31). When we look at them again, we see

FIG. 30.—DEVELOPMENT OF AN ORNAMENTAL CROSS FROM THE CHI-RHO SYMBOL

that five are small and five are large; and then their purpose becomes obvious. They are bread-wafers: and the sculpture is an allusion to the miracle of the Feeding of the Five Thousand, in which the five small loaves were multiplied. When we turn to the other side we find a large Latin cross, under which is an unusually long inscription, with an equal-armed cross within a circle—this time however incised—beneath it. The inscription says *In loc so tanimmarni Ternohc mac Ceran Bic er cul Peter Apstel* —'This place, Ternoc son of Ciaran the Little bequeathed it, under the patronage of Peter the Apostle': the Apostle charged with the duty of Feeding the Sheep with the inexhaustible wafers pictured on the other side of the stone. We do not know who Ternoc was: but we know

FIG. 31.—THE KILNASAGGART STONE

from the Annalists that he died in the year 714 or 716. This is the oldest certainly dated inscription in Ireland—the monument on Inchagoill, an island of Loch Corrib, is probably older, but Petrie's identification of its owner with a nephew of St. Patrick is altogether inadmissible, and we do not know its date. The Kilnasaggart stone is a monument of the working of the leaven of Patrick's teaching, reinforced by the then recent decision of the Synod of Whitby: a stone with a similar dedication to 'the apostle Peter' at Whithorn, the site of *Candida Casa*, is a British counterpart. From a social and legal standpoint, also, the monument is of importance: it gives us an actual example of the making of a bequest, whatever may have been the instrument which took the place of a will: and it also illustrates the possibility of alienating property in land by such a transaction.[16]

The artistic monuments of early Irish Christianity take the form of illuminations on vellum; decorated articles in leather and in various metals, along with settings of enamel, crystal, and precious stones; and sculpture in wood and in stone. In a book of this size it would be impossible to do more than to go over elementary ground already well covered. So far as the analysis of works of Celtic Art is concerned, there are already plenty of books available: and in these latter days the sumptuous publications of the lamented Kingsley Porter, of Françoise Henry, and of the Free State Government under the editorship of Dr. Mahr, have made a large amount of material available for students.[17] But notwithstanding these admirable works, we must emphasize once more the extreme imperfection of our knowledge of this important and immensely wide subject. Almost every single work might be made the subject of a separate monograph. There is hardly a sculptured cross whose pictorial panels can be fully explained: there are riddles, which up to the present have proved more insoluble than that of the Sphinx of old, at Monasterboice, Kells, Old Kilcullen and a dozen other places. And the knowledge which we possess does not as yet qualify us to deal with new discoveries. Every new discovery is a surprise ; the Irish objects in Scandinavian Museums, which formed part of a fascinating exhibition of the 'Art of the Dark Ages' brought together in the year 1931 at the Burlington Fine Arts Club in London, seemed to open fresh vistas of research : as does also the unique but as yet unpublished hanging lamp, discovered in the Harvard excavations at Ballinderry.

We have seen that when we endeavour to trace the history of Celtic Christian art, our first difficulty is to reconstruct the story of its first beginnings. In the later stages of the study we are not much better off, for we are hampered from first to last by baffling chronological difficulties. It is impossible to write a history of any art, or indeed of anything, without knowing how to date the works in which it is manifested : chronology is as necessary to history as a skeleton to a vertebrate. But no tests by which to date early Christian antiquities, either in Great Britain or in Ireland, have hitherto been discovered. Even the two greatest monuments of early sculpture which either island possesses, the crosses of Ruthwell and Bewcastle, have been assigned by various authorities to dates some six hundred years apart—a range which covers practically the entire history of the art of which they are the leading examples. We can best expose our chronological imperfections by enumerating the chief surviving works of Irish art, with the evidence available for dating them.

Let us first take Illuminated Manuscripts. These may be dated by a colophon, appended to the text (in the majority of cases on the last page), giving the name of the scribe, who may or may not be mentioned in some book of Annals or other historical record. It may also mention a datable abbot, secular ruler, or some other authority, under whose auspices the scribe carried out his work. But colophons in current phrase, have a disconcerting way of 'letting us down', as the following enumeration will show :

(1) *Colophon contemporary, perfectly informing, and absolutely trustworthy :* one case only, the *Book of Armagh* (A.D. 807) :[18] a book, however, which is of no significance

for the history of art, though of the first importance in ecclesiastical history and literature.

(2) *Colophon a late addition, and of no secure authority:* the *Book of Lindisfarne*,[19] which is mentioned here because so much importance has been attached to it as a landmark in the history of Celtic art. The colophon assigns the work to a bishop who died in A.D. 721; but this is merely the statement of a man as far removed from the time of that bishop as we are from the time of Queen Anne, and we know nothing of the authority, if any, upon which he based it. Whatever may be the origin of the book itself, its colophon must be condemned as scientifically worthless, in the absence of such knowledge.

(3) *Colophon copied unintelligently from the exemplar which lay before the scribe.* This has happened possibly in the *Book of Moling* (bishop of Ferns), and certainly in the *Book of Durrow*. For the latter we have a minor limit of date, in that according to the inscription on the lost shrine, a copy of which is preserved in a note in the MS. itself, that receptacle was made at the charges of Flann king of Ireland, who died in A.D. 913.

(4) *Colophon a forgery*. This is illustrated by the so-called *Book of Dimma*. There are several colophons in this MS., and in every one of them the name of the real scribe has been scratched out and that of 'Dimma' substituted.[20] The reason for this transaction is obvious. Dimma was a real person—a seventh-century scribe of Roscrea. He was said to have written a gospel-book in a miraculously short space of time. Perhaps he did: but if so it was merely a rough copy for common use. Like Columba's colophon, his scribal note became transferred to an illuminated MS., and *this* book before long came to be regarded as the miraculous product. As such, it was promptly cut up into amulets. The brethren, having thus lost their treasure, had to ransack their library to find another book to take its place.

(5) *Colophon lost*. An outstanding case is the *Book of Kells*,[21] the last leaf of which is missing and presumably the colophon with it. The name of one of the greatest

practitioners of the art of illumination who ever lived is thus for ever unknown. The Trinity College *Liber Hymnorum* also has no colophon.

(6) *Colophon mentions a person who cannot be identified.* The *Stowe St John* [22] is signed in Ogham letters by one Sonid, of whom we know absolutely nothing. The *Rushworth Gospels* in the Bodleian Library is signed by a certain Mac Regol [23] or Mac Reguil (he was a respectable artist, but uncertain as to how to spell his own name). There was a scribe of that name at Birr, who died in 820. The name is uncommon; but as the scribe of the gospel-book does not mention his parentage, we are not entitled to assume that the two persons were identical. We shall see presently that such assumptions sometimes receive rude shocks.

(7) *Colophon gives us details about the history of the book, but no information about its date.* The *Gospels of Mael-Brigte*, now in Lambeth Palace Library, tell us that Mael-Brigte mac Durnain, presumably the Abbot of Iona of that name (891–925), ' dogmatiza[ui]t ' the text, which, I suppose, means collated and approved it; and that Athelstan, king of the Saxons (925–940), having somehow become possessed of it, presented it to the see of Canterbury. This tells us that the book was already in existence about 900, but gives us no further information.[24]

The result of this is the unfortunate fact that, putting aside the *Book of Armagh*, which in any case would not concern us, there is not a single illuminated manuscript of the Celtic period to which we can in absolute security attach a date.

We might have hoped for help from the texts of the MSS. The *Book of Durrow* gives us a very pure Vulgate text, the Books of *Kells* and *Moling* a mixed text, in which Vulgate and Old Latin renderings are intermingled. But apart from the fact that the history of the text of the Latin Gospels is itself an exceedingly thorny subject, the hope is illusory, as a moment's thought will show. The scribes of these illuminated gospels were making works of art, not multiplying texts for practical use. They were applying their art to the glorification of the sacred words. When the *Book of Kells* was finished—so far as it ever was finished, for some of the illuminations are incomplete —it was enshrined in a golden casket and was kept there until the casket was stolen. The actual text which they used was therefore not of much importance: they were artists, not critics. They took the first copy of the Gospels that came to hand, to supply them with the words which they decorated. Consequently a 'mixed' text does not necessarily prove an MS. to be earlier than a pure Vulgate text. In fact the *Garland of Howth*, a fragment of a MS. in Trinity College Library,[25] though it is clearly among the latest and most degenerate of the surviving examples of the art, presents one of the earliest texts. Again, I have some doubt as to whether we can safely assume that the illuminator of a manuscript was the person whom the Annalists would call a *scriba*. The *scriba* of a monastery was the functionary who provided it with books: books that were meant to be handled and read. But the illumination of such a book as the *Gospels of Kells* would occupy a huge cantle out of a man's whole life. He would not be fulfilling the duties of a *scriba* during the time that he was engaged upon it. Still less is it easy to have any faith in a bishop spending his time in illuminating the *Book of Lindisfarne*, as that unfortunate colophon would have us to believe. He might have been a very good artist, but he would have been most reprehensibly neglectful of his episcopal duties.

Nor can we, at least at the present stage of knowledge, put the MSS. in even a relative chronology, in the hope that some later discovery will in the future anchor our sequence to the ordinary framework of history. For we must make allowances for the 'personal equation'; and whatever astronomers can do with their assistants, palaeographers cannot reduce the personal equation of the artists with whom they are concerned to mathematical formulae. The *Rushworth Gospels* is a fine book, but obviously inferior to the *Gospels of Kells*. That may be for any one of three reasons, and we have no guide to enable us to choose among them. The Rushworth book may be older than the Kells book—it may be the product of an art climbing the slope that leads upward to the apex on which the Kells book stands. Or it may be later than the Kells book—the product of an art dropping into decadence after having achieved its supreme triumphs. Or it may be the work of a meritorious artist who was an exact contemporary of the consummate genius who adorned the house of Kells, or Iona, or wherever else the *Gospels of Kells* may have been produced. We can certainly detect the evidence of decadence, and, especially of Scandinavian influence, in such late books as the *Psalter of St Caimin*, the *Psalter of Ricemarch*,[26] and the *Garland of Howth* : the exuberance of animal ornament, and the form of the letters, oblige us to assign these books to the twelfth century. But for the rest, the art of Celtic illuminated manuscripts is a maze as bewildering as its own interlacements, and no one has yet arisen to play the part of that unprincipled and unfilial young person Ariadne.[27]

In metal-work we are rather more fortunate, as there is quite a considerable number of inscribed objects, some of which can be satisfactorily dated. We may mention : [27]

Ballyspellan and Killamery brooches : inscribed, but the names cannot be identified or dated.

Ardagh Cup : the only inscription is the names of the Apostles (substituting Paul for Judas) : no datable inscription.

Shrine of the Gospels of Molaise : datable, by the mention of the name of the abbot of Devenish, to 1001-1025.

Shrine of the Gospels of Clones (incorrectly called *Domhnach Airgid*). Only date of its repair in 1350 recorded.

Shrine of St Patrick's Bell : mentions several persons, whose lives narrow the date to 1091-1105.

Shrine of St Moedoc : no inscription.

Shrine of St Lachtin's Arm : dated by inscriptions to between 1118 and 1127.

Cross of Cong : dated by inscriptions to between 1123 and 1150.

It will be noticed that all the datable examples of metal-

THE MEN OF THE CROSS

work come after the time of the Viking raids. Everything before that time has gone for ever. It will also be noticed that as in the case of the Manuscripts, the most important objects, the Bettystown Brooch and the Ardagh Cup, are undatable. The case of the latter is beyond measure exasperating : for the lettering of its inscription is so closely akin to that of the Gospels of Kells, that if we could certainly date the Ardagh Cup we could date with approximate accuracy the Kells volume also.[28]

Monuments in stone may be architectural or 'sculptural'. And these are as unsatisfactory, chronologically, as all the rest. Certainly this is conspicuously true of the architectural remains of the Celtic Church. We have many little stone churches dotted over the country : primitive cells, with trabeated doorways—though their windows are often cut into an arch shape, showing that their builders knew what an arch looked like, and quite probably could have constructed an arch if they had so desired ; featureless buildings of rubble, or of ashlar mortared or unmortared ; churches with Romanesque ornament, introduced from some foreign source, and flourishing side by side with the native traditions of decoration ; and we cannot with assurance put a date upon a single one of them. Two elaborate Romanesque doorways, at Killeshin and at Freshford,[29] respectively, bear inscriptions. These inscriptions commemorate the persons under whose auspices the buildings were erected, and who were presumably people of substance and influence. But by some fatality, they missed the eyes of the Annalists : among the scores upon scores of names, now empty of all significance, recorded on the arid pages of those chroniclers, we look in vain for the records of these ancient benefactors. Thus, once more, our anchors drag in soft mud, and we drift helpless.

Till recently we flattered ourselves that we had two fixed points for the history of Sculpture : the 'Cross of the Scriptures' at Clonmacnois, and the Cross of Muiredach at Monasterboice. If the cross at Clonmacnois really commemorates Flann, king of Ireland, who died A.D. 913, then we have a fixed point : [30] but the evidence depends upon an old copy of the inscription, which some abominable iconoclast has in later years battered beyond recognition. I have made many attempts to check this copy, but though I have found nothing to discredit it, I cannot verify it. As for the Monasterboice cross, it bears an inscription to say that it was made by, or under the auspices of, a certain Muiredach. There was a distinguished abbot of Monasterboice of that name, who died in 924 : and from the days of George Petrie downward it was assumed that the two Muiredachs were one, and that this cross, which greatly resembles the Clonmacnois cross and might have come from the same *atelier*, was a further testimony to an early tenth-century date for monuments of this type. But ' Muiredach ' has now been found as a stone-cutter on one of the crosses of Kells : and we are forced to conclude that at Monasterboice we have to deal with two persons, an abbot, and an artist in stone, both of whom bore this not uncommon name : and that the abbot's date has no bearing whatever on the date of the stone-cutter and of his handiworks.

In all such cases, identifications based upon a mere similarity of names, unless the parentage of the owners of those names is also recorded, are shaky foundations on which to base a chronological structure : and if as in this Muiredach case, the identification prove illusory, it will bring our Tower of Babel toppling about our ears. It would be ridiculous to tie down a stone inscribed merely with the words ' A Prayer for Colman ' or ' for Cellach ' to any one of the dozens of recorded persons with common names like these : and even if the name should happen to be rare, the identification calls for caution.

The humbler memorial slabs at Clonmacnois can certainly be arranged in a chronological series. A succession of fashions seems there to have prevailed ; and a number of the names, found on the stones illustrating each of these types, can be collated with personages in successive centuries who are recorded as having been worthies of Clonmacnois. Thus we can associate each type with a particular century, and place the slabs in a chronological order which

THE MEN OF THE CROSS 193

may reasonably be accepted as correct.[31] But the scheme breaks down when we travel outside the sphere of influence of Clonmacnois. Not far away, at a place called Clonburren, on the other side of the Shannon, there is a graveyard in which lies a slab commemorating one Mael-Moicheirge : and its style of ornamentation is completely outside the Clonmacnois series, so that Clonmacnois has no light to throw upon its date.[32]

Thus we conclude where we began : that the true history of Christian art in Celtic Ireland is utterly unknown. We know nothing, except what the Mullaghmast stone can tell us, of the evolutionary process by which it came into being. We do not know with complete certainty even the century in which its highest achievements were accomplished. We cannot trace its course or follow out its development. Nothing can show this better than the inconclusive nature of the attempts that have been made to arrange special groups of objects, such as pins, and fibulae or brooches, in an evolutionary sequence.[33]

The problem is not an exclusively Irish problem. The whole early art of Great Britain and of the Germanic peoples is involved with it. The mutual influence of all these peoples has been estimated very variously, some giving the impulse to one, some to another. Some would deny all initiative to the Celtic peoples ; [34] others would make them the teachers of the Teutons—a rash position which no one would now seriously maintain. The ultimate origin of the art has also to be sought for, and we find it in such far remote lands as Egypt, Armenia, Persia, India, as well as in the classical lands of the Mediterranean. A serious complication is introduced by certain sculptured crosses in Wales, bearing inscriptions which would require us to date them comparatively early, and yet showing all the marks of decadence or, at least, incompetence.

Within the small compass of a volume like this we can do no more than this to indicate that every work of ancient Irish Christian art, which we can handle, has thus around it an aura of problems which seem to become more impenetrable the more we are able to discover. What is the date of this ornament? Where did this peculiar technique originate? Where did this design come from? What is the meaning of *this* sculptured panel? *That* sculptured panel obviously represents such and such a familiar scene, Adam and Eve, the Holy Children in the Furnace, the Crucifixion, or what not: but how did it come to represent it in that particular way? What is the meaning of this, that, or the other detail in the treatment of the subject? Why does it differ from other representations of the same scene?—these are only a few of the questions that haunt us; and we cannot answer, save with a shake of the head and a sad *non possumus*.

Some day, perhaps, when politics shall have ceased from troubling and the country is at rest, a library or a museum will be in a position to provide itself with a complete corpus of Celtic and Teutonic art—manuscript, sculpture, metal-work—not in book form but on cards that can be manipulated, shifted, compared, and sorted; with a vast series of reference works on the arts of Coptic and Armenian Christianity, of Byzantium, of India, and of whatever other regions may have a bearing on the subject, as well as technical treatises on the processes of the illuminator and metal-worker: and to maintain an army of students for the purpose of bringing order out of the chaos. If that dream of Utopia were ever fulfilled, we might hope to have some knowledge of the history of Celtic Christian art. Till then, we shall be merely like so many cocks, each scratching his own rubbish-heap, one finding a beetle and another a jewel, but collectively incompetent to formulate a cosmic scheme that shall reconcile these incongruities.

A case in point is the remarkable series of sculptures discovered in the course of works of repair on White Island, in Loch Erne.

White Island is one of the small archipelago situated in Castle Archdale Bay, on the eastern side of the Lower Loch Erne, about three miles south of Kesh. It bears the relics, reduced to their foundations only, of a monastic settlement, and a rectangular church 47 ft 8 in. long and

FIG. 32.—THE WHITE ISLAND SCULPTURES

THE MEN OF THE CROSS

27 ft across. On the south side of this church there is a simple but very elegant Romanesque doorway—which happens to be the only one of its kind in the province of Ulster.

In 1928 the repair of this church was undertaken, involving the clearance of rubbish from the site, and the removal of ivy and other destructive vegetation from the walls.

A series of seven strange carved figures (figs. 32, 33) was then found built into the wall. Three of these figures had previously been known to exist, and had been illustrated so long ago as 1861; they had been found by the proprietor of the island, lying loose in the ruins, and by him had been fixed in the wall. The remaining four were new discoveries: the whole series now stands in a row, and confronts the visitor as he enters the church.

In the style of the carving these figures belong to a school entirely different from any of those which gave us the sculptured crosses or the sculptured doorways. The heavy overhanging brows, the eyes formed by knobs in relief in the middle of deep hollows, the short noses and very long upper lips—some of them in this respect presenting a curious anticipation of the stage-Irish face of the ' comic ' papers—the very prominent cheek-bones and chin, all differentiate these figures from anything that is known elsewhere in the country. The treatment of the hair in two of the figures is also quite peculiar.

Two things are obvious at first sight. The figures were at one time the supports of something, for a mortice-hole is cut in the tops of the heads: and the church-builders who erected the Romanesque building were at once ashamed and afraid of them; for they built them into the walls in such a way that they could no longer be seen, but they did not venture to destroy them.

The first of these figures is one of those strange carvings which so frequently disconcert us with a sense of incongruity when we see them on buildings devoted to sacred use. The silly name ' Sheelanagig ' is established for them, and we need not try to disturb it, as most people know what it means.* The White Island sheelanagig is less disconcerting to, shall we say, Mrs. Grundy, than some of its kindred; but its relationship is unmistakable. And once again we ask ourselves, what are these extraordinary figures for? Are they merely outbursts of frankness on the part of artists of ill-regulated mind, like the carvings sometimes to be seen under the miserere seats of ancient cathedrals? Or are they really meant to avert the Evil Eye? Or to promote fertility? Or to scare away devils, Scandinavian pirates, or other unwelcome intruders? Or what?

We don't know. That is the simplest and the only honest answer. That they do no more than express the sentiments of a sculptor of a grovelling cast of thought is a theory less probable than the others, on account of the general uniformity of the figures. They form a group of related designs, and as such must have a definite and not a merely vague meaning. As that definite meaning is not compatible with Christian ethic, it must be a survival from some preceding Paganism: I feel sure that we must regard all such figures as being, so to express it, idols born out of due time. They prove the truth, if truth were needed, of the statement with which we began this chapter, that the conversion of Ireland to Christianity was a gradual process. But further than this we cannot go: we have no guide but the will-o'-the-wisp of conjecture.[35]

Next come two figures, seated, dressed in long robes reaching to their ankles, with a bordering round the lower hem, and a vertical band of similar material running up in the middle of the front; hidden above the waist, however, by a cape thrown over the shoulders. A flat cap, curved upwards on the brow, covers the head; I do not think that this represents a peculiar hair-clip. One of the

---

* But apparently not everybody: a rapidly increasing number of years ago I came across a play written for children, in the course of which the poor little performers were called upon to introduce themselves to the audience as Sheelanagigs—a word apparently understood by the dramatist to mean some sort of fairy.

FIG. 33.—THE WHITE ISLAND SCULPTURES

figures seems to have his hands in a long narrow muff: the other is holding a short dagger-like sword, in his right hand, and with his left hand touches the side of his chin. Each of these figures wears round the neck what resembles the collar of an ecclesiastical amice more than anything else; but I am not at all convinced that they are intended to represent ecclesiastics. These two figures are not, like the two following, a pair: one of them is considerably larger than the other.

Nos. IV and V are similarly vested, except that the cape is apparently not present and the stripes in front of the tunic in these examples are doubled. The peculiar curly hair of these figures has already been commented upon. One of them grasps two birds, apparently geese, by the neck, one in each hand, and has an interlacing pattern on one side: the other has a short sword similar to that which we have just seen, and a small circular shield. The same form of military equipment appears elsewhere—for example, on the 'David and Goliath' panel on the Muiredach cross at Monasterboice; and if it should ultimately be discovered that we may still date that monument to the early years of the tenth century, this would supply an argument for assigning the White Island figures to about the same time. A large penannular brooch, with broad triangular expansions to the ends of the ring, decorates the left breast of the figure with the sword.

No. VI is an unfinished example, that was merely blocked out: No. VII is a head in relief, by a much more skilful sculptor than the rest. He has contrived to get some character and expression into the face which he has perpetrated—a bad character and an unpleasant expression, but none the less real. A flat cap, resembling the 'smoking-cap' of the mid-nineteenth century, is on the head: I do not think that this, with its ribbing, is merely straight-cut hair.

We have said above that many of the panels on the standing crosses still await explanation. But we may safely prophesy that all of these will be finally written off, docketed, committed to the archives of work accomplished finally and for all time, before we shall begin to understand what was in the minds of the men of White Island when they perpetrated that astonishing sculpture gallery; for what purpose the figures were prepared; in what sort of building did they act as supports: and, again, why the later generation of church-builders had a panic fear of the figures, which withheld them from their destruction; but a bitter shame of them withal, so that they built them facing inward, in the hope that the eye of man would never again rest upon them. And when we have finally solved these problems, even then we cannot take our ease: rather must we step once more into our boat and row to other islands in the same lake, where we shall find other sculptures, different in style, but just as perplexing.[36]

The Gospels of Kells, the Cup of Ardagh, the Bettystown Brooch (ridiculously called ' the Tara Brooch '), such crosses as those of Ahenny, the little chapel of king Cormac at Cashel—all these, each in its own way, stand high among the art treasures of the world. We must not, however, fall into the widespread but fatal error of supposing that the appreciation of art, and the advanced skill in practising it, which produces such works as these, of necessity implies an equally advanced stage of material civilization. Such an assumption is directly contrary to scientific experience: the artistic gifts to which these works bear indisputable testimony are absolutely compatible with uncivilization, even with barbarity. Among the greatest natural artists that have ever been, were the cave-painters of the Old Stone Age, a people not higher in the scale of human civilization than the aboriginal Tasmanians. Ethnological museums are full of the products of the high fantasy and the advanced technical skill of Maoris and other Polynesians, of Central Americans, Africans, and other naturefolk; people whose level of general culture has very little indeed to say for itself.

Indeed it might be possible, though perhaps slightly perverse, to maintain the contrary proposition. The Neolithic folk were far in advance of the Palaeolithic: but

THE MEN OF THE CROSS 199

they could not challenge them in art. The seventeenth century was far in advance of the tenth : but a seventeenth-century monument is a clumsy affair when set beside a tenth-century sculptured cross. A nineteenth-century man who had somehow slipped back into the thirteenth century would be tempted, before a week was up, to escape by suicide from the unspeakable discomforts and limitations of his new life : but a nineteenth-century church makes a poor show beside one of the thirteenth century.

A realization of the 'time-machine' of romance, which would give our *laudatores temporis acti* a few hours' personal experience of the grovelling superstitions of ancient Egypt, the foul immoralities beneath the fair surface of ancient Greece, the filthy barbarities of ancient Rome, the verminous insanitation of the Middle Ages, would be the most salutary invention that could be contrived. If we could look away from the wonderful works of art over which we have been meditating, and could call up a realistic dream-picture of the world in which they came into being, we should very soon be glad to avert our eyes. We should see all the pathological consequences of dirt—scrofula, plague, leprosy, typhus, and whatever disease [37] it was which produced the hideous condition (frequently accompanied by blindness) described as *clār-enech*, 'board-faced'. We have only to read the literature in the original tongue, free from the well-meaning expurgations of translators, to realize that though Ireland was not necessarily any worse off than the rest of Europe in these respects, she was certainly no better. We should see a land populated beyond its economic resources, with the usual consequences —crowds of predatory vagrants, living like foxes, on whatever crumbs they could pick up,[38] and incidentally carrying and spreading these disease germs : frightful famines, far worse than that of 1847, for, as we have already seen, in one of these visitations the inhabitants were actually reduced to cannibalism : and an oppression of the poor by the great such as none in modern times has ever experienced. If we may believe the preface to the hymn

Sēn Dē, in the old Irish *Liber Hymnorum*, the country was so uncomfortably full of people in the middle of the seventh century, that the nobles, with the approval of St Feichin of Fore and other ecclesiastics, petitioned the Almighty with fasting to weed them out!

How can these things be? Well, when all is said and done, what is a work of art more than a product of evolution? The Athenians, in the time of their greatness, lived at the stage of art-evolution which made the Parthenon possible; and accordingly they built the Parthenon. No one else could have done so, either before or since. The mediaeval Europeans lived at another moment of this endless chain of development; and when they set their hands to the construction of mighty temples, Chartres Cathedral or Westminster Abbey took shape as we know them, it is hardly an exaggeration to say, independently of the volition of their builders. In the middle of the squalor of the ninth and tenth centuries a certain man was born whose name we do not know. Through the mediation of those natural laws of heredity, which were contrived from the beginning of Time, but of whose operation we know just enough to underline our ignorance, his Maker had endowed him with an alert and subtle mind, a supreme control over the muscles of his hands, and stupendous eyesight. He had, moreover, the good fortune to live at a time when a mild climatic optimum had restored drooping vitality: it is certainly not a mere coincidence that the highest development of Irish art, and the vast energies of the Irish continental missions, took place at a time when climatologists have determined from other evidence that the atmospheric conditions were for a time slightly more favourable than usual. Wishful to devote his talents to the praise and honour of the Giver, he undertook the task of glorifying, by cunning illuminations, the sacred words of the Gospels. From the moment when he set himself down before the virgin parchment, the 'time-spirit' took him under its omnipotent control: and the Book of Kells was the result. Had the artist lived, say, in the fifteenth century, his work might have been equally wonderful, but it would have been totally different: to have produced the volume which we know would have been a stark impossibility.

Giraldus, in his glowing description of the no doubt very similar Gospels of Kildare, which he was privileged to examine, but which has vanished from the earth long ago,[39] tells us how it was wrought under the guidance of an angel, who laid before the artist a model for him to follow, page by page—St Brigid the while offering up fervent prayer that he should be vouchsafed strength and skill to execute the task. Chronologically, St Brigid is out of the picture, and must be eliminated; but this solecism apart, the fantastic tale tells, in parable form, a very real truth—that these nameless artists were little more than passive tools, in the hands of the Powers, personal and impersonal, by whom the universe is ordered and ruled: so that neither they, nor yet the age and the country which they adorned, can be justified in claiming any excess of credit by reason of the production or the possession of their masterpieces.

In the physical world, Evolution is the law by which Nature, the handmaid of the Eternal, executes His behests. Every biologist knows that one of the most rigid clauses of the Law of Evolution is that which asserts its irreversibility. All things must step forward or perish; but a step forward may never be retraced. The road may never be re-traversed. An extinguished species will never be seen again.

And as in the physical world, so in the world of the soul and the mind. The fruits of the spirit of man, arts, tongues, imaginings, all these are subject to the same inexorable law. We may artificially arrest their doom, but we are powerless to avert it; the man who tries to put a spoke into the wheel of an invincible machine is going to hurt nothing but himself. When they are gone, neither tears nor toil will ever bring them back to permanence. Julian and Decius, who had all the resources of the Roman Empire at their supreme command, laboured with the ardour of fanatic enthusiasm to galvanize the old dead gods of the Roman Republic to life : and they stand for all time, types of pathetic failure.

These truths are hammered into us, whenever we look at the back of the currency note for £1 which has been circulated by the million throughout the Free State for about ten years. It bears an oblong panel of interlacement, at the left-hand end of which the winding band crosses *over* twice consecutively, and *under* twice consecutively—the most heinous of all the crimes that can be committed in this form of design. When the art which it is here sought to revive—uselessly, for like everything else it died for no other reason than that it had already said all that it had to say, or ever could say—when it was a living power, such a mistake would have been scarcely possible ; and its perpetuation, uncorrected for so many years, would have been inconceivable. Once more, they are hammered into us, and with an almost brutal force, whenever we visit some ancient cemetery, containing a superb sculptured cross of the ninth or tenth century, in the midst of a mushroom forest of pitiful modern imitations : the sight is only too familiar. It calls up the picture of the mummy of some mighty Egyptian sovereign, surrounded by a number of inferior waxworks. The Pharaoh is dead : but he has lived ; he has been great ; and even from his poor remains we can acquire a wilderness of knowledge. But these other things never have lived ; they never could have lived ; they never so much as possessed the organs of life. Copies, imitations, revivals, one and all, are subject to the same condemnation. The dead past lies on the dissecting-table. Let us probe it and learn from it what we may, be it good or evil. While we rejoice in the good, by no means may we shirk the evil ; for the evil is part of the truth. And when we have learnt all that we can, let us bury it, earth to earth, ashes to ashes, dust to dust.

He who would seek to revive such things as the atheism of the primaeval ape, or the polytheism of the primaeval European ; the ancient language of Egypt, or the cuneiform script of Babylonia ; the coarse pottery of the Bronze

Age, or the shoddy jewellery of Byzantium; anything else that has served its purpose and been superseded and cast aside, a specimen for the museum or garbage for the scavenger—such a one is like the man who put a clockwork machine inside a dead horse, and, when it trotted on, congratulated himself that he had given it a new life. But at last he realized that the life was merely his own energy, wastefully squandered, with never a hope of respite, on the endless winding of the clockwork; that the horse had been dead all the time, and was going to remain dead for ever and for ever. The Moving Finger writes, and having writ, moves on. . . .

CHAPTER VII

THE MEN OF THE BAYS

LIFE on the coasts of Northern and Western Europe, during the eighth, ninth, and tenth centuries, appears to have been passed under the shadow of an unending terror. And not on the coasts only; dwellers far inland, if a navigable river happened to be in their neighbourhood, were not exempt from its domination. At any moment a long ship might rise over the eastern horizon, to discharge upon the shore a grim and ruthless crew, greedy for gold, greedy for blood, greedy, in lesser measure, for the honour of their ancient gods, as they went forth to do battle against the 'Pale Galilaean' who had challenged the supremacy of their Othin and their Thórr. Driven from their own petty princedoms by the centralizing policy of the kings of Norway, as well as by the limitations of a country unable to support more than a comparatively small population, and at the moment reduced by a sudden climatic deterioration, these raiders had set out to pursue the ancient and profitable industry of piracy. And wherever they landed, with their great swords wrought by cunning artificers, there were scenes of havoc, of throat-slittings, of burnings, of head-breakings, of insatiable plunderings, such as could best be described or imagined by those who saw them re-enacted in the first quarter of the present century.

It is probable that by then most of the portable wealth of Ireland had gravitated into the hands of the monasteries. In a country which had never risen in civilization so far as to circulate coined money, notwithstanding the example of all the neighbouring regions, gifts were necessarily paid in kind; it might be in cattle, it might be in metal ornaments. Sinners, anxiously seeking to purchase salvation, filled the monastic treasuries with bullion, and the expert monastic craftsman melted and re-modelled it into shrines, and vessels, and bookcovers. It cannot be without significance that almost all of the art treasures of the Christian period of Celtic art that have come down to us in Ireland are ecclesiastical in purpose or in origin. Practically the only exception is the long series of brooches, often of great beauty and elegance in form and ornament, but rarely made of any metal more valuable than bronze. This is the more suggestive, when we take it into consideration along with the wealth of gold ornaments which the Bronze Age has bequeathed, and with the description of regal ornaments in the romantic literature that tells us of the pagan Iron Age. Admittedly we must make allowance for exaggerations in the latter; we have already seen that the relics of the Iron Age do not encourage us to look for a high level of general artistic culture: but we might have expected a greater variety and richness in personal adornments than is actually the case. Even if the auriferous gravels had been robbed of all their treasure, the gold must still have been somewhere, bartered from hand to hand. Where did these treasures go, if not into the coffers of the monasteries? And, as though to corroborate the conclusion, it was the monasteries which had to bear the heaviest assaults of the raiders.

Many a precious trinket was carried off. Some of these have been found, in the native land of the plunderer; buried with him in the futile hope that he might carry them with him to the Valhalla which he had forefancied. In the Museum at Copenhagen, to name but one example, there is a shrine which doubtless once contained the bones or other relics of some Irish saint: but it was 'conveyed' by a Viking and gifted to his wife, whom, perhaps, it served as a jewel-case: and the lady's name, Ranuaik, may be read, scratched in Runes on the bottom of the receptacle.[1]

As time went on, the invaders grew in boldness. At

first swoopers, they became settlers. At the mouths of the great rivers they staked out claims, and established cities. It is surely one of the many anomalies in Irish history that the chief towns, Dublin, Waterford, Limerick, owe their origin to these destroying foemen; that the establishment of municipal life is the work of an enemy. From these strongholds, the colonist pirates could ply their trade overseas, and could also sail up the rivers to sites far inland in Ireland itself. Clonmacnois, as far from the sea as she well can be, might have counted herself safe: but the Shannon rolls at her doors, and the Norsemen of Limerick controlled the traffic on the river, so that they could take their toll of Clonmacnois no less than of monasteries more accessible.

In their raiding of the monasteries the gold and the other treasures which the Vikings carried off were the least precious possessions of which they deprived them. Far worse was the robbing of their prestige. The common unlettered people, dwelling round a monastic establishment—people who knew not what to believe other than as they had been taught—these had looked upon the monasteries as being dwellings of men of mystery, who had all the terrors of the unseen world at their call and command. Many were the tales which they had been told, how this or that holy man had been affronted, and how the culprit was forthwith turned into stone, or swallowed up by the earth, or suffered some other monstrous portent of wrath. And lo, before their very eyes, heathens were slaughtering the monks who had impressed these cautionary tales upon them, were penetrating to their most hallowed sanctuaries, were appropriating sacred vessels from their very altars, were burning down houses, towers, and churches indiscriminately: and all the time the blue sky smiled overhead, in a sublime unconcern. We cannot blame these bewildered peasants when we read that their veneer of Christian Faith could not always withstand shocks so severe: that many of them, in the words of the Annalists, 'forsook their baptism',[2] and threw in their lot with the triumphant raiders, whose successes were such admirable advertisements for the might of Othin and of Thórr. A very similar drama has been enacted in these days of ours. The ecstatic devotion of Russian peasant pilgrims in the Church of the Holy Sepulchre at Jerusalem is recorded in graceful and impressive language by Mr. Stephen Graham; and is one of the unforgettable things of life for any one who saw it, less than thirty years before the time of writing this book. But at a stroke, it has all been swept away. They have seen their churches desecrated, their priests murdered; and no Mount Sinai has vomited forth its avenging flames. *Ubi est Deus tuus?* What answer could these poor folk possibly give to the question of the scoffer?

And as the next step, it was very natural for them to ask themselves, Why should these foreigners derive all the benefit of the demonstrated impotence of Deity? If the monastic treasures are really to be had for the taking, why not take them? Whether they argued in these words or not, they certainly acted in accordance with them: there can be no question that a large proportion of the raids, which in those disastrous centuries the monasteries had to endure, were made not by foreign but by native plunderers.

The rape of the Book of Kells is a case in point. This precious volume was kept in a golden shrine that was worthy of it. One night in the year 1006 shrine and book disappeared together from the monastic sacristy.[3] This book is now valued for its illuminations. But a thousand years ago it was the gold cover that aroused cupidity, and, for the sake of this, the theft was perpetrated. The thieves cared nothing for the manuscript; this was found hidden under a sod two months and twenty days afterwards, despoiled of its golden case, which was never seen again. Torrents of raging fury have been poured upon Giraldus Cambrensis for certain unkind criticisms of Ireland and its people, of which he was guilty. But, at least, Giraldus could appreciate the beauty and value of an Irish manuscript, and, as we have already heard, he speaks in the loftiest terms of eulogy of the wonderful book which he saw at Kildare. But the people of Ireland allowed the Kells book to lie out for the better part of three months under their rainy skies, with no better protection than a sod: and as for the Book of Kildare, that has vanished for ever.

What was the inner history of the re-discovery of the book? How did the finders know where to look? Had the informer already made his appearance in local politics? We must fear so. In the year 861 the Norsemen penetrated the great mounds of the Boyne cemetery, and appropriated whatever treasures these may have contained.[4] How did they know that those treasures were there? How did they know where to find the closed-up entrances, which since their time were not discovered till 1699 in the case of New Grange, till the nineteenth century in the case of Dowth, and in the case of Knowth is as yet unknown? Surely some renegade must have told them the traditions of buried wealth, and of the still-remembered places of the doorways: some one who had sloughed off his old superstitions for a superficial Christianity, and who now, with the successes of paganism before his eyes, 'forsook his baptism'. Otherwise the raiders would have been obliged to spend fruitless weeks in excavation, which would have left permanent marks on the mounds themselves.

Undoubtedly the earliest of the raiders were pagans, quite possibly enthusiastic pagans. But paganism rarely breeds a missionary spirit, and it is possible to exaggerate the religious fervour of the raiders. Filthy lucre rather than the honour of Othin and Thórr was their primary objective. And it was not very long before a kind of Christianity began to make some impression upon them. It was a Christianity which turned a blind eye to piracy: but it induced them to found churches, and to respect the lives of priests. It is not impossible, as the late W. G. Collingwood claimed,[5] that some of the numerous churches dedicated in the North of England to St Patrick were founded by Norsemen who had derived their Christianity from Ireland. In a few cases at least it may be that another Patrick is intended ; but they are nowhere to be taken as evidence of the presence, or of the missionary activity, in those regions, of Patrick of Ireland.

Considering the hold that the Scandinavian raiders had upon the country : considering their ubiquity, vouched for by the records of raids which we may read in any of the books of Annals : considering the towns which they built, Dublin, Waterford, Limerick, to say nothing of smaller settlements such as Annagassan : considering the fact that Dublin was for long the seat of a Norse kingdom : considering that a pirate chieftain called Turgeis established a reign of terror in the centre of the country, maintaining a fleet on the great lake called Loch Ree, and even turning the Cathedral of Clonmacnois into the sanctuary of his witch-wife, who gave oracles seated on the High Altar : considering all these things, the relics of the Scandinavians themselves, as yet discovered, are surprisingly few. All round the city of Dublin the country is dotted with names whose Norse origin is obvious : where are the Norsemen who imposed those names ?

We might have expected Viking cemeteries in the neighbourhood of their settlements, and numerous Viking graves in the neighbourhood of their raids : for these cannot always have been carried out without casualties. But only one cemetery is known, if the few graves which were found at Island Bridge on the outskirts of Dublin, and which yielded enough material to fill a single case in the National Museum, can be dignified by such a term.[6] The finds of individual objects of Scandinavian origin are few : a shelf-full of crudely made silver armlets, with simple geometrical patterns stamped upon them : a fine South German sword, bearing its maker's name damascened upon the blade, and another artificer's name on the hilt, from Ballinderry [7] ; but very little else. And yet the influence of the Scandinavian artificers completely revolutionized the art of the native craftsmen, as we can see by comparing the abstract geometrical frets of the pre-Scandinavian Ardagh Cup with the thoroughly Scandinavianized Cross of Cong and its exuberant animal decoration : the earlier 'High Crosses' such as those of Monasterboice and Clonmacnois, with the Scandinavianized Crosses at Tuam, Glendaloch, and Dysert O'Dea ; or the Gospels of Kells and of Durrow with the late Garland of Howth. (Some of the animal figures in the Book of Durrow show pre-Viking Teutonic influence,[8] but not enough to make such a complete inversion of the native styles as we can see in the later works of art.) The native craftsmen must therefore have had models on which their revised ideas of art were based : and where are they ?

In other regions to which the Scandinavians penetrated, they left literary monuments of their presence. Whatever we may think of the Kensington and other inscriptions which have been claimed as memorials of the ancient Norse settlers in America,[9] there is no doubt that inscriptions in Runic letters, testifying to their far-reaching activity, have been found in Iceland, Greenland, the Faerö Islands, England, Scotland, the Isle of Man, and even in the Piraeus. Why is Ireland so empty of Runes, while the Isle of Man is full of them ? Were the Scandinavian dwellers in that small island all (as I once heard it expressed) 'used to usin' a pen', while the builders of Dublin, Waterford and Limerick were illiterate ? It is hardly credible. We actually possess three, at most four, Runic inscriptions : why are there not three or four hundred, as there ought to be, if Ireland had its due proportion as compared with other countries where the Northerners had their settlements ?

This question is the more perplexing, seeing that in other respects the Scandinavian brought a cultural advance into the country. In nothing is this so clearly demonstrated as in the use of coined money. The absence of a coinage, the persistence of a barter system down to as late as the tenth century, in which goods were valued, and fines assessed, on the basis of a graduated standard expressed in terms of weights of metal, cattle, and female slaves—this is one of the most difficult obstacles in the path of those who would claim for the country a highly developed ancient civilization. Romans, Gauls, certain of

THE MEN OF THE BAYS 211

the South British Celtic communities, Saxons, Welsh, all had coined money, and expressed values in terms thereof. But there is no trace whatever of such an institution in the legal documents, where we naturally seek for light on social antiquities. The anomalous bracteate and other pieces, which have come to light from time to time, are too few in number, and too problematic in character, to affect the question; they cannot disturb the conclusion that there was no regular numismatic currency in the country (other than imported Saxon coins of which a few hoards have been found, and which were most likely treasured as mere bullion) before the Norse kings of Dublin stamped silver pennies with crudely drawn images and usually illegible superscriptions.[10]

Nor can we satisfactorily account for the absence of Runic inscriptions by a subsequent iconoclastic vendetta, as we did in explaining the absence of La Tène sculptured monuments. For the evidence of an ultimate Celto-Scandinavian fusion among the ordinary people of the country is too strong to leave room for any such vindictive spirit. The monastic raids were perpetrated by both people alike. The battles were battles of chieftains, not of communities: it would be no more than a mild exaggeration to call even the Battle of Clontarf an incident in a civil war.

From the Annals we gather a monotonous record of plunderings and burnings. Never did a country endure such evils as Ireland did, if we are to accept these records as being the truth, the whole truth, and nothing but the truth. We may, indeed, accept them as the truth. We may even go so far as to concede that they may be nothing but the truth. But we make endless difficulties for ourselves, indeed we reduce the history to incomprehensibility, if we consider that the Annalistic record is the whole truth.

A plundered monastery is not the place to which we should go in search of an impartial description of the plunderers. And the histories which we possess are monastic records, or based upon monastic records, and we cannot blame them if they show a certain bias. Against them we must set the surprising fact that even as the Vikings are raiding, the monasteries are growing in strength and in activity. Clonmacnois, for example, is burnt over and over again, sometimes by the Scandinavians, but quite as frequently by the men of Munster. And yet it goes on, and no one who can see its long series of memorial slabs can doubt that these incidents, exasperating though they must have been, were no real interruption to the corporate life or activity of the establishment; that, after all, they were comparative trivialities. Only one of those inscriptions gives us a moment's pause (fig. 34): it commemorates a certain Feidlimid, who has passed unrecorded by the Annalists—to judge by the style of his monument he lived about the end of the ninth century: and beneath his name we may read the words—

QUI OCCISUS EST
SINE CAUSA

But 'the rest is silence, unrevealed'. There is nothing to show that this man's death was due to Norsemen, any more than was that of MaelMuire, also of Clonmacnois, to whose scribal craftsmanship we owe much of the precious MS., known as the *Book of the Dun Cow*, and who met his death in 1106, long after the Vikings had ceased from troubling, in the endeavour to defend the treasures of his *alma mater* against a band of marauders. Indeed, *qui occisus est sine causa* is merely another way of saying 'this monument was erected by his friends'. In our imperfect world, the application of such terms as 'felon' and 'martyr' reciprocally, to an executed manslayer and to his victim, tell us all that we need to know about the sympathies of the several speakers, but throws no light on the abstract morality of the transaction.

So that in the end we are left, wondering. Were these Viking raids as bad, or as frequent, as they are made out to be? Were they any worse than the native raids, which, no doubt, they were the prime cause in provoking? There are many indications that an assimilation between the Scandinavian settlers and the native Irish began to

FIG. 34.—THE SLAB OF FEIDLIMID

THE MEN OF THE BAYS 213

develop before very long. A native lord may be fighting with the 'Foreigners' in one year, but a page or two later in the Annals we find that he has joined forces with them in order to get the better of some native rival. We shall see an example or two of this in the following chapter. The bewildering matrimonial complications of that remarkable person, the lady Gormfhlaith (pron. 'Gormley') are signs of the extraordinary times in which she lived.[11] They can best be set forth in tabular form. She was—

(1) Sister of a king of Leinster.
(2) Wife of Olaf, the Norse king of Dublin, and mother by him of Sitric Silkenbeard, who killed Niall, king of Ireland, in battle (A.D. 919); and of a lady called MaelMuire, a name (meaning 'servant of Mary') which shows that she was at least nominally Christian.
(3) Wife of MaelShechlainn, afterwards king of Ireland, and mother of his son Conchobar: but by him put away.
(4) Wife of MaelShechlainn's great rival Brian, who likewise put her away. [The reason for these divorces may be gathered from the terse description of her contained in the old Norse Saga of Njál: 'she was excellent in everything that she could not control, but evil in everything that she could control '—in a word, she was good in looks but bad in morals.]

MaelShechlainn, having rid himself of Gormfhlaith, next proceeded to marry his own stepdaughter Mael-Muire (see No. 2 above); thus becoming brother-in-law of one of the chief leaders of the Dublin Norsemen. To add to the muddle, this same MaelShechlainn was the son of Domhnall, king of Ireland, and his kinswoman Donnfhlaith: and this Donnfhlaith also married the Norse king Olaf, and by him was the mother of another of the Norse kings of Dublin, who thus was MaelShechlainn's half-brother!

In conditions such as the anti-Scandinavian monastic historians describe, unions like these would surely have been impossible. A prince on either side, who sought to espouse a princess of the opposition, if indeed he escaped being knocked on the head by the family of the lady so soon as he began to make his advances, would before long be assassinated by his own followers, indignant at what would obviously be a gross act of treachery. We are forced to conclude that the Scandinavians are made into scapegoats by the annalistic chroniclers : that they were not as black as they were painted ; and that they did not seriously change for the worse the existing conditions of public safety. The archaeological and historical evidence would be inexplicable, if the Scandinavians had introduced nothing but turmoil, unrest, and insecurity to the country. These things were there already. The hiding-holes, which we call souterrains, and which are a constant feature of the fortified dwellings so common throughout the country—these are incomprehensible unless we are to suppose that they were made for the safe-keeping of valuables which might at any moment be carried off ; and though I myself have made the suggestion, I must admit that the raiders contemplated by the builders of these 'funk-holes' were not certainly Scandinavians.* The real crime of the Scandinavians was their destruction of the traditional inviolability of the monasteries.

The most conspicuous monuments of the raids of the Northmen are the famous Round Towers, the places of refuge which were prudently provided in anticipation of their attacks, by the builders of the monastic establishments. It were waste of time to recapitulate the floods of lunacy which have been outpoured in reference to these structures : let them fall into their long-overdue oblivion. The round towers are primarily ecclesiastical belfries, nothing more and nothing less. They are not even an exclusively Irish possession, for circular campaniles exist in many places on the continent (that of the Church of Sant' Apollinare at Ravenna, and the 'Leaning Tower' of Pisa are notable examples) and in England (as at Bartlow and Snailwell in Cambridgeshire). Before the Scandinavians came, bell-towers were unknown in the country. The first campanile built in Ireland, wherever that may have been, happened to be built on a circular plan : the others followed its model.

* The most recent research has shown reason to date the origin of Souterrains to a much earlier date than had been supposed.

This is the simple explanation of the Irish 'Round-tower epidemic' as it is not unfair to call it.

There is a practical advantage in the Round Tower plan. It is cheap to build, for there is no necessity to cut well-squared corner-stones. And when it becomes the object of attack, a further advantage comes into view: there are no quoins vulnerable on two faces, and so liable to be prised out with crowbars; and there are not such large areas of the wall entirely out of the ken of the defenders. Doubtless these considerations established the persistence of the circular plan; but fashion was no less potent in maintaining it. Even when the towers rise from the roofs of their churches, as at St. Kevin's and Holy Trinity in Glendaloch, and in the church of Ireland's Ey near Dublin,* where the question of defence does not enter, the Round Tower still persists. The exotic Cormac's Chapel at Cashel, which dates after the Scandinavian period, and a small church on Inis Clothrann (otherwise Quaker Island) on Loch Ree, are the only churches with rectangular towers, dating earlier than the introduction of the Gothic style.

While treating these structures as belfries, we must remember that we are not to think of towers containing large hanging bells, pulled with ropes, as in a mediaeval or a modern church. The only bells known to early Irish Christianity were the rectangular hand-bells, of which not a few examples remain: and these were sounded by a ringer stationed in the topmost floor of the tower. *Bell-windows*, usually, though not invariably, four in number,† encircled this *ringing-loft*. The ringer ascended to his station by means of a ladder: but, as ladders of short lengths are safer, and more easily introduced into such a tower than long ones, the space below the ringing-loft was subdivided into stages or storeys, made of wooden floors supported upon offsets in the interior face of the masonry.

* The two latter towers have now disappeared.

† Eight and two respectively in the two towers at Clonmacnois: eight also at Tullaherin, Co. Kilkenny: six at Kilkenny: five at Kells: exceptionally the Donoughmore tower has *no* bell-windows.

(In the principal tower of Glendaloch the floors were supported upon joists let into the walls of the tower.) These lower storeys, each of which was lighted by a single small window, could be used for storage purposes.

Probably it was by degrees that the value of the tower as a place of refuge was realized. We may suppose that a watcher went up to the ringing-loft, to scan the country and to give notice of the first appearance of an invader: and that when the dreaded signal came, the chief monastic treasures were hurriedly bundled into the store-rooms in the tower, as being less vulnerable than the flimsy wooden dwelling-huts or the small and windowless church. The ruse may have proved successful once or twice: but the invaders must sooner or later have burst the tower door and discovered the hiding-place. This catastrophe suggested the ingenious device, carried out in most of the extant towers, of placing the doorway at a considerable elevation above the ground. The tower of Scattery Island, in the Shannon estuary, has its doorway on the ground-level: its masonry, if we accept the classification formulated by Lord Dunraven and Margaret Stokes, is of the first and presumably oldest type: and therefore it is reasonable to infer that this tower was built before the advantage of the raised door was realized, and that it may actually be the oldest of the extant specimens, which set the model for all the rest. Its imposing dimensions—for it is the tallest perfect example—would carry its fame over the whole country.

Thereafter it was necessary to have a ladder to approach the entrance door. At the base of the tower of Clondalkin, Co. Dublin, there is a stone stairway rising to the doorway, but this is an eighteenth-century addition, and is no real exception to the rule. On emergency, the brethren could enter the tower with their treasures, draw up the ladder, and shut and bolt the iron-sheathed door. Their position was then practically impregnable. Even if one or two of the invaders managed to climb up to the doorway—this is in modern times a favourite feat of the local country boys, greatly to the detriment of the masonry beneath the door-sills—they could do very little damage to the door, which was at the inner end of a tunnel-like archway through the thickness of the wall—some 6 or 8 ft long and not so much as 3 ft across. Only two or three men could stand in such a niche: only one of these could manipulate the door: and no effective use could be made, in so narrow a space, of any form of battering ram. The invaders would have been obliged to heap up a great mole of earth, in order to make an assault upon the tower entrance: and this, in the middle of what would be for the moment an enemy country, would have been impracticable. Only by fire could the defenders be compelled to capitulate. If firebrands were cast through the windows, and not immediately discovered and quenched by the defenders, nothing could save the tower or themselves: if the internal woodwork once caught fire a draught would be established as in a factory chimney, and the whole tower would within a very short time become a roaring furnace.

Under the door-sill of the tower of Timahoe there is a hole running through the wall: perhaps this was meant to allow a stick to be thrust through in order to knock over the ladder of hostile visitors. Otherwise the defenders trusted to casting down missiles from the windows. Except the ringing-loft, whose bell-windows, as a rule, command the country all around, each loft has only one window, and dominates no more than a small sector of the area around the tower: but these windows are set in the wall in such a way that each commands a different sector, so that it would be possible to cast stones down upon the besiegers from the different floors on all sides at once. Doubtless such stones were stored permanently in the tower, in constant readiness: large numbers of them have been found in modern restorations and excavations, fallen with the rotted floors down to the bottom of the tower shaft.

Of other objects belonging to this period none is more interesting or important than the yew-wood gaming-board, found in the rich crannog of Ballinderry.[12] It is a rectangular disc $9\frac{3}{4} \times 9\frac{1}{2}$ in., and about 1 in. in thickness (fig. 35). Above and below project two handles in the shape of knobs, the one longer than the other. Each of these is worked into the shape of a head; the large one a rude but vigorously carved human head with pointed chin, the smaller one much more summary, but apparently a dog, with a collar round its neck. The hair of the human head is parted as with a comb in the middle, but the crown of the head and the back is covered with a coif, or a close-fitting *caputium*. These two projections made the total length of the board 1 ft 2 in. There is a rectangular sinking, $8 \times 7\frac{3}{4}$ in. in the middle of the disc part of the board; it is surrounded with a raised margin $\frac{3}{8}$ in. above the floor of the sinking in the middle of the sides, $\frac{5}{8}$ in. at the angles. The upper surface of this margin is covered with a series of panels of interlacing ornament. Among these the ring-chain pattern is conspicuous. This form of decoration is Scandinavian, and is also found in Scandinavianized parts of England and, especially, on tenth-century crosses, many with Runic inscriptions, in the Isle of Man. In Ireland it appeared only in one tiny panel on the shrine of St. Molaise's Gospels (beginning of eleventh century): though since the discovery of the gaming-board it has been found again, on a fragment of a once very fine crozier, discovered in the Bann drainage works and now in Belfast Museum.

In the rectangular depression there are seven rows of holes, seven in each. These are evidently intended for the reception of pegs, such as are used in the modern game of cribbage. There are irregularly cut grooves along the top and the bottom, presumably for the reception of pegs which have been removed from the board (as in 'taking' a draughtsman). The four corner holes are marked off from the rest by a quadrant of a circle; the central hole has two concentric circles drawn round it.

There is not sufficient information available to make it possible to identify with certainty the game contemplated. It is hardly a chequer game, like chess or draughts. Something more of the nature of solitaire is perhaps indi-

FIG. 35.—THE BALLINDERRY GAMING-BOARD

cated, if we had any information as to the antiquity of this game. Pegs could be placed in all the holes except the corner holes, which would be left empty to allow of the beginning of the leaping-over operation, by which the number of pieces is reduced till the winner is left with a single peg. No doubt complete success required that this should be planted in the specially marked central hole.

We have said that the country has yielded, as yet, three Runic inscriptions. There is, indeed, a fragment of a fourth discovered by Dr. Carl Marstrander of Oslo on the Great Blasket: but it bears nothing but the letters EIK,[13] and so has no information to give us. The other three are anomalous, as is characteristic of Irish antiquities in general. They are quite different from what the records of history would lead us to expect.

One of them is a fragment found in the excavations of the monastery of Nendrum, and seems to show us a Christianized Norseman actually entering the monastic life. But the runes, if they be runes, in which this inscription is written are so eccentric, and the whole inscription is so problematical, that it is well not to attach too much importance to its apparent message, until some future discovery shall help us to elucidate it further.[14] For the present we confine ourselves to the other two.

The first of these is a slip of bronze with an interlacing ornamentation upon its surface, which was meant to be secured to a sword scabbard. It was found at Greenmount in Co. Louth, and is now in the National Museum. If any dispute should arise as to the ownership of the sword, this slip could be taken off, and on the inner surface there would be found a line of Runic letters, announcing, in the old Norse language, that 'Domnall the Seal-Headed owns this sword'. The settling of a similar dispute in a similar way, is told us in an Irish romance, in connexion with the sword of one Socht.[15] This Domnall had an Irish name, and therefore was presumably Irish, or at least had Irish connexions: whether he was Irish or Scandinavian by blood and birth we cannot definitely say, and the mere fact that the doubt exists shows that the relations between the two peoples cannot have been altogether on a Jew-and-Samaritan basis. About the person mentioned in the second Rune, however, there can be no doubt whatever. He was a Norseman, with a Norse and heathenish name, Thórgrimr.[16] He had, however, become a Christian, and (possibly as an act of expiation for his youthful crimes of monastery-plundering) he carved a cross, the stump of which may still be seen in Killaloe Cathedral. On the front of the remaining fragment he tells the world in his native language and script, that he, Thórgrimr, made the cross: on the side he adds a petition in the Irish language and Ogham script, that a blessing may fall on him as a reward for his act of piety. Truly the tables have been turned with a vengeance! No longer do we see trembling Irish saints cowering in dread, thanking their God (as in a well-known epigram, scribbled in the margin of the Saint-Gall copy of Priscian) when the night is so stormy that there can be no fear of a swoop of the heathen sea-raiders.[17] Now it is the man with the Irish name who swaggers about with his sword; it is the Norseman who humbly kneels before the cross which he has fashioned, to pray for a blessing. *Vicisti, Galilaee!*

CHAPTER VIII

MORE SHADOW-SCENES

WE have watched three dramas from Pre-Christian Ireland, so as to judge for ourselves what life was like in those happily vanished days. Let us enter the theatre again and see how the Christians comported themselves.

The play that we shall now follow has a pagan prologue.[1] Tuathal, the king of whom we heard in a former chapter, had two daughters. The king of Leinster wished to marry the second of these: but the father declined to give the junior in marriage before the senior. So the king of Leinster made the best of a bad job, and took the less attractive first-born—only to be met by the taunts of his nobles when he had led her home. Evidently it was notorious that the younger maiden possessed certain personal attractions not shared by her elder sister.

Nettled by his bad bargain and by the rudeness of his courtiers, the king of Leinster conceived a happy thought; to return to his father-in-law, and to inform him that his newly-acquired wife was dead, adding the request that he might now have the girl on whom he had set his desires. We must admit that the king of Ireland took the tragic news very coolly: his attitude in the matter reminds us not a little of Mr. Pecksniff in *Martin Chuzzlewit*, in his pathetic eagerness to unload his objectionable elder daughter Charity upon a suitor. More fortunate than Mr. Pecksniff, king Tuathal had now got rid of the family incubus. And so she was dead: well, well, we can almost hear him muttering, all's well that ends well. Certainly, said he to the suitor, expansively: If I had fifty daughters, you might have your pick of the lot. He was now no longer troubled with scruples about primogeniture!

And so the king of Leinster departed to his palace with his prize, all unprepared for the coming tragedy. The first thing the younger girl saw, on crossing the threshold, was her sister, alive and well. Without a moment's hesitation, she dropped dead from shame. Now to be behindhand, the elder girl, with equal and commendable, though, from such a person as she seems to have been, unexpected promptitude, dropped dead from grief.

In another story we read how a wife chanced to see her husband, who had been bathing, coming unclothed out of the water, and likewise expired on the spot. What does all this mean? Such things do not happen, as a rule. The emotions of shame and of grief are very real, and in excess may possibly have grave psychological consequences: but they are rarely lethal.

It seems to me that we must here see evidence of the existence of the remarkable phenomenon known as *thanatomania*, well known to medical and other observers among the aboriginal peoples of Australia or of New Zealand. A man suddenly becomes conscious that he has broken a tabu. For such a one no consolation has any effect; he has committed an unpardonable sin; his life is forfeit; and, just as certainly as the morrow's sunrise, that man will die—sometimes in strong convulsions.[2] A tabu against, let us say, the simultaneous marriage of two sisters—against seeing a member of the opposite sex undraped—if violated, might produce the like effects upon the culprits, at a similar stage of social development. Cu Chulaind was a person upon whom, for some reason and by some power unspecified, the latter tabu had been imposed: and at least twice in his career a woman presented herself before him in this condition (no less a person than queen Medb herself was one of the delinquents)[3] in the hope that when he should turn away to avoid a breach of it, liers in wait might steal up from behind, to take him unawares. In the Southern Seas, the spell does not usually act so instantaneously as in the case before us, but we may safely ascribe that to the story-teller.

King Tuathal does not impress us as having been an enthusiastically affectionate father while his daughters were alive : and now that they were dead, he turned the affair to profit, seeking the solid consolation that lay in an extravagant weregild. He summoned to his aid the kings of Connacht and of Ulster, who had been foster-parents of the daughters, and in league with them he fought 'a wrathful, ruthless, battle' with Leinster. Leinster could not withstand the united hosts; after the inevitable defeat the province was condemned to pay a tremendous tax, specified as 15,000 cows, 15,000 swine, 15,000 wethers, as many mantles, silver chains, and copper cauldrons, and a quantity of other goods. And this tribute was to be paid, not by the guilty king alone, but by all who should succeed him in the throne, to whomsoever at the time should be king of Ireland.

And so king after king extorted the tribute—not without wars and bloodsheds innumerable, and a rage of hatred that lasted for generations. In the year A.D. 222 the king of Leinster came up against Tara, and found no one at home but thirty princesses, each with her hundred maidens in attendance ; and, in the grip of that mighty rage, he massacred the entire company. When Loiguire mac Neill, the king in whose reign St Patrick came, attempted (now over three hundred years after the original tragedy) to enforce the tax, he was defeated in a great battle, and the heads of his followers were piled up in a cairn on the plain of Moynalvey, where it would be extremely interesting to discover them. He himself was taken prisoner, and was forced to swear an oath by the elements of nature that he would never again exact the tribute. This vow at the end of his life he determined to break ; but on the expedition which he made for the purpose, he was struck by lightning. Thus did the elements avenge their honour against his perjury.

A little more than one hundred years later, Aed mac Ainmirech became king. He had four sons, Domnall,

MaelCoba (a priest), Gabran, and Cumascach. The last named, one day, announced to his father that he proposed to make a circuit of Ireland, and to pass a night with the wife of every king in the country. While we cannot say that the High King gave the proposal his blessing, he raised no objection, and Cumascach set forth.

Brandub was king of Leinster at the time: and when he heard that the unwelcome visitor was on his way, he gave orders that messengers should meet him and his followers: should apologize for his (Brandub's) absence, on the ground that he was gone over to the land of the Britons to collect his tributes; should billet Cumascach's company, man by man, far scattered from one another, over the whole province; and that they should conduct Cumascach himself to the palace, where the queen would be at his service. He further gave instructions that the host of each one of Cumascach's men should privily slay his guest. A house was prepared for Cumascach, and he was received in it.

'Where is the queen?' demanded Cumascach. The lady was promptly summoned, and begged for a boon. 'What is that boon?' said he. 'Give me grace to serve out the feast to the company.' 'So be it,' said he: whereupon she slipped out of the door, and went by devious ways to a place where she could wait in safety.

Meanwhile Brandub, who was at home all the time, served at the cauldron in the guise of a slave. Cumascach's satirist attendant, Glasdam by name, demanded his share: its royal liberality betrayed the king to the discerning satirist, who reported the matter to his master. Brandub, seeing that he was recognized, realized that he must act quickly. He ordered fire to be brought and to be set to all four sides of the house. Glasdam shrieked for quarter: he had already partaken of the king's hospitality, and this, in ancient Ireland as among the modern Bedawin, entitled him to a guest's immunity. 'Climb up then to the roof and jump off, and thou shalt hear no more from me,' said Brandub. 'Quick, master!' cried the faithful satirist to his lord—'take thou these my garments, and hie thee forth.' So Cumascach escaped by the way that had been left open for the satirist, callously leaving the latter to be burnt to death. But he himself was sorely hurt by the leap, and he went limping along till he reached a church called Cell Rannairech. The bailiff of the church came out, found him, identified him, and, we are happy to add, cut his head off. Brandub expressed his satisfaction by making Cell Rannairech free of all imposts: and the Bishop of Glendaloch shared in his sentiments, even though he was king Aed's half-brother, so that the graceless youth had been his nephew. He came to Brandub, and counselled him to send an embassy to king Aed, then at Ailech, far away near the site of the modern city of Derry, apprising him of his son's death.

The king had actually already heard the news: but he recognized that heralds were sacrosanct, and he sent them away with a fitting fee. Thereafter, however, he gathered troops to come to avenge his son, and incidentally to levy the Tribute. Brandub asked the Bishop of Glendaloch* to go the king, with the naïve request that he should hold up his advance till he, Brandub, had collected an army to meet him. The bishop might have foreseen how his angry kinsman would receive him; nevertheless, he faithfully delivered his message. But for the king's reply to the bishop, the reader must be referred to the Irish text in *Silva Gadelica* (not the English translation, which has been adapted for family perusal). Lady Godiva's lord was delicacy itself in comparison. The bishop retorted by specifying the portions of the king's person which he hoped that a she-wolf would devour. 'Such were the ways of those ancient days!' as one of our poets prosily reminds us. In short, the king refused to make any stay; he pressed on, carrying the bishop with him.

* The quaint carving which I have been allowed to reproduce here (fig. 36) may help us to visualize this versatile ecclesiastic. Lady Dorothy Lowry-Corry, who discovered the stone—which has an interest far beyond what appears in the illustration—will shortly publish a full account of it in the *Journal* of the Royal Society of Antiquaries of Ireland.

They arrived at a pass and the king asked its name. 'The Pass of Dun Bolg'—(the Fort of Sacks)—said the bishop. 'Why so called?' 'From the sacks of provender that the Leinsterman shall store there.' They arrived at a flagstone, and the king asked its name. 'The stone of Comart Cnam'—(of breaking of bones)—said the bishop. 'Whose bones?' '*Thy* bones, which to-night shall be broken upon it, and thy head taken from thee.' They arrived at a gap. 'What gap is this?' said the king. 'Berna na Sciath'—(the gap of the shields)—said the bishop. 'What shields?' 'The shields of thy forebears' progeny, which here shall be left this night.'

Then they encamped, and the bishop made off to Brandub to tell him tidings of the king's progress. 'What am I to do?' said Brandub. 'Get thee the largest candle that can be procured, and three hundred teams with twelve oxen in each; place paniers upon the oxen containing young men covered with straw, with a layer of victual over the straw.' While these preparations were being made, Brandub and the bishop went together to spy out the camp of the king of Ireland. The bishop then returned to his clerical duties, after which he came back to his patron, sufficiently recuperated to utter another unedifying curse upon the king of Ireland. After that they took one Ron Cerr, son of a petty lord of Leinster, smeared him with calf's blood and rye dough to make him look like a leper, and sent him limping on a wooden leg to the king of Ireland, to whom he complained that the Leinstermen had ravaged his house in his absence. 'I shall give thee compensation,' said the king, 'only tell me now what do the Leinstermen.' 'They are preparing victual for thee,' said the pseudo-leper, ambiguously. 'Go,' said king Aed to his attendants, 'and fetch me the cowl of Colum Cille.' Years before, Aed had asked that eminent saint how many of the kings whom he had known would get to heaven. 'Only three,' said the saint. He named them, and Aed was not among them. 'What about me?' asked the king. 'Not for any consideration whatsoever shalt thou enjoy the Lord's peace,' was the saint's uncompromising answer.

FIG. 36.—AN IRISH BISHOP, OR ABBOT, AS REPRESENTED ON A STONE AT KILLADEAS, CO. FERMANAGH

FIG. 37.—FRAGMENT OF MEDIAEVAL INTERLACING DEVICE, KNOCKMOY, CO. GALWAY

'But,' he added, 'I give thee my cowl, and what time thou dost wear it, it shall be impossible to slay thee.' And so—'fetch me the cowl of Colum Cille,' said Aed, preparing himself for the fight, for he easily read the riddle of Ron Cerr's words. Then the attendant made a terrible discovery.

'We have left it behind at Ailech,' he cried.

As the crow flies, Ailech was nearly 180 miles away. To send so far for the talisman was quite impossible. Without it, his only shield against certain death and certain Hell, the king must needs gird him for the battle.

And now the oxen, seemingly laden with provision, appeared, coming in a procession headed by the bearer of the gigantic candle. As soon as they reached the camp, from out the baskets rose the young men 'to serve the viands', said the leper grimly. Round the king they pressed, and Ron Cerr, who had discarded his wooden leg, seized him, and on the 'flagstone of the breaking of bones' he hewed off his head. So ended this episode in the age-long struggle for the Tribute : it happened in or about the year 597 A.D.

Eighty more years passed by, and still the Tribute was periodically exacted, though with many wars. Then came a time when Finnachta of the Feastings was on the throne. Twice he exacted the Tribute unopposed : the third time the Leinstermen thought to gather strength to withstand him. The king of Leinster at the time, however, was a man of prudence, and in counsel sought advice of his courtiers as to what he should do—give battle or send a holy man to intervene on Leinster's behalf. The latter course was adopted. St. Moling, the chief ecclesiastic of Leinster at the time, was clearly the proper envoy. He wrote a panegyric on the king of Ireland, and brought with him a poet called Tollchenn to repeat it. On the way they stopped for hospitality at a house : and Tollchenn, incited by some of his professional brethren, and considering it derogatory to be under the service of a mere cleric, slipped away, went on in front, and repeated the panegyric to the king as his own composition. The saint followed, highly indignant: and the king, now apprised of the purpose of his errand, had his young men ready, who received the saint on his arrival with a volley of stones, sods, and sticks. Nothing daunted, however, the saint pressed on into the court, where only two men rose to do him reverence. To them the saint gave his blessing: as for the rest, the son of the king, who had been the ringleader of the hostile demonstration, was killed a few minutes later with a javelin aimed by one of his companions at a deer.

'There,' said the saint to the king, when cries were heard without, 'now hath thine own son died, in expiation of mine honour.'

'Raise him from the dead,' said the king, 'and thou shalt have the price of thine honour.'

'For my poem, for the raising of thy son, for Heaven secured to thyself, I ask only respite of the Tribute till Monday.'

'So be it,' said the king.

'Pledge thee by the Holy Trinity and by the Four Gospels, and that evil may befall thee if thou fail.'

'I pledge me.'

Then the saint began to repeat his poem, but was interrupted. 'Liar!' said the king. 'That is not thy poem: it was made by Tollchenn the bard.'

'If so, let *him* stand and repeat it.'

Up stood Tollchenn; but a spell was laid upon his tongue, so that he could say nothing but gibberish without meaning: and becoming aware of this, he uttered a wild scream, rushed out of the house, and drowned himself. Appalled, the king fell, a humble suppliant, at Moling's feet, and begged once more for the restoration of his son, promising to grant the saint in return everything for which he had come. So Moling stood over the boy and prayed, and his prayers were heard, and the boy rose again: and Moling went his way.

Tidings of these events came to the ears of the great ecclesiastic Adamnan, and he sent one of his followers to summon king Finnachta into his presence. This is a

MORE SHADOW-SCENES

good illustration of the pagan heritage of imperiousness with which the historians love to invest these holy men. The king happened to be playing chess, and he declined to budge till the game was finished.

'Go, tell him that I shall chant fifty psalms; and one psalm among the fifty shall exclude his descendants, and even any namesake of his, from the kingship for ever.'

The messenger returned; once more the king had begun a game, and refused to obey the summons till it should be finished.

'Go, tell him that I shall chant other fifty psalms, and one psalm among the fifty shall give him shortness of life.'

The messenger returned; and the same scene was repeated.

'Go, tell him that I shall chant other fifty psalms, and one psalm among the fifty shall give him Hell.'

Truly the sweet singers of Israel were marvellous cryptographers! In our blindness we had imagined them as uttering songs of praise of overwhelming magnificence, or hymns of penitence of a never-equalled pathos: and all the time they were weaving sinister and secret spells! Unfortunately there is no hint as to *which* are the three baleful psalms: for all we know, a dying Christian, who thinks to comfort himself by repeating this psalm or that, may be unconsciously blasting another in his family, his life, or his eternal welfare!

That useful institution, the chorus of a Greek drama, would here interpose the comment that if Adamnan had possessed the gift of prevision, he would have reserved his curses for the wretched scribbler, shallow-pate dotard or devil-prompted knave, who was destined to put pen to parchment and to charge him with such blasphemous buffoonery. Having heard what the Chorus has to say, we follow the same august Greek precedent, and get on unconcerned with the interrupted story. At the third summons poor superstitious Finnachta threw away his chessmen and obeyed the call. He could put up with the other two curses; but perdition was rather too much, especially after Moling had promised him that apparently very rare boon, an eternity of bliss. At this point a glossator, who must surely have known a great deal more about the Everlasting Mysteries than most of us, has kindly inserted an explanation. It was not so much fear of Hell, as the direct prompting of the Almighty, that had caused the king to obey the summons. For Adamnan's curse would have neutralized Moling's blessing: there would have been a deadlock: and it would seem that even the inner courts of Heaven had reserved no power to deal with such a situation. It was therefore necessary to take steps to forestall anything of the kind.

'Finnachta,' said Adamnan, when the trembling king came into his presence, 'is it true that thou hast promised to Moling a remission of the Tribute till Monday?'

'It is true,' said the king.

'Till *Dia Lūain?*'

'Till *Dia Lūain*,' said the king.

'Then has Moling bested thee. *Dia Lūain* means "Monday"; but it also means "the Day of Judgement",' said Adamnan.

And in this wise the vengeance exacted through so many centuries for king Tuathal's unattractive daughters at last came to an end. For by the oath of Finnachta, damnation awaited himself, or any of his successors, who should presume to continue the extortion—until the Day of Judgement.

Ancient Ireland is one of the most supremely interesting fields for study in the world. There, better perhaps than anywhere else, lies, revealed and unadorned, the primitive background of European civilization. But it must have been an unchancy place to live in! A fairly extensive reading in its literary remains, legal, romantic, and hagiographical, leaves us with a mental picture of a country infested with wild boars, savage wolves and hardly less savage wolf-dogs: infested with the microbes of some of the most unpleasant of diseases: infested with insect vermin—even a sojourner in the monastic guest-house of Cork is represented to us as there encountering fleas more numerous than the sparks of fire or than the sand of the sea:[4] infested with haughty nobles, swaggering in their barbaric grandeur: infested with predatory and dangerous vagabond tramps: infested with lunatics, frequently violent:[5] and if for a single moment we believed what the compilers of hagiographical homilies had to tell, we should be obliged to add, infested with holy men, impiously arrogating to themselves the prerogatives of Deity with their sentences of 'shortness of life and Hell' from which there was, apparently, no appeal either on earth or in Heaven.

It goes without saying that this would be a false, perverted picture—as false as the picture of contemporary life that a visitor from Mars might compile from the daily press. The ordinary citizen's life gives no material either for the ancient romance-writer or for the modern sensation-monger. If these were to exploit nothing but the decencies of normal existence, they would go bankrupt in a week. We have only to compare the Patrick of the *Confessio* with the Patrick of the *Tripartite Life*, to say nothing of later pseudo-biographies, to realize what a world of difference there was between the true saints who really existed, and the hectoring and often dishonest bullies whom their would-be panegyrists describe for us, and who are happily mere fictions. And for the rest, though doubtless there were all the discomforts above enumerated, we need not suppose that Ireland was much worse in these respects than the neighbouring lands at the same time. They were in the established order of things: people took them as a matter of course, and made the best of them.

Let us witness one more drama, from a slightly later time: from the time of the Scandinavian occupation. Let us rapidly follow the career of the last and probably the greatest of the kings of Ireland.[6]

MaelShechlainn II, son of Domhnall, surnamed the Great, succeeded his father in the kingship of Ireland A.D. 980. He was then thirty-one years old. The Norsemen of Dublin had by now at least begun to embrace Christianity; Olaf, son of Sitric, the Norse king of Dublin, went on a pilgrimage to Iona in the year which witnessed the accession of MaelShechlainn, and there he died, ' after penance and a good life '. The occasion for the pilgrimage seems to have been the serious defeat that the new king inflicted on the Norsemen at Tara, in the year of his accession. The victory was dearly bought, however, for the Irish side lost heavily also : but the king was able to follow up his victory. Having repulsed the Norsemen at Tara, he pursued them to Dublin, and there almost anticipated the victory of Clontarf. Hear the comment upon the victory, copied into the Annals of the Four Masters ; those unemotional historians have for once been moved to quote something spiced with human feeling :—

' A great army was led by MaelShechlainn son of Domhnall, king of Ireland, and by Eochaid son of Ardghar, king of Ulidia, against the foreigners of Dublin ; and they laid siege to them for three days and three nights, and carried thence the hostages of Ireland, and among the rest Domhnall the Squinting, king of Leinster, and all the hostages of the Ui Neill. Two thousand was the number of the hostages, besides jewels and goods, and the freedom of the Ui Neill from the Shannon to the sea, from tribute and exaction. It was then that MaelShechlainn issued his famous proclamation in which he said " Let everyone of the Gael go to his own territory in peace and happiness ". This captivity was the Babylonian captivity of Ireland, till they were released by MaelShechlainn ; indeed it was only a degree better than the captivity of Hell ' (about which, we conclude, the historians must have had first-hand information).

After this exuberance, the Annalists resume the usual dry catalogue style of their work, giving us the bones of history, but leaving it to our imaginations to clothe them with flesh. Turn the page, and we may read the following among the events of the year 981 : ' Dál gCais (pronounced something like *daul gash*, a people who occupied the present Limerick and Clare, to which MaelShechlainn's rival Brian belonged) was plundered by MaelShechlainn, and the Tree of the Assembly of the Plain of Adhar was cut, after being dug from the earth with its roots.' No casual reader would guess that this brief sentence looks back to a vast antiquity, and looks forward to the end of Ireland's hope of ever becoming a united people.

For this was no common tree. The Plain of Adhar was the assembly place of the people in whose territory it lay. Here they came together to inaugurate their chieftains. It is a little over two miles from Quin, Co. Clare, on the road to Tulla. The road crosses a little stream, called Hell River, by a bridge, north of which is an amphitheatre formed by crags and enclosed by a low bank. In this area there rises a large flat-topped circular mound, over 20 ft high. On the bank of the stream there is a second mound, much smaller. North of the first mound there is a boulder measuring about 4 by 3 ft with an oval basin cut in its upper surface. Across the stream, 141 ft to the west, there stands a rough slab of limestone, 6 ft 3 in. high, in the line of the two mounds, and of the footway that runs up the great mound. Half a mile to the south-west is a large enclosure with a triple ring of stone surrounding it—perhaps the residence of the chieftain who was here inaugurated.[7]

Far back in pagan times had that great tree been planted, and in some mystic way the life of the ruling family was bound up with the life of the tree. Probably it grew over the grave of the traditional ancestor. To cut down *that* tree was therefore a symbolic act; the man who cut it down was, as it were, pledged to the extirpation of the family whose life centred within it. The cutting down of such a tree would plunge the country in an endless civil war. Nothing could ever bring the old tree back. A new one could be planted, and, as a matter of fact, was planted,[8] but it could never be the same; with every fresh inauguration the sore would be irritated afresh.

When we ask why the king committed this grave act of trespass, the answer lies patent. Among the members of the family whose life centred in the tree, there was one who had already become prominent, and who seemed destined to challenge the rights of the legitimate king. His name was Brian; and he had been born in the year 925. His elder brother, Mathgamhan, was chief of the Dál gCais of North Munster, and had been so successful in his numerous fights with neighbouring princes that they feared that he would establish a supremacy over them, to which they were by no means inclined to submit. Donnoban, the chieftain of the people called Ui Fidgeinte, invited him to a banquet in the year 974, and Mathgamhan, though with misgivings, accepted the invitation. A body of liers in wait was in readiness, and, seizing him, they hurried him off to the mountains, where MaelMuaid, lord of South Munster, awaited them. At his command a sword was thrust into the prisoner's heart.

In Brian, the victim's brother, the treacherous chiefs found that they had caught a Tartar. He at once assumed his brother's authority, and proceeded to avenge him. He plundered Scattery Island, in the face of the Limerick people. Next year he met the king of South Munster and slew him in battle. In the following year he met in battle the Norsemen leagued with Donnoban, and by defeating them he made himself master of Munster. Shortly afterwards the death of the High King, Domhnall, took place : perhaps this event, following so many brilliant successes, put into Brian's head the idea of ousting the lawful heir, and of himself becoming High King of Ireland. Be that as it may, it was to this sole object that he devoted the rest of his life.

And so the great tree was cut down. Brian promptly began reprisals. The year was not over before he had plundered Ossory. Meanwhile MaelShechlainn was busy with a skirmish against the Waterford Norsemen, with whom the king of Leinster had leagued himself (although the Irish king had set him free from their clutches the year before !) In the next year, 983, Brian came up again, and advanced even further, plundering the west of Meath. He had meanwhile greatly strengthened his position in the west and south, so that already Ireland was practically divided among the three rivals—MaelShechlainn in the north and east, Brian in Munster and S. Connacht, and the Norsemen in the coast towns and the districts around them.

In 984 MaelShechlainn overran Connacht, plundered it, destroyed the island fortifications, and reduced the royal residence to ashes. The Connacht men replied by plundering Meath as far as Loch Ennell (near the modern town of Mullingar), where MaelShechlainn had his seat.

In 985 MaelShechlainn was troubled by a revolt among his own people. In the neighbourhood of Ardee there was a community which rebelled against him. He played on them the same trick as he had played on the Dál gCais. In Ardee a shrine of St Patrick was preserved as a treasured possession. MaelShechlainn came and seized it, and bore it away to his own quarters. But the archbishop of Armagh interfered: he adjudged MaelShechlainn to have been guilty of sacrilege, and he compelled him to restore the relic and to pay a heavy fine. In the long run the event proved unfortunate for the king and his kingdom, but meanwhile the rebels were overawed into submission.

Trouble of another kind followed in the next year. A violent storm did untold damage in the region of Louth; and there was an outbreak of a mysterious epidemic, described as ' preternatural sickness brought on by demons in the east of Ireland; which caused great mortality of men plainly before men's eyes. The beginning of the great murrain of cows which had never come before'. This was presumably a visitation of cholera.

However, MaelShechlainn was not altogether unfortunate among these disasters. He had succeeded in alienating the men of Connacht from their allegiance to Brian; in the year of the great storm and of the epidemic, when Brian leagued himself with the Scandinavian enemy and sailed up the Shannon as far as Loch Ree in order to plunder his rival's territory, he was met by his former allies, who slaughtered the Munstermen and their foreign associates with a great slaughter. In the year 988 MaelShechlainn led another army against the Norsemen to Dublin, and besieged that fortress for twenty days. The unhappy garrison were reduced to drinking sea-water, and at the last they were glad to buy off the king with a payment of ' an ounce of gold for every garden in Dublin '.

In 990 died Erard mac Coise, one of the most distinguished poets of his time in Ireland. Certain poems, attributed to him, are still preserved. It is related of him that such was his devotion to God and St Ciaran that he established his residence at Clonmacnois in order that he might be near enough to St Ciaran's Church to hear Mass there daily. But one night an angel appeared to him and told him that he did wrong in fixing his habitation so near to the church, thus making his daily journey thither an easy matter; for the number of his paces in his daily journey to the church were being recorded, and that his pains in the future life would be remitted in exact proportion to the total number of steps taken. The poet accordingly removed his dwelling to the middle of a bog some distance from Clonmacnois—to a place that was still called Mac Coisse's house in the beginning of the seventeenth century—and he took his daily toilsome journey from thence to the church as before. It is to be hoped that the poet profited in the next world from his devotions, for he showed little sign of any very conspicuous regeneration in this. It is on record that king MaelShechlainn had him in great favour, and bestowed upon him an extraordinary mark of the honour in which he held him—nothing less than the emoluments of the kingdom of Ireland for a whole year. When the year had elapsed, the greedy poet refused to relinquish the sweets of office, and told his patron that he would have to fight for his kingdom. Whereupon the king challenged Mac Coisse to fight on horseback, which the poet consented to do. This was foolhardy, for Mael-Shechlainn had the reputation of being the finest horseman in Ireland, if not in Western Europe; it was said of him that he preferred to ride a horse that had never been broken, handled, or ridden till the age of seven years, and that he could manage such a formidable animal as easily as another man could manage an old, tame, and gentle horse. Mac Coisse was no match for such a champion, but (we are told) he felt sure that the king had such favour for poetry that he would never draw his blood. So to battle they went, Mac Coisse in full armour, and the king on a good horse armed only with a headless staff. Mac Coisse attacked the king violently—perhaps he hoped to restore the old pagan custom by which the slayer of the king succeeded him on the throne. But the magnificent horsemanship of MaelShechlainn, and his expertness in defending himself with his staff, easily kept the poet at bay. The king (as the poet had calculated) did not particularly want to hurt him; but at last, when he was tired of the amusement, he knocked him off his horse and contemptuously left him to pick himself up. The poet sneaked back to Clonmacnois, and we are glad to read that in course of time he died there, ' very penitent '.[9]

In 992 the king was obliged to lead another expedition into Connacht, where he took the greatest plunder of cows that king ever took. Brian promptly replied with a raid into Meath, which, however, was a fiasco; he took neither cow nor person, and had to save himself by a secret flight. So say the Annals of the Four Masters, which favour MaelShechlainn: the Annals of Clonmacnois, which are pro-Brianite, say that Brian plundered everything he could lay hands on till he came to Loch Ennell, where the king's house was.

In 994 MaelShechlainn routed the forces of Brian in a battle at Nenagh, and plundered a great part of Munster. Having for the moment given his troublesome rival something to keep him quiet, he once more turned his attention to the Norsemen.

In the possession of the Norsemen of Dublin there was an important heirloom: the ring of Tomar or Tomrar, the ancestor of the Norse kings of Dublin. This person had been killed some 150 years before in a battle near the modern Castledermot in Co. Kildare, and his ring, chain, or collar—whatever it may have been—had been kept in Dublin ever since. MaelShechlainn raided the Norse fortress, seized this treasure, and carried it off—pursuing his usual policy of outraging the sentiments of his enemies in a way which must have made a deeper and more lasting impression than mere slaughter or pillage would have done. As he destroyed the sacred tree of Mag Adair, as he carried off the sacred shrine of Ardee, so he laid hands on the ancestral heirloom of the Dublin Norsemen and carried it off to his home by Loch Ennell. This is the event mentioned in Moore's well-known lines—

> When Malachi wore the collar of gold
> Which he won from the proud invader—

although the hero was an Irish king called MaelShechlainn and not a Hebrew prophet called Malachi, and although we do not know that the 'ring' was actually a collar, or that it was of gold, or that the king wore it after he had captured it.

In 995 Armagh, the centre of the country's religious life, was visited by an appalling thunderstorm. The lightning struck the belfry (a Round Tower) and destroyed it; other flashes set the churches and the houses on fire. A general conflagration followed, which extended even to the woods surrounding the city. Once again the Annalists have been moved to go beyond the dry catalogue form of their narrative; to the record they add the comment: 'there came not in Ireland since it was discovered, and there never will come until the Day of Judgement, a vengeance like to it'. It is wonderful how much they knew! Nothing was hidden from them, past, present, future, or in the timelessness of Eternity.

The Norsemen, enraged no doubt by the loss of the ring, made their way into Meath in the following year, and plundered Clonard and Kells: indeed, their aggressions were now so formidable that the two Irish rivals were for the moment compelled to forget their differences. For once we read that MaelShechlainn and Brian together led an army against them. Coming to Dublin, they carried off hostages and the best of their possessions. What might have happened if Meath and Munster had maintained this allegiance, it is futile to speculate: it was not destined to last more than a year or two. In the next year, 998, the allies met the Foreigners at Glenn Mama in the present Co. Wicklow, and inflicted one of the most crushing defeats which the Foreigners had ever suffered; after which they marched to Dublin and spent a week in plundering and burning it.

In this year, we are told that ' the great stone of Moynalvey in Meath fell, the chief monument of the plain of Bregia, and MaelShechlainn made four millstones of it '. It is not difficult to guess what is behind this curious entry in the Annals. This was one of the rude pillar-stones, many of which are still standing; some of them of great size, often as much as 17 or even 20 ft high. They served partly as grave marks, partly as landmarks, but there is evidence that some of them at least were to all intents and purposes idols, being unshaped representations of pagan deities. It is interesting to notice how often crosses have been cut upon them, as though to dis-harm the paganism in them. This great stone in the south of Co. Meath, was most probably such a pagan monument, and for both politic and religious reasons MaelShechlainn may have been anxious to clear it away. I say politic, for it seems likely that the ecclesiastical authorities of Armagh had not forgiven him for his raid on the shrine of Ardee, and there is some reason to suspect that Brian was opening secret negotiations in that quarter, finding himself unequal to the task of obtaining his desires by open fight : it would, therefore, be in the interests of MaelShechlainn to do something for the cause of religion. The superstitious fears of the neighbours would prevent any interference with this heathen monument so long as it remained standing : but it conveniently fell—and if it was helped to fall, that is no business of ours—and the accident gave MaelShechlainn his opportunity. There could not be much mystery about an idol unable to remain upright, and at least it could be prevented from ever being replaced.

But the rudimentary patriotism then available was impotent to close permanently the rift between the rivals. Just before the battle of Gleann Mama, MaelShechlainn had led a piratical expedition into Connacht, and had taken a large spoil of cattle. The Connacht-men opened negotiations with Brian in 999. Brian was only too willing to listen to them; but he was now conscious of his helplessness against the more youthful energy of his adversary. And so we read without any overwhelming surprise that he patched up an alliance with the Norsemen, and with an incongruous army of Southerners and Norsemen, marched into Meath to meet the king. The latter, however, was ready for him. The Norsemen were in advance and MaelShechlainn made mincemeat of them. Brian got his army as far as the southern border of Meath, but hearing of the disaster to his allies, he turned tail and retreated without striking a single blow.

The king was, however, seriously alarmed by this new development of the complicated story, and determined to lead a punitive expedition into Munster. For that purpose he built a causeway across the Shannon at Athlone in the year 1000. But Brian for once forestalled him: he collected a huge army, and himself took advantage of the new road that had thus been made and marched to Dundalk.

And now a strange thing happened. No battle was fought. No hostages were exchanged. MaelShechlainn quietly, and without a single protest, resigned the High Kingship of Ireland to his rival. It is one of the most extraordinary events in the stormy annals of Ireland.

There are two reasons which may be assigned for this action of MaelShechlainn, which was so different from his usual energetic character. It may have been a carefully-thought-out piece of statecraft. In spite of his matrimonial and other associations with the Norsemen, he seems to have been honestly desirous for their expulsion: but this could never be attained when he was pestered by Brian as by a gad-fly, striving without rest to oust him from his office, and never hesitating even to use the Foreigners to further the personal ends he had in view. Brian would obviously never rest until his ambitions were gratified; but perhaps if he were allowed to have his way, he might then turn his attention to the task of ridding the country from the incubus that for so long had dominated it. But the abdication may also have been due to strong ecclesiastical pressure. MaelShechlainn had never been a *persona grata* at Armagh since his escapade at Ardee; but that may not have been the primarily operative cause. We read that Brian presented 10 pounds of gold to Armagh shortly before his accession, and 20 ounces of gold shortly after that event. In the Annals of Clonmacnois, which as we have seen are pro-Brianite—extravagantly so—we read under this year the following sinister passage: 'Brian Borowa took the kingdom and government thereof out of the hands of King Moyleseachlin *in such manner as I do not intend to relate in this place.*' Then follows a fulsome eulogy of Brian, occupying several pages; but it is badly weakened by the ominous sentence just quoted, which means, to put it bluntly, that the methods by which Brian secured the kingdom were not fit for publication.

However that may be, for the fourteen years that followed, Brian was king of all Ireland—the first and only king of all Ireland since the Creation of the World, before the days of Henry VIII. As was always the case on the accession of a new monarch, his first care was the obtaining of hostages from the different subordinate kingdoms throughout the country. In the necessary expeditions he was loyally aided by MaelShechlainn, who joined him for the purpose of an expedition into Connacht.

We hear but little of MaelShechlainn during the first part of the reign of Brian. In 1006 we catch a glimpse of him trying to restore the old assembly of Tailtiu. In 1011 he led a successful raid into Tyrone—a year in which the country was devastated by a visitation of bubonic plague. Thus encouraged, in 1012 he led his army against the Foreigners: but as Brian had now left them in peace for ten years, they had had time to recover from the blows which they had suffered. He penetrated as far as Howth, but the Norsemen had no difficulty in beating his unofficial army back, and seriously defeating it. In the following year, Brian's son, Murchad, fired by emulation, led a raid into the south of the Foreign territory, and characteristically enough plundered, not a Norse stronghold, but the sacred city of Glendaloch. The Foreigners retorted by a maritime expedition to Cork. Brian besieged them for three months at a place called Ath an Charthainn, now unknown: and at the same time erected fortresses along the line of the Shannon, to check the Scandinavians of

Limerick from sailing up the river on predatory expeditions.

The catastrophe of 1012 had shown MaelShechlainn that in existing circumstances he could do nothing alone, so in the fateful year of 1014 he and Brian once more joined forces. On Good Friday, of that year, the opposing armies met at the fishing-weir on the river Tolka, above Clontarf.

Brian was now no less than eighty-six years of age, and did not venture into the battle himself, but remained at prayer in his tent the whole day, and in great depression because he had seen a banshee who had warned him of impending doom.[10] There he was killed in the evening by one of the Scandinavian refugees. His sons and grandsons gave a good account of themselves, but they all perished at intervals during the day.

The clergy of Armagh came all the way to Dublin to claim the body of their protégé, and they fetched it back and buried it with great pomp in the cathedral of Armagh. The house of Brian was wiped out, in the battle, so that the way was left open for MaelShechlainn to recover his lawful kingdom peacefully. The foreign foe was at least scotched; the rival who had embittered his whole life was dead.

He enjoyed eight more years in the sovereignty. His first step was to settle the troublesome province, Leinster. Having done this, and set over it a king of his own choosing, he proceeded to pick up the threads that had dropped from his hand at his abdication. He must have become reconciled with the authorities at Armagh, for we hear of no more trouble in that quarter. But the Norsemen were not destroyed; during the eight years of his second term in the kingdom, they gave him much trouble. The last recorded action of his life is a great defeat inflicted upon them at the Yellow Ford of Tlachtgha, now called Athboy.

This was on 3 August 1022. Thirty days later, on Sunday 2 September, he died on the little island, now called 'Cormorant Island' on Loch Ennell, just opposite the mounds of Dun Sciath, which are supposed to mark the site of his dwelling. Round him were gathered the abbots of Armagh, Iona, and Clonmacnois, with most of the seniors of Ireland; and they sang masses and hymns, psalms and canticles for the good of his soul. Having received the body of Christ and His Blood, and having made intense penance for his sins and transgressions, and having been anointed by Amhalghaidh, successor of Patrick—*i.e.*, abbot of Armagh: the old quarrel was healed now—the king died in the seventy-third year of his age.

As we take a backward glance over this record of seventy-three years, we find ourselves forced to ask, what chance of progress could any country possibly have had, in circumstances such as are there depicted? Naturally we estimate at its true value all the flamboyant nonsense about 'the captivity of Hell' and the like. We recognize the principle that history records as a rule the abnormal, not the normal, so that a record of intensive fighting *may* mean, in actuality, a high average of peacefulness. We also count the 'great battles' as not exceeding in magnitude the faction-fights of modern times.

Even so: there were too many faction-fights and cattle-raids for a healthy public life. The many who lived and died unnoticed and unrecorded, whose only desire had been to get on with whatever 'jobs' Providence had committed to their charge, must have lived in a state of what we may call 'jumpiness', such as in the long run becomes utterly demoralizing. Even a small raid or fight has its casualties. It is not difficult to imagine some farmer saying to himself: 'Any day these people may come and have a fight in one of my fields; my children or my cattle may be killed, my fruit-trees and my beehives destroyed; and what have I done, that I should suffer from the rivalries of this Brian and that MaelShechlainn? What are these people and their ambitions to me?—They have become so much absorbed in their chess-play each with the other, dredging the country for allies wherever they may find them, that they have completely forgotten its welfare.' It is impossible to withhold sympathy from any decent countryman of a thousand years ago who may have asked such questions as these. As the winner of £30,000 in a sweepstake never remembers the 60,000 families of slum children who have had to go hungry to pay for the 'luck' on which he congratulates himself; so those who sing of the 'Glories of Brian the Brave' never remember the unknown thousands over whom that same Brian trampled, to win for himself the empty privilege of seeing, in the days of his dotage, his own name written into the *Book of Armagh*, where we can read it yet, with *Imperator Scottorum* tacked on to it. Was *Vanitas Vanitatum* ever a more appropriate comment?

In the churchyard of Bromsgrove, in Worcestershire, there is the usual forest of tombstones, shouting the usual conventional adulations of forgotten worthies. But in the midst of them all there stands the monument of one William Blackford, who died in 1808; and by contrast, the inscription carved upon it makes on the reader an impression of almost torturing intensity. In a well-ordered Utopia, that inscription, or something like it, would be cut upon every public memorial: would be solemnly recited at every celebration of a national hero: to remind the citizens that they live in a world of false values and deceptions, of consequential disillusions and disappointments. And here it is—

ENCOMIUMS ON THE DEAD ARE EMPTY SOUNDS AND MOCKERY: THE LAST GREAT DAY ALONE WILL WIPE THE COLOURING OFF, AND MAN'S TRUE STATE WITHOUT A VEIL, WILL STAND DISCLOSED TO VIEW.

CHAPTER IX

THE BUILDERS OF CHURCHES

THERE are many thorny paths in Irish archaeology. But few are more beset with thorns, with quagmires, with impassable ditches spanned by broken and treacherous bridges, than that which lies before the historian of her Church Architecture.

The facts are few and are easily described and apprehended. In the first place, literary evidence, which has been quoted over and over again, and which need not here be recapitulated, leaves no doubt whatever that throughout the ages of paganism, and almost till the eve of the Anglo-Norman invasion, wood, not stone, was the chief building material. We may, if it please us, picture the country as covered with wooden houses and churches, not less fantastically decorative than those which still survive in Norway. The Church of Kildare, which we know from the often-quoted description of Cogitosus,[1] was probably of wood, and seems to have been quite elaborately decorated with the works of the painter and the goldsmith. But fire and decay, tumult and pillage, have swept these hypothetical buildings out of existence with a completeness rare in the annals of destruction. The wooden houses and churches survive only in literature, in imagination, and in the influence which they appear to have exerted on some features in the design of the earliest extant buildings in stone.

The resemblance which the famous oratory of Gallarus[2] near Kilmalkedar, bears in outline to an upturned boat has struck many observers, and it may be more than a mere accident. The early artificers in wood were shipbuilders as well as house-builders, and the one branch of their art might easily have affected the other. When we remember that the currachs were constructed mouth-downwards (not, as in the building of a ship, keel downwards),* we can picture a boat-builder erecting a house in capsized-boat form. The stone-builders afterwards simply translated the wooden structure into the new material.

Secondly, we have at our disposal ruins of the earliest —or, not to beg the question of chronology, let us say the most primitive—stone churches. They are plain rectangular oratories having a doorway at the west end, and a small window at the east. Sometimes, but not always, there are windows in the side walls also. Under the east window is what is left of the altar, a rectangular block of masonry. There is no division of nave and chancel. The doorways are trabeated, that is, they are covered with a horizontal lintel, not with an arch: but this does not necessarily imply that the builders did not know the nature and purpose of an arch, and were unable to make an arch, for we sometimes find (as for instance at Clonamery in Co. Kilkenny) a relieving arch formed in the masonry above the lintel. The windows are small, narrow openings, with what would be the glass-line (if there was any reason for supposing that they had been glazed) always on the outer face of the wall. The external splay, which is sometimes seen in English Saxon work, is rare: there is, however, an example at MaelShechlainn's Church, in Clonmacnois, and perhaps a few more might be found. The inward splay is very wide. These openings are also trabeated; but a curved window head is scooped out of the under side of the lintel so as to imitate an arch: and sometimes the crown of the window is composed of two stones, and may even be built as a true arch.[3]

These buildings are all roofless now: when we try to imagine them as they were when the roof was intact, we must suppose them to have been as dark as burial-vaults, illuminated only by the single ray coming through the narrow window. This would be no more than sufficient

* See the *Illustrated London News* for 3 Dec. 1932.

to give the light necessary for the ministrant as he stood at the altar. There is no evidence of any glazing in the window. It might have been closed in stormy weather with a wooden frame, perhaps containing a translucent pane of horn or of vellum. Sometimes receptacles for the hinges of a wooden shutter are to be seen in the masonry beside the window opening.

Such buildings must have been damp, and they cannot but have been infested with clothes-moths and other insects which would rapidly fret away any textile furniture or decorations. There may have been a plaster covering upon the inner face of the walls, decorated with paint. But unless there was an artificial illumination inside the building, this would scarcely be visible; and as in the case of the ornamental wooden buildings, archaeology has here revealed absolutely no solid facts to limit or to direct our fancies. There is nothing to show that these church buildings were not as severely plain inside, when they were in use, as they are in their present condition of ruin.

We call them 'churches' for convenience: but 'oratories' would be a more accurate name for them. They could never have accommodated a congregation of any size. In many cases we must assume that no one was inside the building except the clergy actually engaged in the ceremonies: the congregation, if any, were outside in the open air, and if they did not hear the voice of the ministrant, at least they heard the sound of his bell.

Externally, the projections of the side walls beyond the line of the gable-walls (the so-called 'antae'); the enigmatical corner brackets: and the 'butterfly' finials crowning the apex of the gables, preserve reminiscences of the wooden model on which these simple buildings were based, with their heavy corner posts, their projecting wall-plate ends, and the crossing principals of their roof trusses.

The masonry of which the walls were constructed cannot be reduced to rule, still less to any chronological scheme.

It depends entirely, if not on the 'taste and fancy' of the mason, at least upon the degree of skill and the nature of the materials, locally available. Dry stone, mud, and (possibly in later buildings) mortar, often burnt from sea-shells; the crudest and most irregular rubble, and ashlar of almost all possible degrees of perfection; in a word, all kinds of masonry that can be imagined, are illustrated in these rude buildings. Except within a single building, where a change of masonry sometimes betrays an addition or a reconstruction, we can make no chronological deductions whatever from the way in which any one of these architecturally primitive churches is built.

It would be a complete mistake to assume that these rude buildings are *necessarily* the earliest stone churches extant, and belong one and all to the centuries immediately following St Patrick's mission. This mistake vitiates much of the invaluable pioneer work of George Petrie. The monastic settlement on the rock called Sgeilig Mhichil, the Greater Skellig, was certainly still in existence in 1044, when the *obit* of one of the Community is recorded in the Annals of the Four Masters: and the remains on this Sgeilig Rock are among the rudest and crudest examples, both of building and sculpture, that are to be seen anywhere in the country.[4] And if it be objected that nothing more could be expected on an isolated rock in the Atlantic, it could fairly be answered that a community marooned in such a place ought to have been only too glad to have had something to do, and that the erection of a worthy building for their devotions ought to have been a welcome occupation for their endless monotonous hours: a necessary prophylactic, indeed, against mental and spiritual atrophy.

Thirdly, there is a group of buildings, architecturally similar to the second group, but differing from them in plan, in that they have a nave and a chancel; a perfectly plain arch of one order dividing the two members of the building. In a few cases a sacristy is added, as in St. Kevin's Church in Glendaloch: and this, as well as its twin structure Holy Trinity, in the same place, has a similar belfry-tower.*[5] In other places the tower is detached: but that it is an intrinsic part of the structure is shown by its proximity to the church building, and by the observance of the usual rule, that the doorway of the church and that of the tower face one another. It is not infrequently the case that the nave and the chancel are in different masonry, showing that the one or the other is an addition to an earlier plain rectangular church. Such are Clara Church, near Kilkenny, and the Church of Mac Duach at Kilmurvey on the greater Aran Island.[6] In the latter, a comparison of the masonry of the two members of the building leaves the impression that the nave is the older part, the chancel the addition; in the former the converse is the case. But though the chancel of Clara Church gives the impression of extreme primitiveness, it cannot really be of very high antiquity, because an Ogham stone has been appropriated to make a sill for the external face of the window. This could hardly have happened if the representatives of the owner of the stone were still alive and active, and therefore we may fix the eighth century as the earliest probable date for this very simple building.

Fourthly, this third group of church buildings passes almost imperceptibly into the Irish Romanesque; and when we approach the problems of Irish Romanesque we find that we are plunged into a maze from which at present we can hardly hope to extricate ourselves.

On a previous page we sketched an outline of the preliminary work that would be necessary before any real progress could be made in the final establishment of the history of Celtic Art and its relation to Teutonic Art. We might almost repeat what was there said, *mutatis mutandis*, in reference to the history of the Romanesque style in Ireland. Every surviving specimen would need to be sought out and illustrated in detail; the west doorway of Clonfert Cathedral (fig. 38) alone would need about thirty plates to illustrate it properly. Then, after a full analysis of the component decorative elements, a similar *corpus* would need to be prepared of Romanesque work

* The tower of the latter structure is now destroyed.

in England, France, and Germany, and of the art-motives that lie in the *Hinterland* : in Italy, Greece, Russia, and Armenia. Then perhaps we should be ready to begin the synthetic work of writing a history of Irish Romanesque. In the meanwhile we have to face the disconcerting fact already mentioned, that the only two inscribed specimens are not datable, and that there is not a single authentic record of the foundation or the building of any structure in the country, which can be identified with an extant Romanesque building. The cathedral at Clonmacnois is known to have been founded in A.D. 904 : but the building in its present form has suffered much subsequent modification, and little that is distinctive in the original building remains. Cormac's Chapel at Cashel [7] is another exception, for that was built by Cormac mac Carthaigh, king of Munster at the end of the first quarter of the twelfth century. But again this does not help us much, for Cormac's Chapel is an altogether exceptional building. It might have journeyed to Ireland, almost as it stands, out of the Rhineland : it was almost certainly built by German builders, or at any rate under German guidance. The square corner towers, the carved tympana over the doorways, the elaborate wall-arcades inside and out, are thoroughly un-Irish. The most characteristically Irish feature about the building is the double roof or 'overcroft', a constructional feature which begins to appear in the third group of Church buildings described above. But even here, Cormac's Chapel is exceptional in providing a stairway for access to this upper loft. In other examples, as in St. Kevin's Glendaloch, St. Flannan's Killaloe, and 'St. Columba's House' at Kells, it is necessary to use a ladder.[8]

For the present, all that we can say about Irish Romanesque buildings—all indeed that it is necessary to say in a study like the present—is a statement of a few general principles. The plans are simple, consisting of nave and chancel only : there are no Romanesque churches with original aisles and transepts, until we come to the transitional transepts of Christ Church Cathedral in Dublin,

FIG. 38.—THE DOORWAY, CLONFERT CATHEDRAL

THE BUILDERS OF CHURCHES 251

another entirely non-Irish building. The only tower is the detached circular campanile. This, in some late examples, as at Timahoe (County of Leix) and Kildare,[9] has a doorway with elaborate Romanesque decoration. The east end of the church is invariably square: an apse is unknown in Ireland. The entrance is most commonly in the west end; but a doorway in one of the side walls is not unknown. Windows are still of small size; but they are more numerous, and we now begin to find them grouped, two or three lights together under a containing arch—the first step towards the elaborate windows of the Gothic period. The east window at Clonfert has a striking treatment of the window-splay on each side with an arcading of two arches;[10] but as a rule the window openings display no ornament other than the mouldings, and these are usually simple. Only by exception are the window arches decorated with the chevrons and other devices which enrich the doorways. These mouldings, it has been observed, frame the window completely, running along the horizontal sill; and are not, as generally in English work, stopped at the base of the jamb.

The walls are usually plain, having no decoration within or without other than an occasional string-course. A remarkable arcading on the external face of the west wall of Ardmore Cathedral, having small figures under the arches, is altogether exceptional.[11] Here again, we cannot say what, if any, applied ornament in the form of hangings, paint, or metal-work may have decorated the building when it was in use. We are again without any evidence of window-glazing during this period.

The builders lavished their decoration chiefly upon the entrance doorways and the chancel arches. These are circular, and are recessed in *orders*—two, three, or more, sometimes as many as six. In the most sumptuous examples, the voussoirs are all richly sculptured, with a resourceful variety in the scheme of decoration: each order being enriched in a way peculiar to itself. Even when the favourite chevron is the dominant motive of the whole design, its treatment varies from order to order.

The finest specimens can challenge comparison anywhere. It would be difficult to match such great arches as the doorway of Clonfert, or the chancel arch of Tuam Cathedral: [12] it is deplorable that we have no evidence to enable us to attach a date to them.

The chevron is the motive of decoration chiefest in favour. Other Romanesque ornaments, billets, bowtells, beak-heads, and so forth, are used more or less freely; but the chevron is by far the commonest. It was set out in every possible way, with the zigzags on the face of the arch and what we may call the 'concertina side' on the soffit: or *vice versa*—a very characteristic Irish Romanesque form, rare in English Romanesque. Or with two zigzag faces on the arch and the soffit, with the points of the zigzags meeting; or with the points of the zigzags alternating. In addition to this variety of arrangement, there is a wide range of ornamental forms in the decoration of the 'background' areas, within the angles of the zigzags.

Another favourite motive of decoration is the human head, which by a graduation of grotesqueness merges into the animal head. These may be found singly, as for instance above the summit of the arch, or in greater or lesser numbers. At Dysert O'Dea, Co. Clare, for example, in the outer order of the arch over the doorway there is a head sculptured upon every voussoir.[13] The corners of the capitals of jamb-shafts are often worked into heads, and when these occur in pairs, on two faces of a wall (as for example on the east and west sides of a chancel arch), the hair and beard of the heads are drawn back and worked into a linkage of fanciful interlacements over the face of the wall underneath the arch.[14] One of the orders in a very fine Romanesque doorway in Killaloe Cathedral has been decorated with a series of human and animal figures in high relief, but it has been at some time most barbarously mutilated.[15]

It is remarkable that the forms of decoration commonly called 'Celtic' are very rarely used in architectural monuments. Either the artists had an instinct that the two

THE BUILDERS OF CHURCHES 253

forms of ornament should be kept apart; or else the church builders had received a foreign training, so that to them the art practised by the cross-sculptors was unfamiliar, or made no appeal. A band of interlacing pattern surrounds the Clonfert doorway, and some key and interlacing pattern is to be seen on the jamb capitals of the chancel arch of the Nunnery at Clonmacnois: but except these two more important examples, and a few trivial odds and ends, there is hardly any other case of the intrusion of 'Celtic' decoration on the domain of Romanesque: and the converse is no less true.[16]

A tall, triangular pediment, surmounting the arch on the face of the wall, is a notable feature of Irish Romanesque doorways. At Clonfert and Roscrea good examples are to be seen.

The most striking proof of a continuity between the ornate Romanesque Churches and the plain buildings described at the beginning of this chapter, is afforded by the treatment of the door-jambs. In a trabeated doorway, it is good policy to set the jambs sloping toward one another to a slight degree: this diminishes the length of the lintel left unsupported by masonry underneath. When the jambs support an arch this expedient is quite unnecessary: but in some Irish work, notably at Clonfert, it is still maintained. In the Clonfert doorway the door-jambs were straightened some four hundred years later, by inserting an incongruous inner order. The perpetuation of sloping jambs is a good illustration of the fact that from whatever source the Romanesque fashion of ornament may have reached Ireland, it was superimposed upon the native tradition of building, and assimilated with it: although it held aloof from the native tradition of art.

The almost total absence of tympana is a special peculiarity of Irish work. Besides the two already mentioned, at Cormac's Chapel, which as probably foreign works hardly count, I know of only one other; a perfectly plain example at Kilmalkedar, near Dingle, in Co. Kerry.

Such, then, was the point to which the development

of ecclesiastical architecture in Ireland had attained, when her independent existence came to an end.

This momentous transformation was much more complex than the crude popular idea of its course as usually stated. We are told that a trumpery king of Leinster ran away with some one else's wife, and was expelled: that the king, to seek redress, appealed to Henry II: that Henry II sent a person called Strongbow (which was not his real name) whose monument is to be seen in Christ Church Cathedral (another popular error),[17] and that Strongbow came, saw, conquered, married the daughter of the king of Leinster aforesaid, and to all intents and purposes reigned in his stead.

But in fact the movement was ecclesiastical at least as much as it was political: and it had been maturing slowly for not less than a hundred years before the galleys of Strongbow appeared in the offing. A hundred years before Strongbow, Lanfranc, Archbishop of Canterbury (encouraged by the allegiance of the Scandinavian Christians resident in Ireland, who thought it beneath their dignity to submit themselves to the Irish bishops), had claimed that Ireland formed part of his diocese: and an energetic body of native ecclesiastics, on their side, were striving, to the utmost of their powers, to complete the fusion in order and discipline between the Christianity of their island and that of the regions round about.

This movement did not begin a day sooner than it was needed. Whatever may have been the origin and antiquity of the abuses, which at the time were only too conspicuous, they had been greatly augmented during the Scandinavian episode, and the consequent loss of the inviolability of the monasteries. With a return of peace, there began intercourse with European countries once more: and the contrast between the comparative order and civilization abroad, and the barbarism at home, was felt painfully by such men as MaelMaedoc (commonly called Malachy), ó Morgair and his associates.

Admittedly, we must always make allowances for the exaggerations of pamphleteers, ancient and modern: and

THE BUILDERS OF CHURCHES 255

St Bernard's historically valuable (but, as a work of literature, insufferably tedious) life of MaelMaedoc partakes of the nature of a pamphlet.[18] Gerald the Welshman himself could hardly have excelled St Bernard in his uncompromising condemnation of the inhabitants of Ireland, their manners, customs, and morals. 'A barbarous people'; 'A nation not holy'; 'A people rude and lawless'; 'Not men but beasts'; 'Shameless in morals, dead in rites, unclean in life'; 'Christians in name, pagans in fact'—these are some of the pearls of language set down by Bernard of Clairvaux, presumably based on information imparted to him by his friend MaelMaedoc himself. Making every concession, it is impossible to evade the conclusion that ecclesiastical rites had fallen into abeyance, that immorality was rampant, and that many abuses, such as hereditary abbacies, had become firmly established. So firmly indeed were the people rooted in their own ways, that a reformer, however zealous he might be, would have stood little chance of success, if he had trusted only to his own resources, and had neglected to enlist the powerful aid of the Church in the regions beyond the seas. Ireland had too long remained in isolation; Ireland must now, for her own sake, strengthen the bonds that linked her to the rest of the Church in Europe. The monasteries of native growth must now give place to plantings of the great European orders. Synod after synod must sit, under direct Papal auspices, and must bring to an end abuses in ecclesiastical government and in public morality. This process of breaking down the isolation and self-sufficiency, which had brought nothing but corruption, lasted throughout the twelfth century: the escapades of the king of Leinster merely precipitated the end, which would have come about, exactly as it happened, even if he and his paramour had never been born.

The Cistercians entered Ireland in 1142, in which year Mellifont was founded, the first house of the Order in the country.[19] The foreign name given to the new establishment was a symbol. Ireland might never again live a life of aloofness: the culture of Europe must be accepted as it comes. The spade that turned over the first sod at the building of Mellifont wounded to the death the art, the traditions, the language, all the exclusive possessions of Ireland : it was the penalty she had to pay for her moral shortcomings. The victim might linger for centuries ; but the wound was mortal. Palliatives might delay the end : but long before this present century will have joined its predecessors in the grimy Archives of Time, the work of destruction, begun eight hundred years ago at the hallowed 'Honey-fountain' in its peaceful valley, will have been completed in the flaunting palaces of the less sacred 'Holly-wood'—with the powerful aid of those weird ethereal vibrations of which we have just begun to learn the mystery, and which may yet develop in ways transcending our wildest fancies.

In accordance with the Cistercian system, a network of daughter houses began to spread over the whole of Ireland (fig. 39). In this genealogical linking of the Cistercian houses lay the strength of the Order. Each house was directly in union with its mother house : all, as it were, formed one single family, and all looked to Citeaux as their source of inspiration.[20]

The predominance of the Cistercian Order in mediaeval Ireland had important consequences. There was only the slightest local architectural initiative. The Masons' Guilds, which evolved the Gothic styles on the Continent and in England, had scarcely any direct influence upon church building in Ireland. She has nothing to set beside the wonderful series of parish churches which adorn every county of England ; she never would have had them, even if the storms of the sixteenth and seventeenth centuries had never raged. The Cistercian builders set the fashion which was copied by the local builders : Cistercian principles are followed, even in structures not directly connected with the Order. The rule of the Order enjoined austerity. Unnecessary ornament was forbidden : and the cold bareness which this produces—and which may often be deeply impressive—extends in Ireland far beyond the Cistercian structures themselves. In any case the Irish builders were

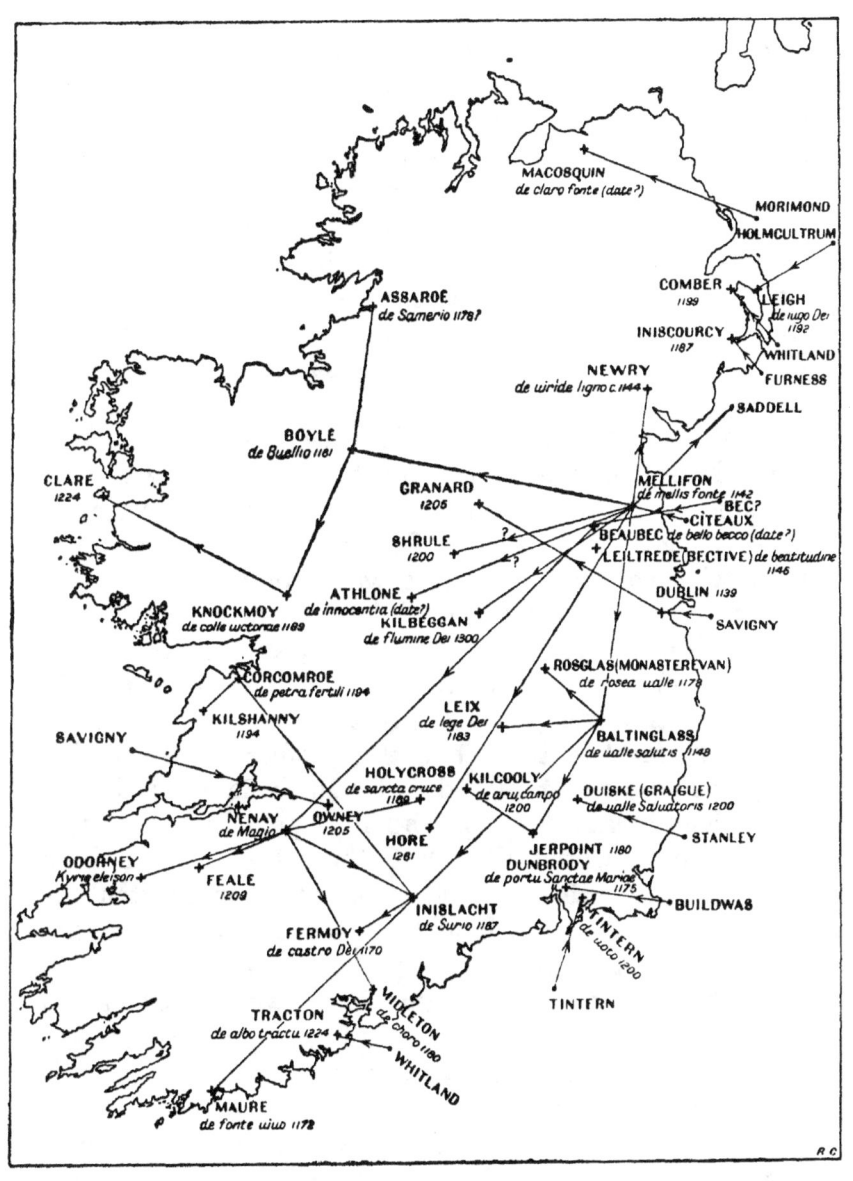

FIG. 39.—THE NETWORK OF CISTERCIAN FOUNDATIONS IN IRELAND

handicapped by the absence of soft, easily carved building stone like the clunch of East Anglia, suitable for interior decoration. In the hard stones of Ireland delicate work could not be executed except with enormous toil, and, perhaps, with no very satisfactory results.

A dogged conservatism is the most striking characteristic of Irish Gothic. In England each century—we might almost say each quarter-century—has its own styles, so that the dating of a Gothic church is comparatively easy. But ornamental and other details sometimes continue in Ireland for a couple of centuries after they had become obsolete in England. The builders seem to have no feeling of incongruity in erecting a fifteenth-century wall with a window of a thirteenth-century style and a fourteenth-century type of doorway. In England we occasionally meet with such archaisms, as when some notable tower or window is copied by the builders of later churches : but the mouldings always conform to their own age ; they never fail us, and they keep us safe from chronological pitfalls. A thirteenth-century tower might have been imitated in the fourteenth century, but the profiles of the earlier mouldings are never reproduced. In Ireland this key to chronology breaks down beyond all hope. In a few buildings, such as Christ Church Cathedral in Dublin, built under English influence and even, to a large extent, of English materials, the mouldings are of orthodox forms. But outside this small group, they are either absent altogether, or else they prove intractable when we endeavour to reduce them to a system. Any one who attempts to sort them out will sooner or later relinquish the task, in utter bewilderment.

A very good example of the eclectic nature of Irish Gothic is presented by the Franciscan Friary at Askeaton, none of which can be earlier than 1389, the date of its foundation. The east window of the choir is the usual dull cuspless interlacement of forked mullions. In the north wall, however, there is a cusped window with Curvilinear tracery, while the cloisters, which are well preserved, show Geometrical mouldings—certainly not the deeply undercut Lancet mouldings—but adorned with the characteristic Lancet dogtooth. The foliage ornament approximates in style to the stiff foliage of the Rectilinear period, though it is not quite identical with it in type: some of the stems on which the leaves are mounted show a subconscious reminiscence of Celtic interlacement.

These facts cause unending embarrassment to the student of architectural history in Ireland; and this is doubtless why the history of Gothic architecture in Ireland has yet to be written. The large and handsome quarto entitled *Irish Ecclesiastical Architecture*, by Arthur Champneys, is of great value, but it falls short of the requirements of a final study. It is too summary in the treatment of plans and moulding-profiles, the backbone of the study of Gothic architecture. In these respects, as well as in window tracery and sculpture, Irish Gothic is absolutely unique: and no one has yet grappled seriously with its peculiarities and its many problems.

There are two possible reasons for this neglect. The earlier, pre-Norman remains of Irish Church history are admittedly more attractive, on grounds both of sentiment and of artistic beauty: while for a student whose chief interest is architectural rather than historical, the Irish buildings cannot compete with the wonderful monuments of architecture in England or on the Continent. Irish Gothic buildings are bizarre rather than beautiful: they lie in a provincial backwater, rather than in the main stream of European development. This situation, as we have seen, induces a conservatism, the like of which we can find nowhere else, and which naturally complicates any serious study of the subject. In no country are documents more necessary to a chronological study of the architectural monuments than in Ireland; and so, once more, we are confronted with the empty ruins of the Dublin Record Office, and with the endless volumes of unexplored history which were there annihilated by a single act of senseless wickedness.

Champneys has done his best to reduce the resulting

chaos to order, and his book is a creditable work for one man to have accomplished. But the task is beyond the reach of a solitary student. Until by the completion of the Archaeological Survey the scattered material can be adequately brought together, within the four walls of a library, it will be impossible to establish this important branch of Irish history on a systematic basis.

But let it not be supposed that Irish Gothic buildings are to be despised. There is hardly an example that does not contain something surprising, unexpected, and even beautiful. In their roofless condition we cannot look for wall paintings; faded traces at Knockmoy and Ross Erilly, Co. Galway, at Holycross, Co. Tipperary, on Clare Island off the West Coast, show us that a whole chapter of the history of Art of the country has been torn away by the troubles which brought the buildings to ruin.[21] The windows, with their quaint cuspless tracery (as in fig. 40)—desperately monotonous as a whole, but sometimes showing astonishing flashes of originality—have been despoiled of their glass, and here, once again, a chapter in the history of art has been annihilated. It is the small things that count in the study of Irish mediaeval architecture. Even the plainest structures, however uninspiring they may look from the outside, cannot be neglected: they are often found to have at least one agreeable surprise inside. It is this element of complete *unexpectedness* which is the chief source of pleasure in studying Irish mediaeval architecture. There are many handsome buildings, but no really great buildings: but on the other hand there are few which are entirely destitute of little points of detail that make the structure well worth the trouble of a visit. These can hardly be reduced to rule: a treatise on Irish ecclesiastical or domestic mediaeval architecture would easily tend to become a mere catalogue of the pleasant little freakishnesses of individual buildings. That dear little sculptured owl, who gazes down at us out of the church tower of the Franciscan Friary of Kilconnell, is worth a whole monotonous wilderness of painted St Christophers.

FIG. 40.—WINDOW, KILCOLMAN, CO. KERRY

THE BUILDERS OF CHURCHES

He has no business there at all. He is meaningless, out of place: yet in his own way, as we gaze upon him, he contrives to slide into our souls a subtle sense of mystery, of knowledge unknowable, of a vastness and purposefulness behind his apparent insignificance and needlessness. There are many, many, preachers in the world a great deal worse than that little owl.

The custom of providing a chamber walled off from the church as a residence for the officiating priest is common in Ireland. Usually this is at the west end of the church; in MaelShechlainn's church it was in an upper loft above the west end, and the holes for the joists which supported the roof are to be seen in the wall. The most remarkable case is that of St Duilech's, a short distance to the north of Dublin. The present church is modern, and need not detain us. The tower is a self-contained monastic or anchoretal structure, first erected about the year 1230, though altered in subsequent years. In its present form it contains seven chambers, united by three stone staircases: the effect to a stranger visiting it for the first time is rather like that of a labyrinth in three dimensions! Among the chambers was the abode of an *inclusus*, an immured anchorite. One Eustace Roche was there enclosed in the year 1406, for a letter of indulgence, providing for his maintenance, is extant. A ruined church, probably of the fourteenth century, at Kilronan near Clonmel, also has an ankerhold, in the east wall.

During the Middle Ages, if we define that vague period as lying between 1200 and 1500 A.D., there were two opposing attitudes toward 'Celtic' art. The scribe maintained the tradition as best he could: for such of the manuscripts, written during those years, as have any ornamental writing at all, are decorated with 'Celtic' scrolls and interlacements. This does not mean very much, for the literary matter in these manuscripts was all copied from earlier sources: there is nothing new: and the decoration appears to have been copied also, often in a very faltering hand. Contrariwise, some of the ancient reliquaries were covered over with metal plates, with engraved or repoussé decoration in the Gothic styles—always very feeble, both in design and execution—which conceal the original 'Celtic' adornments. Examples are the *Cathach* and the so-called *Domhnach Airgid*, which bear bad fourteenth-century enrichments (figures under Gothic canopies, &c.). The shrine of the bell of Scattery Island, and that of the Stowe Gospels, have had all of their interlacement-panels overlaid, or actually replaced, with plates of metal engraved with wyverns and other grotesque semi-heraldic animal figures in the one, with extremely barbarous figures of the Crucifixion, the Virgin and Child, a bishop, and another personage unidentified in the other.[22] All of these shrines show, by this later treatment, a complete indifference to the appeal of 'Celtic' Art. But the old tradition sometimes breaks forth (as in fig. 37), or in occasional knot-work treatment of the stems of foliage, and of the lettering and devices sometimes found in sculptured memorial slabs of the sixteenth and seventeenth centuries. These late survivals of the tradition are never very complicated, and they never display originality—this would indeed be impossible, as the resources of this form of ornament had been exhausted before their time. They are fossils of an earlier time, in the world of art something like giraffes and elephants in the present-day world of living organisms—creatures that have survived as pathetic relics of an earlier age into a world where they seem pitifully incongruous.

The monumental antiquities of mediaeval and early modern Ireland pass through well-defined phases of fashion. The thirteenth and fourteenth centuries show us flat, or slightly hog-backed slabs, with floreated crosses and marginal inscriptions, exactly similar to the contemporary cross-slabs of England. The inscription is sometimes, though rarely, on the stem of the cross. It is occasionally in Norman French, gradually giving place to English: usually in Latin; never by any chance in Irish. Indeed, there are only three or four mediaeval inscriptions in Irish throughout the whole country. The letters are usually of the kind called 'Gothic': 'Lombardic' letters are also

THE BUILDERS OF CHURCHES 263

used, but much less frequently in proportion than in England. Seldom, if ever, do we find any reason to believe that these letters were inlaid with brass; monumental brasses are extremely rare in Ireland. At one time there was a considerable number of mediaeval ecclesiastical memorials of this kind in St Patrick's Cathedral in Dublin, and rough sketches of them by the traveller Dineley, who toured in Ireland in 1680-1, are in existence.[23] But the brasses themselves, and in almost all cases even the matrices, have disappeared. A few square plates of the sixteenth and seventeenth centuries survive in the Dublin Cathedrals: there is another in Santry Church, near Dublin; there are a few empty matrices in Old Leighlin Cathedral; and this, so far as I am aware, completes the record. Altar-tombs, often of great elaboration, though seldom of very high artistic or technical merit, are common. They are usually carved on the three upright faces (the fourth being against the wall) with a series of canopies decorated with stiff foliage, under which stand figures, as a rule representing the twelve apostles or other groups of saints, identified very conspicuously by their conventional emblems, more rarely by their names. These figures are often extremely grotesque; but they are very valuable documents for students of the history of costume. A recumbent effigy may lie upon the altar tomb in the vestments of an ecclesiastic, or in the armour of a warrior, as the case may be; but the figure is often merely incised on a flat slab. Sometimes for the figure a cross is substituted: this may bear a portrait head of the person commemorated (examples at Kells, Co. Kilkenny). A favourite device is a series of representations of the instruments of the Passion, which are sometimes extremely interesting: notably when the cock whose crowing awakened the conscience of St Peter is represented as standing on a pot—in reference to a silly legend that the bird was dead and being cooked when the event took place.[24]

The earlier monuments are aristocratic. It does not appear that the commoners commemorated their dead: at least there are not many monuments, coming down from the early mediaeval centuries, to those whom modern stump orators, with untoward ambiguity, describe as 'the plain people'. From about 1450 onward these become more frequent: and between that date and about 1650 there lies a long series of incised slabs, much more interesting, because less stereotyped, than the monumental brasses whose place they take. These sepulchral monuments commemorate tradesmen, ploughmen, smiths, and so forth, and they announce the fact unashamedly by bearing the instruments of their owners' crafts upon them. Very rarely indeed do they adventure into portraiture. The central ornament is usually a cross, with the sacred initials I. H. S.; knot-work, and plait-work, perhaps suggested by the model of early sculptures, frequently decorate these monuments; in one group, found in about half a dozen churches, south of the city of Dublin, and probably all the work of one artificer, the inspiration seems to have come from some cup-and-circle bronze-age rock-scribing. The inscriptions on these slabs are in Latin or English, never, or at least hardly ever, in Irish.

In the course of the seventeenth century the flat slabs give place to erect tombstones of a more ordinary kind. These often display quite remarkable efforts at decoration, with the symbolic figures conventional at the time, angels with trumpets, winged hour-glasses, Reaper Deaths, and the like. Irish is sometimes found on these erect seventeenth- and eighteenth-century tombstones: and the publication in 1785 of the (spurious) Mount Callan Ogham stone, the first Ogham inscription to get into print, inspired a few people to use that ancient script for their memorials, towards the end of the eighteenth century.

Tombstone poetry is far less common in Ireland than in England; very rarely indeed (except in the larger centres) do friends commemorate their dead in verse, and it is but seldom that these verses are of the psychological interest which an English graveyard so amply supplies. Perhaps an exception is presented by James Keally (1640) at Gowran, Co. Kilkenny, who had been married twice, and having caused a burial vault to be constructed for his family in the parish church, expressed his purpose thus—

> Both wives at once alive he could not have,
> Both to enjoy at once he made this grave.

On the whole it is just as well that epitaph-writers restrained their poetic fervour.

CHAPTER X

THE BUILDERS OF CASTLES

A CASTLE is the defence of a man who is obliged to mistrust his neighbours. An Anglo-Saxon lord—even an Anglo-Saxon king—lived among his own people, with nothing more than a hedge or a ditch to separate him from those who were subordinate to him. A Norman baron, like his Celtic or Teutonic predecessor, who had seized upon lands to which he had no hereditary right, was under the necessity of protecting himself against those whom he had dispossessed. In England, castles were unknown in the social order till just before the Norman conquest : certain Norman protégés of Edward the Confessor appear to have erected structures of this kind somewhere about 1048. Not till after the Conquest had been accomplished, however, did a fever of castle-building begin.

It is not to be supposed that these early castles were comparable with the imposing structures of Plantagenet times. They were, indeed, nothing more than wooden towers, erected on the tops of earthen mounds, surrounded by an enclosure of earth and palisading. The enclosure was called *basse-cour*, base-court, or *ward*, the 'guarded place' : or else *ballium*, bailey, the 'palisaded place'. The mound, which was usually at one side of the bailey, conical in shape, and flattened on the top, was called the *mote* or *motte* (not *moat*, a word which should be confined to the water-ditch of later fortifications). The wooden tower was known as *bretesche*.

Castles of this kind were suitable to the conditions which called them forth. Castles, to serve as military bases, were essential to Norman methods of fighting : and there-

THE BUILDERS OF CASTLES 267

fore in subduing a new country, at each military centre a castle had to be run up hastily. Even if the conception of stone castles had evolved in the eleventh century—and the Tower of London, which appears to have been built of stone from the first, shows that such structures were not impossible even at so early a date—the Conquerors could not have afforded the time to wait until they had been erected.

But when the Conquest was completed, the castles could never remain at such a rudimentary stage of development in the turbulent conditions of eleventh-century society. Building with wood is easy and rapid, but it is dangerous; wood can be easily burned, and determined assaults by fire are difficult to deal with effectively. Stone very soon took the place of wood, and the essentially temporary houses, in which the new lords had lodged themselves, gave place to permanent fortified habitations, strong to resist the puny munitions which were then the sole resource of the attackers. This change took place in England during the century that intervened between the victory of William the Conqueror and the Anglo-Norman invasion of Ireland; indeed, by the time of the latter event, the large fortified keep, with its surrounding walls, had become an established feature of the English landscape. The motte-and-bailey stronghold was already, in England, a thing of the past.

But history repeated itself when Ireland was invaded; the same conditions were met with once more, and the old devices were revived to cope with them. Once more the invaders had to run up castles rapidly, to serve as bases for the reduction of a hostile country. Once more they had to deal with a people among whom castles were unknown, and with a land where warfare took the form of hand-to-hand fighting. Once more the fortifications of the newcomers took the form of wooden bretesche-towers, erected on the tops of earthen mottes, to raise them above the range of the arrows which were the most formidable weapons in the hands of the enemy. Once again the structures were temporary, to suit the immediate emergency; and were superseded by strong buildings of stone so soon as the reduction of the country had been sufficiently accomplished. As the new stone structures were built to conform to the contemporary styles of England—though on a smaller scale—Ireland cannot show any examples of the intermediate stages of the evolution, which in England ran its course between 1066 and 1172.

There are motte-and-bailey earthworks in plenty through the country, especially in the places where the Anglo-Norman lords established themselves most firmly. These take the form of conical flat-topped hillocks, resembling in outline a gigantic Turkish 'fez' more than anything else. The flat top distinguishes them from the rounded hillock-tumuli wherein the magnates of the Bronze Age were buried; but otherwise there is little external difference between them, and there is some excuse for the early antiquaries who could not understand that all earth-works are not necessarily prehistoric. Indeed, it may be that an ancient tumulus was sometimes adapted to the purpose of the motte-builder, by having its rounded top flattened down: such a transaction could be exposed by an excavation bringing to light a bronze-age burial in the heart of the mound. It is difficult to believe, for example, that the enormous mound of Knockrafann, near Cahir in Co. Tipperary,[1] was erected from the first as the foundation for a Norman bretesche, although in outline it conforms to the motte model.

The results of excavation would, however, have to be interpreted with judgment. A find of bronze-age objects in the soil of a motte would not in any way justify us in dating the structure to the Bronze Age: on the contrary, its evidence would be definitely unfavourable to such a conclusion. It would mean nothing more than that they happened to be lying in one of the parcels of earth which the motte-builder appropriated for his own purposes, and that they were heaped up with the earth, unnoticed or disregarded in the haste with which the operation had necessarily been carried through. It is in this way that we interpret the discovery of a stone hatchet-head, and

THE BUILDERS OF CASTLES 269

the slip of bronze inscribed with the Runic inscription of Domnall Seal's-head (*ante*, p. 219), in an incongruous union within the motte of Greenmount, Co. Louth.

Though we may pardon the earlier writers for misinterpretating the nature of the mottes, there is now no excuse for doing so. It is not difficult to distinguish at a glance between true prehistoric structures and these Norman erections. The flat top is the invariable criterion: and such mounds as those of Kilfinnane, Co. Limerick; Castletown Geoghegan, Co. Westmeath (a superb example); Clonard, Co. Meath; are object lessons, a sight of which is worth pages of description, to teach the student to discriminate these works from any other. Other criteria can be found at individual sites. The complete Norman establishment includes a bailey at the foot of the motte—an enclosed court, surrounded by a defence now reduced to an earthwork and ditch, though once, no doubt, strongly palisaded: and when this remains (as at Castletown Geoghegan) no doubt can possibly be left as to the purpose of the structure. Again, place-names may often help us to assign a mound of the kind to its proper use and period. The Norman word *motte* was borrowed, in the form *mōta*, by the Irish, and sometimes reappears in topographical nomenclature. The town of Moate, Co. Westmeath, contains within its area a mound resembling in size and shape the motte now called 'Castle Hill' at Cambridge: this structure has obviously given its name to the town, and the name helps to explain the structure. There is another name which reappears several times on the map of Ireland, and is equally instructive: this is *Brittas*, a corruption of *bretesche*, the name of the wooden tower which once stood on the motte. Of such a structure nothing ever remains but the memory, enshrined in the name: but if at a place called Brittas we find an earthen mound, we are obliged to explain it as a Norman motte unless there be unshakeable evidence to the contrary.

In addition to the palisading surrounding the bailey, there was a further rampart of the same kind surrounding the bretesche on the summit of the mound: and the first stage in the evolution of the stone castle was the conversion of this inflammable defence to a wall of stone. Such a wall, however, would be very insecurely founded on the top of a recently heaped mound of earth: and the consequential abandonment of the motte became inevitable. For the motte with its summit-palisade was substituted a circular wall within the bailey, inside which stood the wooden house of the lord of the castle. This *shell-keep*, as it is called, characterizes the castles of the end of the eleventh century: and in consequence shell-keep castles are unknown in Ireland. By the time stone castles began to be built in Ireland, the shell-keep had evolved into the mediaeval stone keep, the strong house of stone in several storeys, wherein the master with his family and servants had their habitation.

From the thirteenth to the seventeenth century, castle-building was one of the chief industries of the country. The number of ruined 'castles' is enormous. We must, however, enclose the word thus, within inverted commas, because, although it is the term commonly used to denote the structures indicated, it is in most cases a misnomer—almost as bad as calling a hedgehog, a porcupine. The great majority of the buildings so designated are merely family houses, fortified as an act of precaution in a country liable to political and other disturbances; they have little in common with the lordly baronial establishments, housing an army of retainers, and dominating an extensive territory of serfs, to which the name should properly be confined.

This plethora of fortifications is a severe practical embarrassment to the Irish antiquary, especially to those charged with administrative duties in connexion with the preservation of ancient monuments in Ireland. It is an impossibility to undertake the care of them all, for many of them need constant attention, and often expensive repair or conservation works. And yet they should not be allowed to perish unrecorded. Once more, as we contemplate these ancient structures, many of which will disappear before the road-maker or house-builder within the coming century, we realize the need of an official Survey of ancient monuments, by which the special points of interest of each structure could at least be recorded on paper. There is no one of these buildings that has not had a history—a history of joy and grief, romance and tragedy. But once again, they have been struck dumb by the hand which fired the Record Office, and thus condemned the people of Ireland, for all time, to grovel in a bovine ignorance of vast tracts of the history of their country.

Notwithstanding the wealth of the material, it cannot be said that any adequate study of the castles of Ireland has ever been made.[2] Individual specimens have been described with more or less accuracy: but there is no synthetic work tracing the history of the development of the fortified dwelling, from the motte-and-bretesche through the mediaeval castles and the Tudor houses, to the manorial dwellings of the seventeenth and eighteenth centuries. Many of the latter, in recent years, have been wantonly destroyed, along with an untold treasury of contents in furniture, books, pictures, and family and other historical documents, to the permanent impoverishment, not so much of their individual owners (who presumably obtained at least a nominal compensation by insurance or otherwise) but of the nation at large. Never did the people of Ireland cut off their noses to spite their faces so assiduously as in those troubled years. The material for the study of civil history is now much less than it was, so recently as the beginning of the present century: by so much is the need for preserving what is left all the greater.

In fact, the true castles in the country are not really so very numerous. The early thirteenth-century fortress of the De Lacys at Trim is the most imposing, with its huge square keep, each side having a square projection —thus making the unusual form of a twenty-sided building. Outside is the bailey wall with numerous towers, enclosing a space of about 2 acres. Thirteenth-century castles with circular keeps are found at Dundrum, Co.

Down (De Courcy's) and at Nenagh (Butler's). The former structure still retains part of the barbican. The extensive fourteenth-century castle of the Desmonds at Askeaton, Co. Limerick, which is among the most elaborate of its kind in the country, is erected on an island on the river Deel. The outer bailey covers the whole island, and is adapted to its shape. It encloses an oval inner bailey, at the north end of which is the keep, a complex three-storeyed structure.[3]

Very interesting is O'Brien's Castle of Carigogunnell, Co. Limerick, which was probably built early in the fourteenth century, but its history has been as complicated as it is obscure.[4] The special peculiarity of this structure is that it is a native attempt to imitate the defences of an English castle, without any real understanding of the strategic principles which dictated their design. The gate is at the worst possible place—at a *corner* of the outer wall, which in any case is poor and thin, and would yield without much labour to a battering-ram: and there is no tower to defend the gate, so that besiegers could operate against it unchecked. The outer wall, again, has no towers: there is therefore no means of preventing stormers from attacking it with their battering or undermining tools. Strangest of all, the keep is actually in the wall, so that it could be captured without the necessity of taking the bailey at all!

The remarkable hybrid structure at Bective calls for passing notice. This was a Cistercian House, founded in the year 1150. It had fallen on evil days in the fifteenth century, and for some reason had to be rebuilt, on a smaller scale: the foundations and other details of the larger building can be traced enclosing the smaller structure. In due course it was suppressed, along with the rest of the monasteries, and after lying derelict for a while it was sold, and after passing through several hands was adapted in the sixteenth or early seventeenth century to serve as a mansion.[5] As a balance to Bective, a dwelling constructed from a Cistercian building, may be set the Franciscan Friary of Quin, Co. Clare, built on the ruins of the

De Clare Castle, which was destroyed in 1286. The bastions of the fortress are still clearly visible under the ruins of the monastic church.

These structures, to which others might be added (such as Limerick, Bunratty, Maynooth, and Carlingford), are imposing either by their architecture or their picturesque position; though none of them can compete with the huge structures of Great Britain. The gigantic fortress on the rock of Dunamase might perhaps have challenged comparison with some of these, if it were not in such a desperate condition of ruin. But the overwhelming majority of the so-called castles are mere pele-towers—towers to protect a pale or boundary (fig. 41). These structures vary in detail, but in general they may be described as oblong on plan, with an entrance usually in one of the narrow sides. Sometimes there is a loophole through the jamb of the door, by means of which an unwelcome visitor could be attacked. On the right-hand side of the entrance there is a lodge for the porter. It has a window commanding the approach to the entrance, an opening to the entrance passage, and another doorway leading into the basement chamber. On the opposite side of the entrance a spiral staircase leads to the upper chambers. Over the entrance there is often a room with a hole in the floor, which served for dropping stones upon the heads of undesirable intruders. Small sleeping-chambers are also provided in the wall above the doorway, which for the purpose is made of great thickness. This part of the tower often rises in one or more turrets. Behind the thick front wall there are usually two or more storeys, each storey containing one large chamber which served as kitchen, store-room, common hall, &c. There is a very large number of such structures, for the greater part erected in the fifteenth–seventeenth centuries. They are so uniform in structure, and so devoid, as a whole, of any feature of interest, that a visit to one is quite as profitable as a visit to a score of them. But the architectural student cannot neglect them: occasionally he is surprised by finding a fancifully carved chimneypiece or an interesting corbel.

Or a building, in itself unattractive, may occasionally have become enriched with graffiti of real interest scrawled on the plaster of the wall. The very remarkable series of drawings of seventeenth-century ships scratched on the plaster in one of the chambers of O'Brien's Castle near Cork, is a case in point.

Of later residential buildings in the country a special notice is due to the very handsome, but much-decayed Ormonde mansion at Carrick-on-Suir, built in the early sixteenth century adjacent to an Edwardian castle—and thereby affording an instructive contrast in domestic appointments. The walls are decorated with stamped plaster, a form of ornament of which few examples remain in the country. 'Myrtle Grove', the residence of Sir Walter Raleigh at Youghal, is an excellent late sixteenth-century building, with some admirable carved oaken chimneypieces; while the Jacobean mansion called Donegal Castle, presents valuable examples of early Stuart ornament.

In spite of centuries of destruction, it would still be endless to enumerate all individual examples of special interest that remain to us: we can but mention a few representative specimens of each type.

The record of 'Ancient Ireland' may be said to end with the eighteenth century—that courtly, squalid, period, so near to us in time, so remote from us in its every outlook: a period of contrasts, when little girls embroidered upon their samplers rhymes like this (by Elizabeth Usher of Waterford, 1780, aged seven)—

> Reasons whole pleasure all the joys of sense
> Lie in 3 words health peace & competence
> But health consists in temperance alone
> And peace oh virtue peace is all thy own

while husbands and fathers wrote rhymes like this, which I succeeded in deciphering upon a window-pane, amid the scratches wherewith a later hand had endeavoured to obliterate it—

FIG. 41.—A PELE-TOWER, DUNGOREY, CO. GALWAY

THE BUILDERS OF CASTLES

> The Crab of the Wood is Sauce that is good
> For the Crab that resides in the Sea:
> The Wood of the Crab is Sauce for the Drab
> That will not her Husband obey.*

But perhaps this inscription, carved on a block of stone which stands by a roadside outside the town of Tuam, Co. Galway, is about as good a summary of the eighteenth century as any that Ireland can offer—

> THIS . STONE . WEIGHING
> 27 . HUNDRED . VNWROVGHT
> ON . A . WAGER . LAID . BETWEEN
> THE . RIGHT . HONOVRABLE
> FRANCIS . LORD . BARON . OF
> ATHVNRY . AND . TIMOTHY .
> DVNNE . ESQUIRE . THEN . SVF
> ERAIN † . OF . TVAM . WAS DR^{A}WN (*sic*)
> ON . A . COMMON . WHEEL-CART
> FROM . THE . PARISH . CHVRCH
> YARD . OF . TVAM . TO THIS
> PLACE . BY . A . MULE . AGED . THIR
> TY . YEARS . BELONGING TO
> THE . SAID . TINOTHY (*sic*) DVNNE
> ON . THE . 27th . DAY OF IVNE
> 1715

Can we not picture the scene? The two local magnates, doubtless half-tipsy: mentally as vacuous as their poor old mule: the idiotic wager: the useless performance: the callous indifference to the feelings of the wretched brute, who, we doubt not, was scourged almost to death to minister to the selfishness and folly of its masters: and

---

* The date of the house containing this elegance is 1769, so that the rhyme has at least the mild interest of giving us a later authority for the pronunciation of final *ea* than Pope's oft-quoted couplet about Queen Anne's tea. I can make no comment on the rhymester's culinary predilections: my gastronomic enterprise is unequal to experimenting on the lines suggested.

† Sovereign, *i.e.* Mayor. The inscription ends with a reference here irrelevant, to the building of a bridge by Timothy Dunne in the same year.

the shamelessness of the carving of the inscription which records the story for the scorn of posterity. Or may we quote as one further illustration that other inscription, which we may still read on a house in Athlone—

> Let not Satan's agents enter
> 'Will-o'-Wisp' and 'Jack ye Printer'

—a hymn of hate put up by a former owner of the house against his next-door neighbours. All three have been dust and ashes a hundred years ; only the hate remains.

These are trivialities : some readers may perhaps feel irritated by their triviality. But the important things are already well recorded, in books easily accessible : the trivialities help to fill in the background, and to make the picture complete.

It was a period of splendid wealth and art ; of horrible poverty and misery. A gay time of high revel ; a grisly time when it was unsafe to go for an evening stroll unattended, for fear of footpads—nearly every number of the volume of a Dublin newspaper, running through the year 1784, which I happen to possess, reports the holding-up of citizens, even on the very outskirts of the city. We have gained much since those vanished days. But we have also lost much. Life in the bungalows that have spread like a rash over the fair face of the countryside is possibly happier, and certainly healthier than the life in the lofty mansions, adorned inside and out with wonderful iron-work, carved marble chimneypieces, plaster-work ceilings—museums of beauty in miniature, which are recorded for posterity in the sumptuous volumes of the Georgian Society. But it is quite safe to prophesy that there will never be a George-Fifth-ian Society to record the beauties of the bungalows !

From the beginning of the century between that time and this comes the Nelson monument in Dublin, one of Ireland's greatest art treasures ; which surpasses every other monument of its kind, in all Europe, in its absolutely perfect proportion, its dignified detail, its magnificent monumental lettering, and its impressive adaptation to its surroundings. It stands with solemn, almost awe-inspiring aloofness, in the midst of a once stately street which in these cinema-besotted days we have vulgarized beyond endurance with glaring electric-light signs.* From the other end of the intervening time there comes a forest of monuments scattered through the country, commemorating various celebrities, from Queen Victoria downward. All that need be said about these is, that the promised removal of Queen Victoria's monument will be a great national act of homage to her late Majesty; and that it is to be hoped that the other victims will in time be honoured in the same way.

As we cast our eyes backward over the history which we have traced, we see only too clearly the helplessness of Man in the grip of the Eternal Destinies. Look at this diagram (fig. 42); it is the key to the history of Ireland.[6] The central line is the standard of climate prevailing at the present moment: the curve falls to the left, or rises to the right, according to the evidence for good climate or bad in the days of old. When the climate was at the best at which it ever was, after the Ice Age, in the Upper Forestian Period, the country was empty: it was, indeed, too full of forest-land to afford a habitation. Somewhere about 2000 B.C. there was a climatic decline, when the forests began to disappear: just at that time, and doubtless in consequence, Europe and Asia were stirred into a ferment, in which the Pictish Halberd-Folk were flung on the shores of Ireland. The climate was still, however, much more favourable than it is to-day; and the Halberd-Folk were in consequence energetic and pushful in commerce. But, some time about 1300 B.C. (why, none can tell us) there was a sudden and violent drop. Immediately Europe was plunged into confusion: and the devouring Goidelic Sword-Folk burst out of England and crushed

---

* It is a curious illustration of what was said on a previous page (p. 200) about the artist being a child of his own time, that the distinguished Dublin architect, Francis Johnston, who designed this superb monument, made such a pitiful hash when he adventured into Gothic for the Chapel Royal in Dublin Castle.

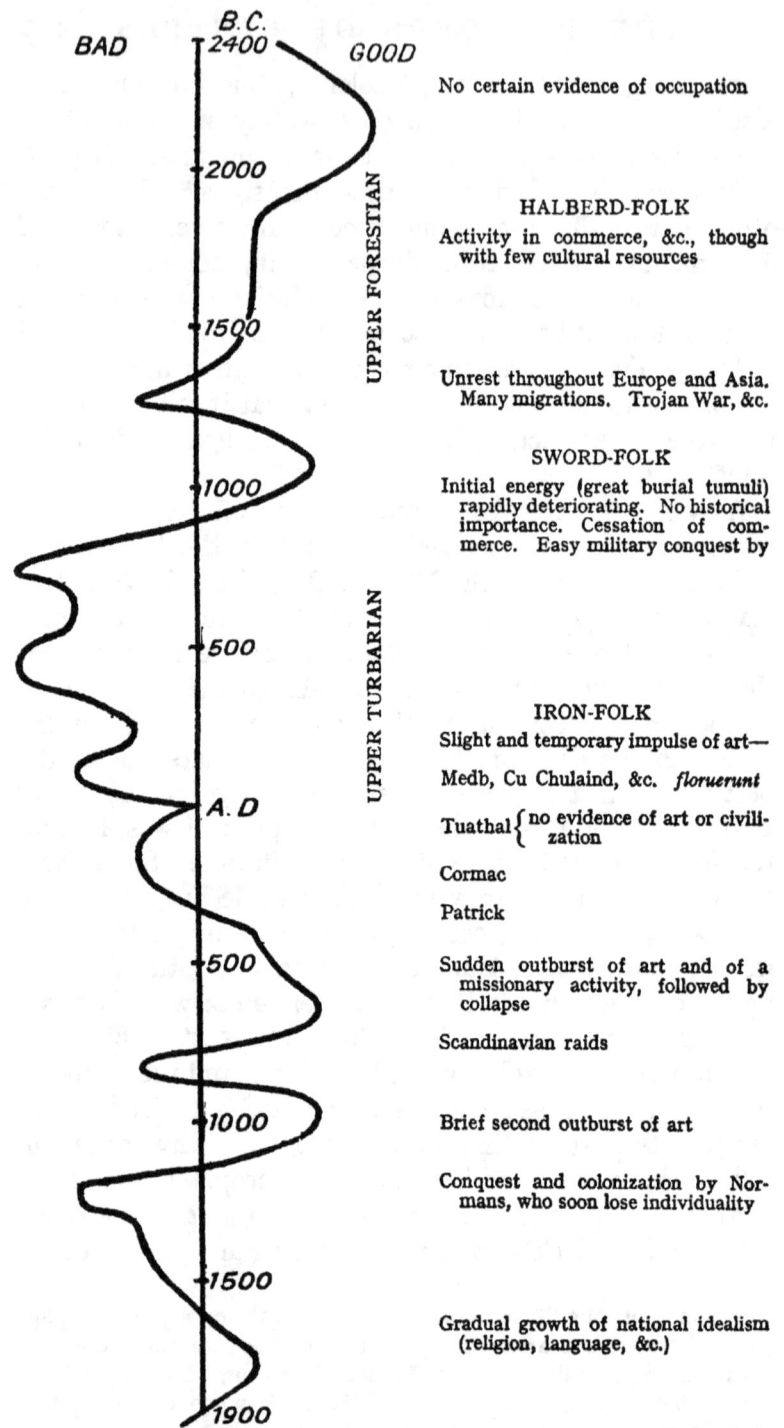

FIG. 42.—THE CLIMATE-CURVE AND THE HISTORY OF IRELAND

THE BUILDERS OF CASTLES

the Halberd-People. The climate improved and in the initial energy of that new optimum the Sword-Folk built their great tomb-sanctuaries: but after that there followed a period of unrecorded barbarism, as the climatic curve declined steadily. The Teutons, under their leaders Eremon and Eber, now arrived, presumably driven out from their own country by the hard conditions. There was a slight recovery about 250 B.C., at which time a few artists, such as the maker of the Turoe Stone, managed to pick up a living: but once again there followed a time of unrelieved squalor. Then came another recovery, about the beginning of the Christian era: but, if we may believe the testimony of the *Táin* story, the resultant energy was dissipated in warfare, especially in the aggressions of Connacht upon the other kingdoms; stimulated, it may be, by news of the ever-widening conquests of Rome. Another time of obscurity follows: then a slow climb upward. The energetic Cormac mac Airt, the first real personality in Irish history, begins a career of conquest. This improvement reaches its climax in about the year 650: and not very long afterwards, there comes the first blaze of Christian art, which culminated in the Ardagh Cup and in the Gospels of Kells. [It is natural that the beneficent effect of an optimum, the maleficent effects of a 'pessimum', should be felt *slightly after* the culminating point is reached.]

About this time Christianity had become completely dominant. Christianity ever brings its message of freedom to the serf: through its influence, the enslaved aboriginal folk, the Picts, were at least partially relieved from the burden of oppression that had crushed them down to the dust. Is it a mere coincidence that this emancipation is synchronous with the sudden manifestation of art? Have the Celts been usurping a glory which is not theirs? Are the Ardagh Cup and the Gospels of Kells the thankofferings of a people long enslaved, and come to their own once again?

But once more there is a sudden drop. Scandinavia cannot sustain her people—they burst over the neighbouring lands, and under their iron heel the arts languish.

There is then a second optimum, and correspondingly a second efflorescence of Art, when the tamed Scandinavians unite with the native craftsmen to give us the Cross of Cong and the later sculptured crosses.

And then come the Anglo-Normans—and what follows? They almost immediately lose their individuality: they become—as those who had sent them forth complained—more Irish than the Irish: and once again the climate is at fault. There is a sudden shift to the left, and the Normans lose their Norman souls.

From that onward there is an upward climb, and with it the growth of a national idealism, ever steadfastly moving towards a fixed goal. The historian records a dismal series of rebellions, savagely perpetrated, savagely crushed: the expression, withal, of a tide of hope and aspiration, rising with the rising curve of climate. But the curve is falling now; and the future must decide whether the disquieting events, at present recorded almost daily in the newspapers, are the foreshadowings of the physical, moral, and material atrophy which an adverse fluctuation of climate *must* produce, in a country with Ireland's unfortunate geographical situation.

On the monument to Charles Stuart Parnell in Dublin there is an inscription to the effect that no one may set bounds to the march of a nation. Beside it there is the effigy of a harp, with its two principal strings attached to the pedestal and not to the soundboard: it is not necessary to know very much about harps to understand that this would set very decided bounds to its utility as a musical instrument. Herein lies a parable. The Omnipotent Creator Himself has taken up the boastful challenge. By His mighty engine, the drift of the hot winds and waters of the Atlantic, *He* has set bounds to the march of the Irish nation. The moist, hothouse atmosphere which these generate makes the land a green and flowery paradise: but it poisons human energy with the mechanical efficiency and the impersonal ruthlessness of a leaky gas-pipe.

However Ireland and England may quarrel, they are necessary to one another: they were wedded when they first became islands, and they cannot be divorced. Neither of them can stand alone: it is beyond the power of man to make it possible that either of them should stand alone. It matters nothing who inhabits either country. It matters nothing what government rules either country, or what relations exist between them. At all times and in all circumstances England must be the barrier-reef for Ireland against invasion and exploitation, if only in self-defence. At all times and in all circumstances Ireland's situation compels her to act, whether she will or not, as the barrier-reef for England against the hot Atlantic drifts; absorbing their poison, and deflecting their course to the north, thus neutralizing in Scotland the icy breath of the Arctic. Were Ireland to sink under the waves, the people of England would immediately begin to develop all those shortcomings which they are now so ready to find in the Irish; the people of Scotland would be frozen down to the cultural and economic level of the Eskimo. Thus Ireland must renounce all hopes of independent greatness: but it is Ireland alone which makes possible the greatness of Great Britain, and in compensation for the enforced self-sacrifice, she is entitled to a lion's share of that greatness. There are people in both islands to whom the situation may be disagreeable: but to change it is outside their competence and jurisdiction. Whoso would seek to do so must fight, not against men, but against the Architect of the Universe.

NOTES AND REFERENCES

[*A. of I.* = the author's *Archaeology of Ireland* (Methuen, 1927). R.I.A. = Royal Irish Academy.* R.S.A.I. = Royal Society of Antiquaries of Ireland. *I.N.J.* = *Irish Naturalists' Journal.*]

CHAPTER I

¹ On the subject of this paragraph, and on the post-glacial geological and biological history of Ireland in general, consult : W. B. Wright, *The Quaternary Ice Age* (London, 1914) ; G. A. J. Cole and T. Hallissy, *Handbook of the Geology of Ireland* (London, 1924) ; R. Ll. Praeger, ' Recent Views bearing on the Problem of the Irish Flora and Fauna ' (*Proceedings*, R.I.A., xli, § B (1932), p. 125 : extensive bibliography).

² For the discoveries in the Kilgreany cave see : E. K. Tratman and others, ' Report on Excavations in Ireland ' (*Proceedings*, Spelaeological Society, University of Bristol, iii (1928), p. 109 ff.) ; S. P. Ó Ríordáin, ' Palaeolithic Man in Ireland ' (*Antiquity*, v (1931), p. 360) ; also a report by A. W. Stelfox, *I.N.J.*, iii (1931), p. 118.

Postscript. I have allowed this paragraph and the foregoing note to stand, partly because some reference to the Kilgreany skeleton may be expected by the reader, and partly to avoid distributing the type unduly : but the most recent researches in this Cave have virtually withdrawn from the Kilgreany Man the scientific importance at first attributed to him. Pending the publication of the results of this work see *The Irish Times*, 23 November, 1934.

³ On the subjects touched upon in the foregoing paragraphs consult : G. Fletcher (editor), *Ireland* (Cambridge University Press, 1922) ; Idem, *The Provinces of Ireland*, 4 vols. (same publisher and date) ; W. FitzGerald, *The Historical Geography of Early Ireland* (' The Geographical Teacher ', supplement No. 1, George Philip, London, 1925).

⁴ On the distribution of metals in Ireland, see : G. A. J. Cole, ' Memoir and Map of Localities of Minerals of economic Importance and Metalliferous Mines in Ireland ' (Memoirs, Geological Survey

---

* The volumes of *Proceedings* of the R.I.A. are divided into three sections, separately paged. Section C is devoted to History and Archaeology, and it may be said once for all, that this is the section referred to throughout, unless one of the others be specified.

of Ireland, Dublin, 1922) ; T. Hallissy, a note on tin in Ireland, appended to a paper by E. C. R. Armstrong in *Proceedings*, R.I.A., xxx, p. 524 ; Idem, *Gold Resources of the Irish Free State* (No. 20 of ' Gold Resources of the World ', *Fifteenth International Geological Congress*, South Africa, 1909).

[5] See *Calendar of Oengus* (Henry Bradshaw Society), p. 40.

[6] The principal line of this rampart is laid down on the map (*frontispiece*). For the minor ramifications, which are of some elaboration, reference must be made to the papers on the subject, published by De Vismes Kane in *Proceedings*, R.I.A., xxvii, p. 301 (1909), xxxiii, p. 531 (1917). For a fine air-photograph and plan of the Dorsey, see *Antiquity*, 1930, pp. 454-5. An air-photograph of the ' Dane's Cast ', a travelling earthwork running across the eastern end of the ' Black Pig's Dyke ', will be found in the same communication.

[7] For a summary of this controversy, with a full bibliography, see J. K. Charlesworth and R. A. S. Macalister, ' The Alleged Palaeolithic Implements of Sligo ' (*Proceedings*, R.I.A., xxxix (1930), p. 18).

[8] See the Map of Raised Beaches in W. B. Wright, *The Quaternary Ice Age*, p. 422.

[9] G. Coffey and R. Ll. Praeger, ' The Antrim Raised Beach, a contribution to the Neolithic History of the North of Ireland ' (*Proceedings*, R.I.A., xxv (1904), p. 143), is the standard work on the subject of the foregoing paragraphs. It is well illustrated. A further bibliography will be found in *A. of I.*, pp. 30 ff.

[10] On the general subject of the Campignian Culture see P. Salmon and others, ' Le Campignien ' (*Revue Mensuel* de l'École d'Anthropologie de Paris, viii (1898), p. 368) ; W. C. Brögger, ' Öxer av Nöstvettypen ' (Norges geol. Undersög. No. 42) ; A. P. Madsen and others, *Affaldsdynger fra Stenaldere i Danmark* (Copenhagen, 1900) ; M. C. Burkitt, *Our Early Ancestors*, pp. 27 ff. On the Asturian Culture see H. Obermaier, *El Hombre Fósil* (Madrid, 1916), p. 334 ; Burkitt, *op. cit.*, p. 24. At the time of writing (July 1934) there has been nothing of special importance on the subject of these cultures in Ireland published, since the bibliographical notes in *A. of I.*, which see.

Chapter II

[1] G. Keating, *History of Ireland* (Irish Texts Society), i, 110.

[2] Keating, *op. cit.*, i, 140 : *Book of Fermoy*, folio 4, col. 2, quoting a lost authority called *Cin Droma Snechta*.

[3] This will be found in the forthcoming edition of the *Book of Invasions*.

[4] On Whitepark Bay see *Journal*, R.S.A.I., xliv (1914), p. 191, and references there.

[5] See the evidence for this collected in the author's *Ireland in Pre-Celtic Times*, p. 42 ff.

[6] For the association of flint instruments with early iron-age pottery, see C. Blake Whelan, *I.N.J.*, ii (1928–9), pp. 94 ff.

[7] E. Crofton Rotherham, ' On Stone Implements found in Meath ' (*Journal*, R.S.A.I., xxxii (1902), p. 139).

[8] See the bibliographical particulars given in the footnotes in *A. of I.*, pp. 38 ff., supplemented by reference to the various headings in the index volumes of the publications of the R.I.A. and the R.S.A.I.

[9] On the prehistoric relationship between Ireland and Spain, which will come into view more than once as we proceed, we refer here once for all to the exhaustive essay by P. Bosch-Gimpera, ' Relations préhistoriques entre l'Irlande et l'ouest de la Péninsule Ibérique ' (*Préhistoire*, ii (1933), p. 195). Good illustrations of the rhomboid javelin-head will be found in the British Museum *Stone Age Guide*, 3rd edn., plate viii, esp. fig. 9.

[10] R. A. S. Macalister, ' On some antiquities discovered upon Lambay ' (*Proceedings*, R.I.A., xxxviii (1929), p. 240).

[11] *A. of I.*, p. 45.

[12] *Arrowheads* bound with gut have been found: see *A. of I.*, p. 42.

[13] O. G. S. Crawford, *Man and his Past* (1921), p. 150. See further Idem, ' The distribution of early bronze-age settlements in Britain ' (*Geographical Journal*, xi (1912), p. 184). The map here given is partly based on maps contained in this paper, with Mr. Crawford's kind permission.

[14] W. Bremer, *Die stellung Irlands in der vor- und früh-geschichtliche Europas*. (In a series of essays published by the Museum of Mainz, 1926.) English Translation, *Ireland's Place in Prehistoric and Early Historic Europe*, Dublin, 1928, p. 15. For Irish objects in Cornwall see H. O' N. Hencken, *Cornwall and Scilly*, London, 1932 (pp. 64, 68, 79, 92 and the index).

[15] See *A. of I.*, pp. 56 ff., and references there.

[16] For further details see *A. of I.*, p. 63, and references there.

[17] See *A. of I.*, pp. 94 ff., and references there: also plate I in the same work.

[18] See *Journal*, R.S.A.I., xxxiv (1904), p. 271 ff., for the discovery of this vessel. It is now in the National Museum.

[19] For numerous illustrations of lunulae, see the *Catalogue of Irish Gold Ornaments in the Collection of the Royal Irish Academy*, in which every specimen in the collection to the date of publication is figured. See also literature referred to in *A. of I.*, pp. 64 ff.

[20] G. Coffey, ' Gold Lunulae in Ireland and North-Western Europe ' (*Proceedings*, R.I.A., xxvii, p. 252). He seems to have abandoned the theory later, as the passage quoted is deleted in the reprint of this paper in his *Bronze Age in Ireland*. It was, how-

ever, revived independently by Mr. J. H. Craw (' On a jet necklace from a Cist at Poltalloch, Argyll ': *Proceedings*, Soc. Antiq., Scot., 1928-9, p. 154).

[21] For this map, on which the distribution map contained in the present volume is based, see the literature quoted in the preceding note.

[22] William C. Borlase, *The Dolmens of Ireland* (3 vols., London, 1897), is a compilation which, notwithstanding some faults, is an indispensable companion to the study of these monuments. It contains many statistics as to the sizes and weights of the component stones.

[23] *Ancient Laws of Ireland*, i, p. 202.

[24] See *Silva Gadelica*, vol. i, p. 118; vol. ii, p. 128. Incidentally the story gives us an admirable example of the practice of *sati*: for with the buried warrior, Salbuide son of Feidlechar king of Munster, not only his treasures, but 'thirty hounds, thirty attendants, and thirty warriors' had been walled up.

[25] Ed. O'Kelleher, pp. 72-3.

[26] C. Smith, *Ancient and Present State of the County and City of Cork* (Dublin, 1750), ii, p. 403; *A. of I.*, p. 130.

[27] W. G. Wood-Martin, *Rude Stone Monuments of Ireland* (Dublin, 1888), p. 185, fig. 146.

[28] One of these, long ago lost, was found in a carn at Mount Stewart, and is known only from a poor woodcut in the *Dublin Penny Journal*, 29 September 1832. The other is a recent discovery in a place called O'Neill's Hill; a fragmentary specimen, not yet published, but displayed in the Belfast Museum.

[29] Betham, *Etruria Celtica*, i, 173; Borlase, *Dolmens of Ireland*, i, 301; Rev. C. Hudson, C.C. in *County Louth Archaeological Journal*, iii (1912-15), p. 149.

[30] See Borlase, *Dolmens*, vol. i, p. 291, where Mr. Stopford's description is reprinted from a Dublin newspaper of 1841. The plan did not accompany the newspaper description, but was sent separately to John Windele of Cork, and is preserved among his MSS. in the R.I.A. Library.

[31] See W. Wulff, ' Carnagat ' (*Journal*, R.S.A.I., lii (1922), p. 38).

[32] Borlase, *Dolmens*, vol. i, p. 191 and reference there.

[33] Borlase, vol. i, p. 119 ff. and references there.

[34] *Proceedings*, R.I.A., xxix (1912), p. 323.

[35] W. F. Wakeman in *Journal*, Roy. Hist. and Arch. Assn. of Ireland, xvi (1883-4), p. 162.

[36] W. F. Wakeman in the same *Journal*, xi (1870-1), p. 579. Compare also a Carn at Bighy, Co. Fermanagh, same *Journal*, xvi, p. 169.

[37] *Ireland in Pre-Celtic Times*, p. 348.

[38] Borlase, *Dolmens*, vol. i, p. 134; W. J. Hemp, ' Leac Con Mic Ruis ', *Antiquity*, v (1931), p. 98.

³⁹ See Spencer and Gillen, *Northern Tribes of Central Australia* (London, 1904), pp. 239 ff., 737 ff.

⁴⁰ The principal literature on the subject of sculpture in Ireland will be found in *A. of I.*, p. 94 ff. A few examples of minor importance have been discovered and partly published since.

⁴¹ On ancient mines in Ireland see *A. of I.*, p. 52 and references there.

⁴² The Drumkelin house was first described by W. Mudge in *Archaeologia*, xxvi, p. 361; see also Wood-Martin, *Lake Dwellings in Ireland*, p. 39 ff. For the Bog of Allen Road, see *Journal, R.S.A.I.*, lxii (1932), p. 137.

Chapter III

¹ On the duration of the Beaker in England see the relevant sections of Hon. John Abercromby, *A Study of the Bronze Age Pottery of Great Britain and Ireland* (Oxford, 1912).

² Examples of brachycephalic skulls recently found: Galbally (*Proceedings*, R.I.A., xxxvi, p. 150); Annaghkeen (*Journal*, R.S.A.I., 1924, p. 173); Corroy (*Journal*, R.S.A.I., 1929, p. 101); Stonepark (*ibid.*, p. 107); Carrownacon (*ibid.*, 1934, p. 77).

³ The *Book of Invasions*, of which a modern version has already been published, but the older versions still remain in MS. (an edition is in preparation), is the most convenient compilation of all these quasi-historical traditions. See also Keating's *History of Ireland*, published in four volumes (the fourth an invaluable analytical index) by the Irish Texts Society.

⁴ The best accounts of the Aran forts are those contained in papers by T. J. Westropp (*Proceedings*, R.I.A., xxviii, pp. 1, 174). See also the *Guide* contained in the *Journal*, R.S.A.I., xxv (1895), p. 239 ff.

⁵ The standard work on the subject is G. Coffey, *New Grange and other Incised Tumuli in Ireland* (Dublin, 1912). See also Borlase, *Dolmens of Ireland*. Reference may also be made to an illustrated paper on the excavation of a carn on Seefin Mountain, Co. Wicklow (*Journal*, R.S.A.I., lxii (1932), p. 153).

⁶ Further references will be found in *A. of I.*, p. 124 ff.

⁷ On Ballon Hill see a number of references in the Index Volume of the R.S.A.I. *Journal*, vols. i–xix. On Drumnakilly, see the same *Journal*, xii, p. 499.

⁸ The Bunbrosna interment is described, with illustrations, in *Proceedings*, R.I.A., xl, p. 308.

⁹ *Tripartite Life of St Patrick*, ed. Stokes, i, p. 90; *Revue Celtique*, xvi, pp. 35–6 and references there. For the topography of Mag Slecht see J. P. Dalton, 'Crom Cruaich of Magh Sleacht' (*Proceedings*, R.I.A., xxxvi, p. 23).

[10] The best account of the Loch Gur group of structures is contained in Sir Bertram Windle's paper (*Proceedings*, R.I.A., xxx, p. 283). Most of what has been written elsewhere on the subject is best forgotten.

[11] Illustrated in the *Journal*, Cork Hist. and Arch. Soc., 1903, p. 24, 1909, p. 105 ff. The Aberdeenshire relationship of the stone is pointed out by Admiral Boyle Somerville at the latter reference.

[12] See Armstrong's *Catalogue of Irish Gold Ornaments*, p. 40 and references there. On the Messingwerk hoard, see G. Kossinna, *Der germanische Goldreichtum in der Bronzezeit* (Mannus-Bibliothek no. 12, Würtzburg, 1913).

[13] On the subject of bronze-age trumpets, their origin and manufacture, see Hubert Schmidt's long and elaborate paper, 'Die Luren von Daberkow' (*Prähistorische Zeitschrift*, vii (1916), p. 85.

Chapter IV

[1] On these see the instructive pages of Dottin, *Manuel pour servir à l'étude de l'antiquité celtique*, pp. 35 ff.

[2] *Les premiers habitants de l'Europe*, ii, p. 278 ff.

[3] *Histoire de la Gaule*, vol. I, chap. vi.

[4] *Antiquity*, iii (1929), p. 33.

[5] On this figure and the excavation which revealed it, see *The Antiquaries' Journal*, 1934, p. 180; *Journal*, R.S.A.I., 1934, p. 139.

[6] On Hallstatt objects in Ireland, see Armstrong's paper, *Journal*, R.S.A.I., liv (1924), pp. 1, 109.

[7] Two earrings, dated by their archaeological context to *c.* 1500 B.C., are figured in *Illustrated London News*, 9 July 1932; four others, dated *c.* 2000 B.C. in the same journal, 16 June 1934. On chronological grounds their attribution to Ireland is impossible. But they have the importance of knocking one more nail in the coffin of the more extreme 'diffusionist' theories.

[8] On the etymology of *Fomoire* see Kuno Meyer, *Zur keltische Wortkunde* (Sitzungsberichte der kön. preuss. Akad. der Wissenschaften, 1914, p. 635). The equation Conaing = Koninga was suggested to me in conversation by Prof. E. Mac Neill.

[9] See *Archaeologia*, vol. lxxx, p. 1 ff.

[10] See W. B. Stevenson, 'The First Crusade' (*Proceedings*, Royal Philosoph. Soc., Glasgow, 1913).

[11] Beside the standard works of Brooks and Ellsworth Huntington, the reader may refer to Oswald Spengler, *Untergang des Abendlandes* (1908; English trans. 1926), but reading at the same time the trenchant essay by R. G. Collingwood in *Antiquity*, i, p. 311. See also Sir F. Petrie, *Revolutions of Civilization* (1911, third edn., 1922), and O. G. S. Crawford, 'Historical Cycles' (*Antiquity*, v, p. 5, where further references will be found).

[12] *Hist. Nat.*, xvi, i. On lake-dwellings on the Continent, see the standard works of Keller, Vouga, and Munro.

[13] The standard work on Irish lake-dwellings is still Wood-Martin's not very satisfactory compilation *The Lake-dwellings of Ireland* (1886). Further literature will be found in *A. of I.*, p. 182: the results of the investigation of the Ballinderry sites, which are the most important that have been made in recent years, still await full publication.

[14] The chief authority will be found in the Rolls Series publications of *Ancient Laws of Ireland*, ii, 194–341: but there are facts of importance to be gleaned throughout the whole of this important but soul-petrifying literature.

[15] See R. J. Moss, 'A Chemical Examination of the Crucibles in the Collection of Irish Antiquities of the Royal Irish Academy' (*Proceedings*, R.I.A., xxxvii, p. 175).

[16] For a detailed description of the objects in this hoard, see *A. of I.*, p. 148, and references there. In Armstrong's Catalogue of the gold objects in the collection of the R.I.A. every normal type of gold object found in the country is illustrated.

[17] For analyses of La Tène art see the British Museum *Guide to the Antiquities of the Iron Age, passim*; the relevant volumes of Déchelette's *Manual d'Archéologie*; E. T. Leeds, *Celtic Ornament in the British Isles down to* A.D. 700 (Oxford, 1933), with numerous fine illustrations and further references.

[18] On this site see *A. of I.*, p. 153 and references there.

[19] On La Tène in Ireland, see Armstrong's paper, *Journal*, R.S.A.I., liii, p. 1. The Turoe and Castle Strange stones were first described by Coffey (*Proceedings*, R.I.A., xxiv, p. 257); the Turoe Stone has frequently been reproduced since. The Killycluggin stone is described in *Journal*, R.S.A.I., lii, p. 113.

[20] Some fine results have already been achieved in Northern Ireland: see *Antiquity*, iv (1930), p. 483.

[21] See, for example, E. Cecil Curwen, 'Prehistoric Agriculture in Britain' (*Antiquity*, i (1927), p. 261).

[22] Full report in *Proceedings*, R.I.A., xxxviii, p. 69.

[23] Full report on the excavation in *Proceedings*, R.I.A., xxxix, sect. C, p. 54.

[24] See the report on this excavation, published as a separate Monograph by the Society of Antiquaries of London (Oxford, 1932).

[25] On the Lochcrew site see *A. of I.*, pp. 127–8 and references there. Further references in the index of the same book.

[26] These opinions, with an illustration of the monument, will be found set forth in the author's book on *Tara*.

[27] See *Aarbōger for Nordisk Oldkyndighed og Historie*, 1881, p. 383; Oscar Almgren, *Nordische Felszeichnungen als religiose Urkunden*, p. 65. The Shercock figure has been illustrated, with a

short notice by Dr. Mahr, and some other references, in *Antiquity*, iv, p. 487.

²⁸ Facsimiles of these alphabets will be found in E. S. Roberts, *An Introduction to Greek Epigraphy*, vol. i, p. 17.

²⁹ In a forthcoming work on *The Secret Languages of Ireland* the matter of the foregoing paragraphs is discussed with greater fullness.

³⁰ Poseidonius (in Diodorus, v, 32) is especially emphatic on this subject, for he uses 'the Britons who dwell in Ireland' as a standard of comparison with other cannibals in the region of Scythia (φασί τινας ἀνθρώπους ἐσθίειν, ὥσπερ καὶ τῶν Βρεττανῶν [lege Πρεττανῶν] τοὺς κατοικοῦντας τὴν ὀνομαζομένην Ἴριν). See the discussion of all these passages by C. S. Greaves, 'Cannibalism in England' (*Archaeological Journal*, xxxvi (1879), p. 38). For cannibalism during famine see *Annals of Clonmacnois* (A.D. 695); *Annals of Ulster* (A.D. 699).

³¹ H. Bradley, 'Ptolemy's Geography of the British Isles, (*Archaeologia*, xlviii, part ii, p. 379); G. H. Orpen, 'Ptolemy's Map of Ireland' (*Journal*, R.S.A.I., xxiv, p. 115).

Chapter V

¹ The text has been edited, with a German translation, by Prof. Windisch, in the series *Irische Texte*; an edition of the *Lebor na Huidri* copy, without translation, by Prof. Strachan and Mr. J. G. O'Keeffe. English translations by Miss W. Faraday (Grimm Library) and by Mr. Joseph Dunn (Nutt, London, 1914) are available.

² Sir W. Ridgeway's paper, 'On the date of the first shaping of the Cuchulainn Saga' (in vol. ii of the *Proceedings* of the British Academy), shows this clearly.

³ For an analysis of this list of tales, with particulars as to the extent to which they have been preserved, see Brian O'Looney, 'On Ancient Historic Tales in the Irish Language' (*Proceedings*, R.I.A., Ser. II, vol. i, p. 215).

⁴ See Dottin, *L'Antiquité celtique*, p. 150, and references there.

⁵ In the story before us: see Windisch's edition, pp. 440, 441.

⁶ See Stokes, *Lives of Saints from the Book of Lismore*, pp. 322, 323.

⁷ Poseidonius in Athenaeus, iv, 151.

⁸ *Lives of Saints from the Book of Lismore*, pp. 62, 209.

⁹ For the objects in silver found in Ireland, see Armstrong's edition of Wilde's Catalogue (*Proceedings*, R.I.A., xxxii, p. 287).

¹⁰ Diodorus, v, 31. For Medb's auguries on Samain (1 November) see *Agallamh*, ed. Stokes, line 3863 (*Silva Gadelica*, ii, p. 202).

¹¹ A large number, including the example here quoted, are collected together in a paper by Sir S. Ferguson in *Proceedings*, R.I.A., xv, 355.

[12] Caesar, *De Bello Gallico*, iv, 33. See the discussion of the use of Chariots in Rice Holmes, *Ancient Britain and the Invasion of Julius Caesar*, p. 674.

[13] The story is told under the title *Ces-noinden Ulad*, 'Childbirth pains of the Ultonians'. See Best's *Bibliography of Irish Philology and Literature*, p. 88, for references.

[14] *Ancient Laws of Ireland*, iv, pp. 338–9.

[15] *Ancient Laws and Institutions of Wales* (Record Commission), p. 119.

[16] See the Preface to the hymn in the Irish *Liber Hymnorum;* also *Tripartite Life*, i, 46.

[17] Frequently illustrated: an easily accessible representation will be found in M. C. Burkitt, *Our Forerunners* (Home University Library), facing p. 210.

[18] *De förhistoriska Perioderna i Skandinavien*, pl. 15, fig. 1 ; also in his longer work on the *Civilisation of Sweden in Heathen Times*, in which the same plates are repeated.

[19] For further illustrations, see Frazer, *Taboo and the Perils of the Soul*, index s.v. Name, Names.

[20] *Ancient Laws of Ireland*, iv, p. 150.

[21] See Th. Reinach, 'Les Chars armes de faux chez les anciens Gaulois' (*Revue Celtique*, x, p. 122), with a wealth of references ; Rice Holmes, *Ancient Britain*, p. 675.

[22] Such towers are described by Vegetius, *Epitoma Rei Militaris*, iv, 17.

[23] The version here followed is that printed (without translation) in *Irische Texte* (vol. I) from the *Book of Leinster*. See Best's *Bibliography*, p. 92, for further literature. Zimmer's study, *Der Kulturgeschichtliche Hintergrund in den Erzählungen der alten irischen Heldensage* (Berlin *Sitzungsberichte*, 1911, p. 174), is of high importance in this connexion.

[24] On Diarmait and Gráinne, see the literature cited in Best's *Bibliography*, p. 103.

[25] References in Best's *Bibliography*, pp. 90, 91.

[26] Rivers, *Social Organization*, p. 162.

[27] Iliad, vii, 321 ; 1 Samuel ix. 22 ff. Poseidonius in Diodorus, v, 28, and again in a passage cited by Eustathius from Athenaeus (Müller, *Fragmm. Hist. Graec.*, iii, p. 259, no. 24).

[28] *Táin Bó Cúalnge*, ed. Windisch, pp. 896–7.

Chapter VI

[1] *Senchus na Relec* : printed in Petrie's *Round Towers and Ancient Architecture of Ireland*, p. 97 ff.

[2] *Tripartite Life of St. Patrick*, ed. Stokes, ii, p. 272.

[3] The unforgettable picture drawn by R. L. Stevenson (*The Ebbtide*, chap. v) might serve almost as it stands, for a picture of the

establishments of scattered communities of Christians among the Pagan populations in Ireland and elsewhere. The scene is a schooner on the South Seas, manned by a native crew under the command of three disreputable whites. 'Upon the Sunday each brought forth his separate bible and they would all join together in the singing of missionary hymns. It was thus a cutting reproof to compare the islanders and the whites, to see these poor souls, so faithful to what they knew of good.' Doubtless on such an occasion some very queer theology would be propounded, and there would be mingled with the Christianity many strange reminiscences of their former ways of thought. It would therefore not be surprising if no uniform ecclesiastical order and discipline should exist in Apostolic and sub-Apostolic times: the ancient literary evidence collected in such a work as B. H. Streeter's *The Primitive Church* (London, 1929) is conclusive on this point. But it is really unnecessary to go further than *The Acts of the Apostles*, which gives us a picture of a community of Christians in Ephesus, ignorant of the doctrine of the Holy Spirit (xix, 1–4): these must have been theologically just such a company as the Kanakas of Stevenson's story. As it took an appreciable time for the varieties of local churches to fuse into one organic whole, a community of Christians who had not developed an episcopate, on a predominantly pagan island at the end of the world, need not cause the slightest surprise—especially as they were outside the jurisdiction of the Empire of Rome. Doubtless their treatment of Palladius, an emissary from Rome, was at least partly prompted by a fear that Ecclesiastical domination would be only the prelude to Imperial domination.

[4] See his elaborate volume, *Pelagius in Irland*. Harnack's *History of Dogma* (vol. v, English trans.) is chiefly occupied with the history of the Pelagian controversy. See also *Encyclopaedia Britannica* (eleventh ed.), s.v. *Pelagius*, and references there.

[5] Bury's *Life of St Patrick* is the principal authority on the historical setting of Patrick's career, which is all that concerns us in the present study. There is an enormous Patrick literature, ancient and modern, but for the greater part it may be regarded as the literary equivalent of a slightly monotonous musical *tema con variazioni*—the *tema* being St Patrick's *Confessio*, the *variazioni* what the different authors read into it, with occasional inharmonious counterpoints from Muirchu and other gossip-mongers. See Kenney's *Sources for the Early History of Ireland*, index s.v. Patrick.

[6] See the author's interpretation of the enigmatical *Silua Focluti*, *Journal*, R.S.A.I., lxii, 19.

[7] Deut. xviii. 20; Acts v. 34.

[8] Fantastic though this reconstruction of the history may appear to some, it is not without precedent. Who would have believed that a bishop of another province having had a dream that he was

to become bishop in Jerusalem, promptly went thither, ostensibly to visit the Holy Places : and that certain of the Christians of Jerusalem, having in their turn dreamt that this man was to be made their bishop, went out and welcomed him, refusing to let him depart from among them ? And yet this strange story is told in all seriousness by Eusebius (*Hist. Eccl.*, vi, 11). The leading cases of certain Old Testament dreamers gave a sanction to the importance attached to dreams as revelations of the divine will.

[9] *Tripartite Life*, ii, p. 272.

[10] *The Rule of Tallaght* (ed. Gwynn, *Hermathena*, xliv, pp. 20, 48).

[11] By G. Coffey, in *Proceedings*, R.I.A., xxiv, p. 257.

[12] For 'The Priest's House', Kilmalkedar, see *Journal*, Roy. Hist. and Arch. Assoc. of Ireland, xi (1870-1), p. 577 ff. For St Columba's House, see Lord Dunraven's *Notes on Irish Architecture* (vol. ii, p. 50), where plans, sections and a photograph will be found.

[13] Descriptions of the ruins of High Island (Ardilaun, Ardoilean) will be found in *Proceedings*, R.I.A., x, p. 51 ; *Journal*, R.S.A.I., xxvi, p. 197.

[14] *The Rule of Tallaght* (ed. Gwynn, *Hermathena*, xliv, pp. 10, 11).

[15] Refer (with caution) in connexion with these monumental slabs to Petrie's *Christian Inscriptions in the Irish Language* (two vols. : numerous plates, but not very accurate). The Clonmacnois slabs have been published by the Royal Society of Antiquaries under the editorship of the present writer.

[16] The Kilnasaggart and Inchagoill stones are both discussed in Petrie, *op. cit.*, vol. ii, pp. 10, 27. The latter has been made the subject of several papers : see the indexes to the *Journal*, Royal Society of Antiquaries of Ireland, s.v. Inchagoill. For the Candida Casa (Whithorn) stone see the illustration in Romilly Allen's *Early Christian Monuments of Scotland*, and references there.

[17] The reader may be referred to the following works : J. Romilly Allen, *Celtic Art in Pagan and Christian Times*, and the same author's *Early Christian Symbolism* ; Margaret Stokes, *Early Christian Art in Ireland* ; G. Coffey, *Guide to the Celtic Antiquities of the Christian Period in the National Museum* ; A. Kingsley Porter, *The Crosses and Culture of Ireland* ; F. Henry, *La sculpture irlandaise pendant les douze première siècles de l'ère Chrétienne* ; H. S. Crawford, *Carved Ornaments from Irish Crosses* ; J. A. Bruun, *An Enquiry into the Art of the Illuminated MSS. of the Middle Ages*, part i ; Stanford F. H. Robinson, *Celtic Illuminative Art* ; A. Mahr (editor), *Christian Art in Ancient Ireland*. A large number of papers on individual objects, too numerous to be catalogued here, will be found in the proceedings of the principal societies : and naturally the student cannot afford to neglect the studies that have been made on cognate arts in neighbouring countries.

[18] This MS. has been published (in typography) by the Royal

Irish Academy. A facsimile of the Patrician documents is in preparation.

[19] The British Museum has issued a monograph upon this MS. with facsimiles of many of the illuminated pages.

[20] This fact was first noted by Dr. R. I. Best. See *Hermathena*, vol. xx, p. 84.

[21] A number of the pages, with a preface by Sir E. Sullivan, have been reproduced in colour by the publishers of *The Studio*.

[22] Collotype facsimiles published by the Henry Bradshaw Society.

[23] See Rev. S. Hemphill, 'The Gospels of MacRegol of Birr' (*Proceedings*, R.I.A., xxix, p. 1).

[24] No recent study of this book has been published; particulars will be found in the antiquated works of Westwood and Bruun.

[25] Coloured facsimiles of a couple of pages from this MS. will be found in the Monograph on *Ancient Irish MSS.* published in the *Vetusta Monumenta* of the Society of Antiquaries of London.

[26] For the Psalter of St Caimin, see Mario Esposito's paper (with photographic facsimiles), *Proceedings*, R.I.A., xxxii, p. 78. The Psalter of Ricemarch has been published in facsimile by the Henry Bradshaw Society.

[27] For the story of Celtic Illuminated MSS., Zimmermann's gigantic work *Vorkarolingische Miniaturen* is indispensable; other literature is indicated in the bibliographical notes to *A. of I.*

[28] Photographs of all these objects are given in Coffey's *Guide to the Celtic Antiquities of the Christian Period*. See also the Free State Government's publication, *Christian Art in Ancient Ireland*, which comprises a fine series of plates. Facsimiles of the inscriptions will be found under the several heads in Petrie's collection.

[29] For these doorways, see Petrie, *Christian Inscriptions*, vol. ii, pp. 85–9. Killeshin has been fully described by H. G. Leask and H. S. Crawford in *Journal*, R.S.A.I., lv (1925), p. 83.

[30] See Petrie, *op. cit.*, vol. i, p. 42, plate xxxiii, for the Clonmacnois Cross. The Monasterboice Cross is fully illustrated in the present writer's monograph, *Muiredach, Abbot of Monasterboice*, though the discovery described in the text puts that work in some respects out of date.

[31] This is worked out in detail in the author's *Memorial Slabs of Clonmacnois*, published by the R.S.A.I. in 1909.

[32] The Clonburren stone is illustrated in *Journal*, R.S.A.I., 1912, p. 28.

[33] See *Archaeologia*, lxv, p. 223, lxxii, p. 71. Further references in *A. of I.*

[34] As for instance Bernhard Salin, in his monumental work, *Altgermanische Tierornamentik*.

[35] For some references on the subject of these figures, see *A. of I.*, pp. 348–9, to which add M. A. Murray, 'Female Fertility Figures'

(*Journal*, Royal Anthropological Institute, lxiv, p. 93). For a fuller description of the White Island Figures see a paper by Rev. Canon McKenna and Lady Dorothy Lowry-Corry in *Journal*, R.S.A.I., lx (1930), p. 23.

[36] Described by Lady Dorothy Lowry-Corry in *Proceedings*, R.I.A., xli, p. 200.

[37] Possibly lupus: hardly syphilis, as suggested in Plummer's *Vitae Sanctorum Hiberniae* (I, p. cxi), for I am informed by medical historians that this disease was unknown in Europe till Columbus and his successors brought the taint from the aborgines of the New World. Some painful pathological details were exposed in the excavation by Messrs. Hencken and Movius at Knockast, Co. Westmeath (*Proceedings*, R.I.A., xli, p. 232). It may be mentioned here that if nothing has been said in the foregoing pages about this important work, it is because I feel that we are not yet in a position to traverse the ethnological vistas which it seems to open out before us. Much further research will be necessary before we can claim the franchise of that labyrinth.

[38] *Sindach brothlaige*, 'crumb-fox', was actually a technical term for a tramp: see *Ancient Laws*, Glossary, s.v.

[39] *Topographia Hiberniae*, II, 38, 39.

Chapter VII

[1] For the history of this period, see *A. of I.*, chap. viii, and references there. To the references on the Ranuaik (Copenhagen) shrine add now Mahr's *Christian Art in Ancient Ireland*, vol. i, plates 16, 17.

[2] Three Fragments of Irish Annals, ed. O'Donovan, pp. 126-7.

[3] *Annals of the Four Masters*, under the date indicated. For examples of native raids on the Monasteries, see the table of the history of Clonmacnois at the end of the author's Monograph on the Memorial Slabs at that place.

[4] *Annals of Four Masters* under date specified.

[5] 'Christian Vikings' (*Antiquity*, i, p. 172).

[6] See Coffey and Armstrong, 'Scandinavian Objects found at Island Bridge' (*Proceedings*, R.I.A., xxviii, p. 107). For the silver objects, see Armstrong's edition of Wilde's Catalogue of these, *ibid.*, xxxii, p. 287.

[7] See A. Mahr, ' Ein Wikingerschwert mit deutschen Namen aus Irland ' (*Mannus*, VI, Ergänzungsband (1928), p. 240).

[8] See on this Nils Åberg, *The Anglo-Saxons in England*, p. 177 ff.

[9] On which see *Antiquity*, vi (1932), pp. 420 ff.

[10] For ancient coinage in Ireland, see references in *A. of I.*, p. 342.

[11] For the evidence for these, see Todd's *Wars of the Gael and the Gaill*, index, s.v. 'Gormfhlaith'. The reference to *Njál's Saga* for the lady's character will be found in paragraph 154 of Valdimar

Ásmundarson's edition of the text (in Sigurðr Kristjánsson's convenient series) and at section 153 of the English edition in *Everyman's Library*, which is now more easily accessible than Dasent's original publication, referred to by Todd.

[12] See H. O'Neill Hencken, ' A Gaming Board of the Viking Age ' (*Acta Archaeologica*, iv, p. 85).

[13] Information derived from Dr. Marstrander personally. I have not seen his publication of the inscription (*Norsk Geografisk Selskaps Årbok*, 1908–9, p. 129), but borrow the reference from his paper quoted in note (16) below.

[14] H. C. Lawlor, *The Monastery of St Mochaoi of Nendrum*, p. 70.

[15] The story is narrated (from the *Book of Ballymote*) in O'Curry's *Manners and Customs of the Ancient Irish*, ii, p. 322 ff. For the Greenmount Rune, see *Journal*, Roy. Hist. and Arch. Assn. of Ireland, xi, pp. 279, 471.

[16] When *A. of I.* was written the stone was still built into the wall where it was discovered. It was afterwards taken out, when the Ogham was discovered. See R.I.A. *Proceedings*, xxxviii, p. 236, and, for a correction, the Minutes of the same body, 1930–1, p. 40. See also C. J. S. Marstrander, Killaloekorset og de norske Kolonier i Irland (*Norsk Tidsskrift for Sprogvidenskap*, iv, p. 378).

[17] See the text in Stokes and Strachan, *Thesanous Palaeohibernicus*, ii, p. 290.

Postscript. In August 1934 the author had the good fortune to discover another Runic inscription, which, so far as he has been able to decipher it, appears to be parallel to the Killaloe inscription. It is, however, very difficult, and will require a much more prolonged examination than he was able to give it at the time before even a tentative reading can be offered.

CHAPTER VIII

[1] The story that follows is that of the *Boraime* or ' Tribute ' contained in the *Book of Leinster* (also a fragmentary copy differing in some respects, in the Book of Lecan). Text printed in S. O'Grady's *Silva Gadelica*, vol. i, p. 359 ff.; translation, headed ' Here begins the story of the Boromean Tribute ', in vol. ii of the same work, p. 401 ff.

[2] For examples, see Frazer, *Taboo and the Perils of the Soul*, chap. iv.

[3] *Mesca Ulad* (Todd Lecture Series), pp. 52, 53, *Fled Bricrend* (I.T.S. Edition), pp. 66, 67.

[4] *Vision of Mac Conglinne* (ed. K. Meyer), pp. 10 ff.

[5] The necessity of stopping to secure such a lunatic is admitted as one of the few sufficient excuses for a delay in giving notice of

completed distraint, which otherwise was required to be done immediately after the transaction. See *Ancient Laws*, i, pp. 268-9.

⁶ The following paragraphs are chiefly compiled from the *Annals of the Four Masters*, of *Ulster*, and of *Clonmacnois*.

⁷ For further particulars see T. J. Westropp's paper on the site, *Proceedings*, R.I.A., xx, p. 55.

⁸ It was cut down in its turn in 1051, according to the Four Masters.

⁹ These curious anecdotes are narrated in the *Annals of Clonmacnois* under date 990.

¹⁰ *Wars of the Gaedhil and the Gaill*, pp. 200-1.

CHAPTER IX

¹ See *A. of I.*, p. 239.

² Illustrations of this building are a commonplace in works in Irish archaeology and architecture. The latest and perhaps the best is in Mahr's *Christian Art in Ancient Ireland*, i, plate 12.

³ Numerous examples of these early churches are represented among the fine photographic illustrations in Dunraven's too modestly named *Notes on Irish Architecture*.

⁴ Good illustrations of the Skellig buildings appear in Mahr's *Christian Art in Ancient Ireland*, i, plates 2-4. See also Dunraven's work cited in the preceding note. Further illustrations and a full description of the site will be found in the *Journal*, R.S.A.I., 1892, p. 277.

⁵ Illustrations of both buildings in Dunraven. St Kevin's is frequently reproduced.

⁶ There is a very summary notice of the Clara Church in *Journal*, R.S.A.I., xxiii, 207. For Mac Duach's church see Dunraven, *op. cit.*, as well as a short notice in *Journal*, R.S.A.I., xxv, p. 259.

⁷ Illustrations of the Cathedral of Clonmacnois will be found in a short pamphlet on Clonmacnois by the present writer, published by the Catholic Truth Society of Ireland. There is much about Cormac's Chapel at Cashel scattered through Petrie's *Ecclesiastical Architecture* and Stokes's *Early Christian Art in Ireland*, but we still await an authoritative monograph on this important building with proper measured drawings. (Some measured drawings, but hardly sufficient, will be found in Brash's *Ecclesiastical Architecture of Ireland*, plates 31-35.) For its German affinities see C. McNeill, 'Affinities of Irish Romanesque Architecture' (*Journal*, R.S.A.I., xlii, p. 140). Good photographs of this and most if not all of the buildings mentioned in this and the following chapter are published by Mr. Thomas Mason of Dame Street, Dublin, and Mr. Welch of Belfast.

⁸ Illustrations in Dunraven, *op. cit.*

[9] The Timahoe doorway is illustrated in Dunraven, *op. cit.*, and in fuller detail by H. S. Crawford and H. G. Leask in *Journal, R.S.A.I.*, liv (1924), p. 31.

[10] Measured drawing in Brash, *Ecclesiastical Architecture of Ireland*, plate 15.

[11] Illustrations in Champneys, *Irish Ecclesiastical Architecture*, pl. 64; *Journal*, R.S.A.I., xxxiii (1903), p. 369, where the figures are more clearly represented, and in the accompanying letterpress are identified so far as may be.

[12] Illustration in Dunraven, *op. cit.*

[13] Illustration in *Journal*, R.S.A.I., xxiv, p. 152.

[14] Examples are to be seen at St Saviour's, Glendaloch (see the fully illustrated monograph on this site published by the Irish Board of Public Works), at Timahoe (*Journal*, R.S.A.I., 1924, p. 38) and numerous other places.

[15] For an illustration see *Journal*, R.S.A.I., xxii (1902), p. 409.

[16] See H. S. Crawford's paper on the Clonfert doorway (*Journal*, R.S.A.I., xxxii (1912), p. 1 ff.) for details of this ornamentation. A photograph showing the 'Celtic' ornamentation on the Nunnery Arch will be found in my pamphlet on Clonmacnois above quoted. The Dysert arch, referred to in the preceding note, affords another illustration.

[17] The heraldry of the shield borne by the effigy commonly called Strongbow's contradicts the identification. It would link the figure to the earldom of Drogheda: and it has been suggested that the effigy was a Drogheda monument stolen from the parish church of that town to substitute it for the genuine Strongbow monument which was destroyed by a fall of the cathedral roof.

[18] This document can be most conveniently studied in H. J. Lawlor's scholarly translation, with an elaborate historical introduction and notes, published by the S.P.C.K.

[19] Actually the Abbey of St. Mary, Dublin, said, with doubtful authenticity, to have been founded as a Benedictine house in the tenth century, was slightly earlier than Mellifont, for it joined the allegiance of Citeaux in 1139.

[20] The document known as *Triumphalia Chronologica Monasterii Sanctae Crucis*, edited by Rev. D. Murphy in 1895, is authoritative for the history of the Cistercians in Ireland. But as yet there is no satisfactory monograph on mediaeval monasticism in Ireland: Archdale's *Monasticon Hibernicum* does not satisfy modern requirements. The work would be beyond the power of a single scholar, unless he had his whole life to spare, and was willing to devote it to the task exclusively of all other interests.

[21] Other examples of wall-painting, no longer traceable, have been recorded at the Franciscan Friary at Adare (*Journal*, R.S.A.I., xlv, p. 151) and at Corcomroe (*ibid.*, xxx, p. 302).

[22] For illustrations of these shrines see Coffey's Guide to the

Christian Antiquities of the Celtic Period, under each article. Good illustrations of the figures on the Stowe Missal Shrine in Mahr's *Christian Art*, i, pl. 65. For the Scattery Bell Shrine see Westropp's paper on this object, *Journal*, R.S.A.I., xxx, p. 237.

[23] Dineley's journal, with facsimiles of his rough sketches, is published in several of the early volumes of the *Journal* of the R.S.A.I. See also H. J. Lawlor, *The Monuments of the Pre-Reformation Archbishops of Dublin*, *ibid.*, xlvii, p. 109. The Santry brass is figured in the same journal, xv (1879–82), p. 482, and the Old Leighlin matrices in *Proceedings*, R.I.A., xvi, p. 424 ff. and associated plate.

[24] See Seymour's paper on this tradition and its iconography, *Journal*, R.S.A.I., li, p. 147.

CHAPTER X

[1] Illustration in *Journal*, R.S.A.I., xxxix, p. 275.
[2] There are books on the Castle of Ireland by C. L. Adams and by J. S. Fleming; the latter has also written a monograph on the *Town Wall Fortifications of Ireland*. These works are collections of descriptions of individual specimens rather than a record of evolutionary history. A list of the descriptions of castle buildings scattered through the Journals of Societies would fill a long bibliography, and when it was completed it would be found, first that scores of buildings have so far escaped description, and secondly, that very little is really known about Castle architecture in Ireland.
[3] There are no adequate monographs on Trim and Nenagh, though particulars as to the former, at least, can be found with the help of the Indexes to the *Journal*, R.S.A.I. For Dundrum Castle, see the same *Journal*, xxxv, p. 294, and for Askeaton, *ibid.*, xxxiv, p. 116.
[4] See an illustrated description in *Journal*, R.S.A.I., xxxviii, p. 141.
[5] See a fully illustrated monograph by H. G. Leask, *Journal*, R.S.A.I., xlvi, p. 46.
[6] It is based on data collected in the works of C. E. P. Brooks, especially his *Climate through the Ages*.

Trim Castle; add the description in the Programme of the Summer Meeting of the Royal Archaeological Institute, 1931, p. 42.

The Cistercians; add A. H. Thompson, A. W. Clapham, and H. G. Leask, 'The Cistercian Order in Ireland' (*Archaeological Journal*, Vol. 88).

INDEX

Adamnan, 228 ff.
Aed mac Ainmirech, King of Ireland, 223 ff.
Agriculture, 99
Ahenny Crosses, 198
Ailech, 225, 227
Ailill, 129
Altartate, Co. Monaghan, 85, 86
Amatus, Bishop, 171
Animal gods, 134
Ankerholds, 261
Annagassan, 209
Annaghclochmuilinn, 38
Annals of Clonmacnois, 237, 241
Annals of the Four Masters, 232, 237, 248
Antae, 247
Antrim, shore sites of, 8, 15
Aran Is., 34, 57, 58, 249
Ardagh Cup, 190, 198, 209
Ardee, St Patrick's Shrine at, 235
Ardmore Cathedral, 251
Argei, 116
Arreton Down dagger, 72
Art, Christian, in Ireland, difficulties of study, 176
Askeaton, Castle at, 272
Askeaton Friary, 258
Assaroe, 145
Assemblies, 102
Asturian Culture, 13
Athboy, Battle of, 242
Athlone, Inscription at, 276
Attecotti, 123
Australia, Scribings in, 48

Bailey, 266

Ballinderry, 186, 209, 217
Ballintoy, figure from, 80
Ballon Hill, 66
Ballyglass, Co. Mayo, Monument at, 46
Baronies, origin of, 90
Barr of Fintona, Carn at, 45
Basse-cour, 266
Beads, 31, 63
Beaker People, 29, 36, 54, 78
Beakers, 36
Bective, Castle at, 272
Bell, John, 38
Bell-beakers, 36
Benignus, St, 35
Bernard of Clairvaux, life of Mael Madoc, 255
Bettystown Brooch, 191, 198
Black Pig's Dyke, 6
Blasket, Great, 219
Bog of Allen, 50
Book of Armagh, 172, 186, 188, 244
Book of Dimma, 187
Book of the Dun Cow, 212
Book of Durrow, 167, 187
Book of Invasions, 18
Book of Kells, 187-9, 198, 200, 207
Book of Kildare, 201, 208
Book of Leinster, 128, 154
Book of Lindisfarne, 187, 189
Boyne Tumuli, 59
— Plundered by Norsemen, 208
Brandub, King of Leinster, 224 ff.
Brasses, Monumental, 263

Brehon Laws, 35, 93, 111, 139
Bremer, Walther, 29, 71
Bretesche, 266
Bretha Comaithchesa, 149
Brian Borama, 90, 213, 232 ff.
Bricriu, Feast of, 156
Brigid, St, 129, 201
Britain, its relation to Ireland, 7, 12, 281
Brittas, 269
Broighter gold hoard, 95
Bromsgrove, Inscription at, 244
Bronze Weapons, 72
Brooches, 190
Brugh na Boinne, 62, 63 ff.
Brythons, 77 ff.
Bull-fighters, 147
Bunbrosna, Westmeath, 67
Bunratty Castle, 273
Butterfly finial, 247

Caelestius, 163
Caithness, 37
Calder Stones, Liverpool, 69
Calendar of Oengus, 284
Campignian culture, 12, 13
Cannibalism, 123, 199
Capa, Luigne, and Luasad, 18, 56
Carlingford Castle, 273
Carnagat, 41
Carrigogunnell, Castle at, 272
Carrowkeel, Cairns at, 44, 62
Carrowmore, 36
Castles, 266
Castle Saffron, 36
Castle Strange stone, 98, 129
Castletown Geoghegan, Motte at, 269
Cattle Raid of Cualnge, 126
Cauci, 91
Cauldrons, 84
Caverne des Trois Frères, 145
Celtic Art in Mediaeval times, 261
Celtic Languages, 76
Celts (people), 76, 82
' Celts ' (tool), 25

Cemeteries, Early Christian, 165
Cenn Cruaich, 69
Ceremonial implements, 27
Cesair, 56
Champion's Morsel, 156
Champneys, Arthur, 259
Chariots, 137
Chert, 23
Chevrons, treatment of, 252
Chi-rho Symbol, 184
Christ Church Cathedral, 253, 258
Christianity in Ireland, 160 ff.
Churches, early, in Ireland, 181, 191, 245
Churches, Palladian, 162
Ciaran, St, 101
Cistercians, 255
Cists, 66
Clais tarsna, 182
Clara, Kilkenny, 249
Clare Island, 260
Climate, influence of, 6, 50, 73, 89, 200, 277
Clonamery, 246
Clonard, 238
—, Motte at, 269
Clonburren, 193
Clondalkin, Round Tower at, 216
Clonfert Cathedral, 249, 251-3
Clonfinloch slab, 31
Clonmacnois, 183, 191-2, 206, 209, 212, 215, 236, 246, 250, 253
Clontarf, Battle of, 242
Coffey, George, 33, 65
Cogitosus, 182, 245
Coinage, 210
Collingwood, W. G., 208
Colloquy of the Ancients, 35
Columba, Colum Cille, 35, 87, 167, 226
Conaing, 83
Confessio Patricii, 166, 168, 169, 170
Cormac mac Airt, 161
Cormac's Chapel, 198, 215, 250, 253

INDEX

Corner Brackets, 247
Cornwall, relations of, with Ireland, 22, 29
Cosmogonies, ancient, 56
Cotswolds, 37
Crannogs, 23, 92
Crom Cruaich, 69
Cross of Cong, 190, 209
Crusades, 88
Cualnge, 129
Cu Chulaind, 140 ff., 222
Cullamore, 42
Cumascach, 224 ff.

Dane's Cast, 284
D'Arbois de Jubainville, H., 77
Deerpark Monument, 46
Derdriu, Deirdre, 153
Devil's Bit Mountain, golden bowl from, 73
Diarmait and Grainne, Chase of, 154
Diodorus Siculus, 123, 136
Disc Brooch, 80, 109
Divisions of Ireland, 6, 21, 37, 71, 239
Dolmens, 34
Donard, Cup marked stone at, 47
Donegal Castle, 274
Donoughmore, Round Tower at, 215
Doohat, Carn at, 45
Dorsey, 6
Dowth, 66
Drumbeg, stone circle, 70
Drumkelin, House at, 50
Drumnakilly, 66
Drunkenness, 129, 135
Dublin, founded by Scandinavians, 206, 209
— Norsemen of, 235 ff.
Duels, 148
Duilech's, St, Dublin, 261
Duk-duk, 145
Dunamase Castle, 273
Dundrum, Castle at, 271
Dunraven, Earl of, 216

Dun Ruadh, Greencastle, 45
Dysert O'Dea, 252

Earliest Settlers in Ireland, 8
Eber, 83
Epidemic, 235
Epitaphs, 264
Erard mac Coise, poet, 235 ff.
Ériu, meaning of name, 6
Erne, Loch, 116

Fairies, 143
Fāl, Stone of, 112
Feasts, 135
Feidlimid, Monument of, 212
Fer Diad, 129
Fergus mac Roig, 139
Ferguson, Sir Samuel, 130, 161
Fertility Ceremonials, 115
Finnachta, King of Ireland, 227 ff.
Fir Bolg, 56, 101
Flann, King of Ireland, 187, 191
Flat axe, 27
Flint, distribution of, 8, 24
— implements, 22
— nature of, 9
— use of, in Ireland, 22
Flood Myths, 56
Fomorians, 56, 83, 140, 142
Freshford Church, 191

Gailioin, 139
Gallarus, 245
Gaming-board, 217
Garland of Howth, 189-90
Gaulish raids in Rome and Delphi, 79
Gaza, gold earrings from, 81
Geography, Physical, of Ireland, 4
Germany, halberds from, 30
Giraldus Cambrensis, 201, 207
Glendaloch, 215, 248, 250
Gleninsheen, gorget from, 73
Glenn Mama, Battle of, 238
Goidels, 77 ff.

Gold in Ireland, 6, 19, 31, 55, 72, 75, 94
Gorgets, 72
Gormfhlaith, 213
Gospels of Clones, 178
Gospels of Mael Brigte, 188
Gothic Architecture in Ireland, 258
Gowran, Co. Kilkenny, 264
Greek Alphabet, ancient, 119
Greenmount, Motte at, 269
— Runic Inscription from, 219

Halberds, 30
Hallstatt in Ireland, 80
Harnack, 163
Harps, the Fair-Lucky, 144
Hatchet, Stone, 25
Head-hunters, 152
Heads as Ornaments, 252
Henry, Mlle Françoise, 185
Heralds, inviolability, 136
Heremon, 83
Highwood, 44
Holderness, boat from, 114
Holly, Magical use of, 149
Holycross, 260
Horned Carns, 37, 63
Hospitality, Laws of, 156
Houses, fortified, 270, 271
Howth, 125

Ice Age, 1
Iconostasis, 182
Inchagoill, 185
Inis Clothrann, 213
Inscriptions of the Eighteenth century, 274 ff.
Invasions, Book of, 18
Invasions of Ireland, 56
Ireland's Ey, 215
Iron, 75
Island Bridge, Scandinavian Cemetery at, 209
Island Magee, 12

Jambs, sloping, 253

Jar-Burials, 36
Jerome, St, 123, 163
Johnston, Francis, Architect, 277
Julius Caesar, 78, 121, 122, 127, 137
Jullien, Camille, 77

Keating, Geoffrey, 18
Keenogue Cemetery, 66
Kells, Co. Kilkenny, Memorial Slabs at, 263
Kells, Co. Meath, 185, 192
—, Chert Implements from, 23
— plundered by Norsemen, 238
—, Round Tower at, 215
—, St Columba's House, 181, 250
Kilconnell Friary, 260
Kildare, 251
—, Early Church at, 182, 245
Kilfinnane, Motte at, 269
Kilgreany man, 1, 283
Kilkenny, Round Tower at, 215
Killadeas, Sculpture at, 225
Killaloe, 252
—, Runic inscription in, 220
—, St Flannan, 250
Killeen Cormac, Kildare, 119
Killeshin Church, 191
Killycluggin Stone, 98
Killygarvan, 85
Kilmalkedar, 245, 253
—, the Priest's House, 181
Kilnasaggart, inscribed stone at, 183
Kilroot, early remains at, 10
Kings, function of, 71, 112
Kitchen-midden Axe, 13
Knockmoy, 260
Knocknarea, 62
Knockrafann, Motte at, 268
Kraft, Georg, 77

Lake dwellings, 91
Lambay, 24
Land movements, 2, 10
Larne, shore deposits, 10, 12

INDEX

La Tène Art and Civilization, 82, 84, 95 ff., 110, 127, 178-9
Leask, Mr. H. G., 181
Leeds, Mr. E. T., 85
Legends of Irish History, 55
Limerick, Castle at, 273
— founded by Scandinavians, 206, 209
Lisalea, Clones, 31
Lisnacrochera, Lake-dwelling, 97
Literature, Irish, 117, 126
Loch Corrib, 185
Lochcrew, 62, 110
Loch Ennell, 235, 242
Loch Erne, 195
Loch Gur, Stone circles at, 70
Loch Ree, 125, 235
Loiguire mac Neill, 223
Lunulae, 31
Lydney Park, 109
Lynchets, 101

Macha, Story of, 138
MaelMadoc ó Morgair, 254
MaelMuire, 212
MaelShechlainn II, King of Ireland, 213, 231 ff.
—, Abdication of, 240
Mag Adair, tree of, 232 ff.
Magic, 140, 155
Mag Slecht, 69
Mahr, Dr. A., 67, 116, 185
Manapioi, 78
Manuscripts, Illuminated, 186
Matriarchate, 33, 132
Maynooth Castle, 273
Medb, Queen, 62, 129, 222
Megalithic Monuments, 34, 68
Mel, Bishop, 129
Mellifont, 255
Mesolithic Period, 9
Messingwerk, 73
Milesians, 57, 82
Millstones, 100
Mines, Ancient, 49
Moate, Motte of, 269

Moling, St, 227
Monasterboice, 185, 191-2
Montelius, Oscar, 147
Morrigu, 150
Mother goddess, 80
Mottes, 266 ff.
Mouldings, Gothic, 258
Movements of Peoples, 88
Moynalvey, 223
— Stone of, 239
Muc-Inis, 84
Muirchu maccu Machtheni, 162, 171
Mullaghmast stone, 179, 193
Mull Hill, Isle of Man, 45
Myrtle Grove, Youghal, 274

Name-tabu, 147
Nature-Worship, 113 ff.
Nelson Monument, 276
Nemed, 56
Nenagh, Battle of, 237
—, Castle at, 272
Nendrum, 219
Newbliss, 41
New Grange, 59, 64
Nigg, Ross-shire, 51
Nöstvet, 13

O'Brien's Castle, Graffiti in, 274
O'Curry, Eugene, 126
O'Donnell, Manus, 35
Ogham Script, 117
—, Magical use of, 140 ff.
Oghams, 52, 249
Olaf, King of Dublin, 231
Old Kilcullen, 185
Old Leighlin Cathedral, 263
Omens, 136, 170
Ormonde Mansion, Carrick-on-Suir, 274

Pains of Ultonians, 138
Palladius, 162
Paradoxes of Ireland, 4, 5
Parnell Monument, 280

Partholon, 56
Patrick, St, 35, 69, 144, 146, 155, 165 ff., 208, 223, 231
Peat, 3, 5
Pediment, Architectural, 253
Pelagius, 163
Pele-towers, 273
Penrith, Stone circle at, 69
Periodicities, Historical, 87 f.
Petrie, George, 112, 192, 248
Pictish Language, 52
Picts, 33, 51, 78
Pillar stones, 140, 144, 146, 150, 152
Ploughing, 100
Plutarch, 137
Porter, A. Kingsley, 185
Portrush, Early remains at, 10
Poseidonius, 127, 135, 151, 157
Pottery, 31, 40, 63, 98
Pre-Patrician Christians, 173, 174
Prettanic Islands, 78
Princesses of Tara, Massacre of, 223
Prosper Tiro, 162
Psalter of Ricemarch, 190
Psalter of St Caimin, 190
Ptolemy, 78, 123, 160
Purification rites, 116

Quartz, 61, 63
Quin, Friary at, 272

Races of Mankind in Ireland, 12, 21, 55, 136
Raised Beaches, 10
Ralaghan figure, 114
Record Office, destruction of, 14, 259, 271
Ring of Tomar, 237
Ring-chain pattern, 218
Roadways, Ancient, in bogs, 50
Rock-scribings, 46 f., 60, 64 f.
Romanesque, Architecture in Ireland, 249
Roscrea, 253

Ross Errilly, 260
Rosses Point, 9
Rotherham, E. Crofton, 23
Round Towers, 214
Runes, 210, 219
Rushworth Gospels, 188–9

Sacrifices, human, 70, 116
Sanctuaries, 107 f.
Santry, Dublin, 263
Sardinia, 46
Scandinavia, Irish Objects in, 186, 205
Scandinavian influence on Irish Art, 210
Scandinavians, 204
Scattery Island, 234
—, Round Tower at, 216
Scythed Chariot, 151
Secondary interments, 34
Senchus Mór, 132
Sepulchral Monuments, early Christian, 183
—, Mediaeval, 262
Sepulchral Slabs, 264
Serfs in Ireland, 76, 93
Sheelanagigs, 195 f.
Shell-heaps of Denmark, 11, 13
Shell-keeps, 270
Ships, 95, 115 ff., 245
Shrines, 190
Sickles, 101
Silver, 102, 136
Sir Gawayne and the Green Knight, Lay of, 149
Skellig, the Greater, 248
Slievemore, Achill, dolmen at, 44
Social organization, 33, 52, 59, 129
Souterrains, 214
Spain, relations with Ireland, 13, 18, 21, 22, 24, 31, 36
Stokes, Margaret, 216
Stone Circles, 68
Stonehenge, 69
Stories, Traditional Irish, 128
Stowe St John, 188

INDEX

Strabo, 123
Strongbow, 254
Sub-Atlantic Period, 50
Sub-Boreal Period, 50
Sunwise turn, 137
Survey, Archaeological, necessity for, 17, 23, 41, 194, 260
Sword of Light, 75
Swords, 141, 147, 209

Tailtiu, Assembly of, 241
Tallaght, Monastery of, 174, 182
Tara, 71, 157, 223
Tara Brooch, *see* Bettystown Brooch
Tarvos Trigaranos, 147
Teutons, 82
Thanatomania, 222
Timahoe, Round Tower at, 217, 251
Tin, absence of, 6, 22, 27
— Use of, in Bronze Age, 27
Togherstown, Co. Westmeath, 80, 107
Tollchen, poet, 227
Tombe dei Giganti, 46
Tornant, inscribed stone at, 47
Trackers, 141
Trade, Irish, 28 ff., 33, 49
Tranchet, 13
Tribute, the Leinster, 223
Trim, Castle at, 271
Trumpets, 73
Tuam Cathedral, 252
—, inscription at, 275
Tuatha, 90

Tuatha De Danann, 57, 58, 82
Tuathal, King, 104, 221
Tullaherin, Kilkenny, Round Tower at, 215
Tumuli, 58 f.
Turgeis, 209
Turoe Stone, 98, 113, 179
Turret siege-engines, 152
Twin gods, 134, 150
Tympana of Church Doors, 253

Uisnech, 16, 99, 101
Upper Forestian Period, 50
Upper Turbarian Period, 50
Urnfields, 66
Usnech, Exile of Sons of, 153

Vallancey, Charles, 38
Ventimiglia, sculptured figures near, 30, 100
Victoricus, 166

Wales, Sculptured stones of, 193
Waterford, founded by Scandinavians, 206, 209
Wheeler, Dr. R. Mortimer, 109
Whitby, Synod of, 185
White Island, Sculptures at, 194
Whitepark Bay, 15, 20
Whithorn, 185
Windle, Sir Bertram, 70
Women in Military Service, 131
Wright, W. B., 283

Zimmer, Prof., 129, 163

For Product Safety Concerns and Information please contact our EU
representative GPSR@taylorandfrancis.com
Taylor & Francis Verlag GmbH, Kaufingerstraße 24, 80331 München, Germany

www.ingramcontent.com/pod-product-compliance
Lightning Source LLC
Chambersburg PA
CBHW060551230426
43670CB00011B/1771